**Illinois Central College
Learning Resources Center**

The Multiplicity of Dreams

The Multiplicity of

Dreams

Memory, Imagination, and Consciousness

Harry T. Hunt

Yale University Press
New Haven and London

Designed by James J. Johnson
and set in Electra types by Huron Valley Graphics, Inc.
Printed in the United States of America by
The Murray Printing Company, Westford, Massachusetts.

Library of Congress Cataloging-in-Publication Data

Hunt, Harry T., 1943–
  The multiplicity of dreams: memory, imagination, and consciousness / Harry T. Hunt.
      p.   cm.
  Bibliography: p.
  Includes index.
  ISBN 0–300–04330–9 (alk. paper)
  1. Dreams. 2. Dreams—Research. 3. Cognitive psychology.
I. Title.
  [DNLM: 1. Dreams. 2. Psychoanalytic Interpretation. WM 460.5.D8
H941m]
BF1078.H86 1989
154.6′3—dc19
DNLM/DLC
for Library of Congress   88–27908
                                                                    CIP

*The paper in this book meets the guidelines for permanence
and durability of the Committee on Production Guidelines for
Book Longevity of the Council on Library Resources.*

10 9 8 7 6 5 4 3 2 1

Contents

Preface

In what follows I have synthesized recent developments within the study of dreams, from cognitive and dynamic psychologies, anthropology, and neurophysiology to our growing realization of the actual multiplicity of the various forms of dream experience.

Among these perspectives the "cognitive" is inevitably the most prominent, since whatever else dreaming is, it is an expression of mind—in all cultures dreams have posed the question of their potential "meaning." For all that, the study of dreaming and related states has far more to offer current "cognitive science," with its narrow emphasis on memory and language, than the other way around. As useful as certain "mainstream" models of memory and story grammar may be for some aspects of dream formation and some forms of dreaming, it is precisely the more striking, if infrequent, forms of lucid dreaming, dreams based on mythological, spiritual themes, and nightmares, that push us toward more pluralistic frames of mind based on image and metaphor, closer to aesthetics than "computation" and requiring a more organismic-holistic perspective on symbolic cognition.

It has finally occurred to me that, so far at least, there are really only two theories of dreaming. The first approach, common to Freud, the neurophysiologists Hobson and McCarley, and the cognitivists Antrobus and Foulkes, holds that dreams result from a competition between a coherent organizing system—whether termed ego, cortex, left hemisphere, or narrative intelligence—and a more primitive and ultimately disruptive tendency: unconscious, brain stem, right hemisphere, or diffuse memory activation. The resultant compromise is then seen as semantically meaningful or randomized nonsense depending on one's understanding of the disrupting agent. The alternative view, common in very different ways to Jung, Hillman, Jones, Gendlin, and a host of contemporary "dream workers," holds that the emergent sources of dreaming, at least much of the time, are not "primitive" or "disruptive" at all. Rather they constitute the spontaneous expressions of a symbolic intelligence alternative to standard representational thought and variously termed "imagistic," "affective," or "presentational." By distinguishing between narrative and visual-kinesthetic metaphor as sources of dream formation, and between different forms of dreaming, I attempt to mediate between these positions.

Yet there are dangers within even this alternative organismic perspective, semantic and for all I know empirical. Cognition is endlessly fascinated with "structures" and too often fails to address the more dynamic, energetic, and/or affective expressions of symbolic intelligence, as if the former were somehow disembodied and the latter lacked any intrinsic organization. I have tried to avoid such fictionalizing by including an affective-kinesthetic dimension within my discussion of the visual-spatial side of dream formation, on the notion that spontaneous imagery seems so often self-referential or autosymbolic of ongoing emotional concerns. Another might equally well have chosen to speak of three strands in all dream (and symbol) formation—visual imagery, narrative sequence, and kinesthetic-affective embodiment.

Along these lines, and speaking of convenient fictions, I would not want anything that follows to imply an adherence to rigid "dual code" models of human intelligence, which tend to distinguish an abstract verbal capacity from a more rudimentary imagistic one. Not only is the latter fully capable of its own line of abstract development, as seen in certain dreams, alterations of consciousness, and aesthetics, but each of these "frames" seems capable of endlessly complex interactions at all levels of their potential unfolding. Rather, it would be precisely the cross-modal "synesthetic" fusions of patterns from the separate senses that would, with different weightings and emphases, create both language and the vivid imagistic expressions of some dreams. These cross-sensory syntheses would constitute the organismic basis of current speculations about the "holographic" operation of the cortex (see also Globus, 1987). In fact it is precisely research on the multiplicity of dream forms that offers some of the most convincing evidence for the potential unity amidst endless diversity that constitutes the human mind.

Acknowledgments

Acknowledgments are difficult. Too few and you are an egotistical hermit, too many and the author emerges as a sort of academic sociopath.

I would like to thank the teachers who encouraged my work on dreaming—Eugenia Hanfmann, Richard Jones, and Paul Seligman—and the many students who have participated with me in the research that lead into this book: Ernie Atalick, Kathy and Denis Belicki, Paul Kelly, Theresa Casteels, Barbara McLeod, Coralee Popham, Roc Villeneuve, Maya Polywjanyj and Aurelia Spadafora. Colleagues who were especially helpful with support, advice, and information include Jayne Gackenbach, Kathy Belicki, Alan Moffitt, Robert Ogilvie, George Gillespie, Sebastian Fazzari, Carol Munschauer, Alan Hobson, and John Antrobus. Brief conversations with Endel Tulving and Martha Farah were also useful and clarifying. I am indebted to the Analytical Psychology Society of Western New York (and Paul Kugler) and to the Center for Advanced Study in Theoretical Psychology, University of Alberta (especially Paul Swartz and Leendert Mos) for providing settings in which I could present preliminary versions of this material.

My department chairman, Jack Adams-Webber, and Brock University offered much needed moral and financial support, and I am grateful to Deborah Bray and Joanne Gazzola for the typing and preparation of the manuscript. Without question the efforts of Jeanne Ferris at Yale University Press and of Stephanie Jones, who edited the manuscript, contributed immensely to the quality of the final product.

Finally, I wish to express my thanks for the editorial help and personal support offered by my new wife, Kate Ruzycki-Hunt. She saw the best and worst of it and this book is dedicated to her.

PART I

Contemporary Theory and Research on Dreaming

All things are so inter-related that, though the difference between a fruit and what is commonly called a vegetable seems obvious, there is no defining either. . . . In an existence of the hyphen, it is impossible to be altogether wrong—or right. This is why it is so hard to learn anything. It is hard to overcome that which cannot be altogether wrong with that which cannot be altogether right. I look forward to the time when I shall refuse to learn another thing, having accumulated errors enough.

—Charles Fort, *Wild Talents*

CHAPTER 1

Dream Studies and the Fundamental Question of Meaning

The Contemporary Self-Deconstruction of Dreaming

DREAM research, both experimental and clinical-phenomeno-logical, has arrived at a point of historical hiatus. Research on the psychophysiology of the REM (Rapid Eye Movement) state, once widely heralded as a means of testing Freudian dream theory and settling mind–brain controversies, now faces skepticism, disillusionment, and lack of funding. True, a great deal has been learned about the unique physiology of the REM state as a periodic, chemically mediated condition of arousal in mammalian sleep, but the anticipation that understanding REM will explain dreaming has been shaken as researchers realize that dreaming involves far more than the specific conditions of the REM state. Dreaming appears not only in the lighter levels of non-REM (NREM) sleep and in the hypnagogic period of sleep onset, but also under hypnosis (where dreams can be directly suggested), in "daydreaming" as studied under laboratory conditions, and in the "waking dreams" or guided fantasies characteristic of various therapeutic traditions.

At the same time, and independent of the psychophysiological laboratory, several attempts have been made to include dream experience and dream formation within the current "cognitive revolution" in psychology and related

3

fields. Cognitive psychologies of dreaming range from the attempts of David Foulkes and John Antrobus to subsume dreams under mainstream "cognitive science," centered as it is on models of memory and linguistic processes, to the heterodox theories of James Hillman, Charles Rycroft, Calvin Hall, as well as my own, that understand dreaming in terms of organismic-holistic approaches to imagery, imagination, and metaphor. A generally unremarked feature of the attempt to modernize dream psychology as an aspect of cognitive science is that it represents a return to the diverse and complex dream theories developed in the nineteenth century. There we find the very "faculty psychology" approaches that Freud both scorned and synthesized in his still controversial, still foundational *Interpretation of Dreams*, published in 1900.

In addition to this increasingly heterogeneous mix of dream theories and research findings, over the past twenty years our understanding of potential variations within the dream experience itself has considerably expanded. An earlier anecdotal literature on lucid dreaming (in which one realizes that one is dreaming while the dream continues and attempts to observe and/or control its course) has been augmented by experimental-cognitive, neuropsychological, and phenomenological studies. These have had the potential virtue of so confounding basic assumptions about dreams that they have drawn equal and uneasy criticism from all major practitioners of dream research—clinicians, psychophysiologists, and cognitivists. In a parallel development with potentially similar consequences, interest has revived in the anthropology of dreaming in tribal peoples—with a corresponding emphasis on the cultural relativity and malleability of dreaming and the suggestion that there may be multiple types of dreams.

Meanwhile, on an organizational level, the Sleep Research Society (SRS) and its small cluster of researchers focusing on physiological, neurocognitive, and content analysis approaches to dreams have been supplemented by a more eclectic organization, the Association for the Study of Dreams (ASD). Within ASD, a diverse group of Freudian, Jungian, existential, and other psychologists interested primarily in dream interpretation and "dreamwork" has banded together with others attempting to relate dreams to altered states of consciousness and transpersonal psychology, and a small number of SRS experimenters.

All this adds up to a postmodern "self-deconstruction" of dream psychology. In short, all the major descriptive, theoretical, and research approaches to dream studies seem equally open to new questioning, which affords us an unparalleled opportunity to take a fresh look at the full varieties and range of dreaming. At the same time this deconstruction of dream research stands as an object lesson in the necessary relativity and perspectivism of the human sciences. Indeed, part of the promise of the cognitive era in modern psychology is its potential to address the full extent of the human symbolic capacity, as reflected in the multiple "frames of mind" through which human intelligence is manifested—language, imagery, interpersonal relations, mathematics, aesthetics, and religion. It would be tragic for a "cognitive science" to remain focused only on those computational and technical capacities that can be functionally circumscribed and computer simulated—thereby making psychology the unwitting architect of a science of mind excessively restricted to the artificial and domesticated. It is never clear in the human sciences whether we lead society to new discoveries or are merely led in turn by its pervasive ideologies of power and order (see Foucault, 1978; Sampson, 1981).

Accordingly, it is important to interrogate critically the standard history of dream research, which asserts its familiar linear progression from the pre-scientific era of psychoanalysis to the psychophysiological study of the REM state, and thence finally to contemporary cognitive science approaches. As one might expect, reality is not that simple.

First, although Freud's dream theory has set the standard against which all others are compared, we cannot forget the contrastive clinical theories and techniques of interpretation of Jung, and an equally intriguing eclectic tradition that includes Herbert Silberer, who influenced both Freud and Jung; Samuel Lowy, a student of Stekel, who in many ways anticipated both REM state physiology and Eugene Gendlin's approach to "felt meaning"; and Medard Boss, who developed a phenomenology of the multiplicity of dream forms within an existential perspective. This clinical tradition has not simply been supplanted by laboratory physiology but has continued to develop in its own right. This is attested within the eclectic tradition by recent publications by Charles Rycroft (*The Innocence of Dreams*, 1978), Boss (*I Dreamt Last Night*, 1977), Richard Jones (*The Dream Poet*, 1980), and Liam Hudson (*Night Life*, 1985), along with more popular dream books written by Ann Faraday, Gayle Delany, and Montague Ullman. Meanwhile, the psychoanalytic tradition has produced Jones's earlier *New Psychology of Dreaming* (1970), Palombo's *Dreaming and Memory* (1978), and numerous studies by Greenberg and Pearlman and by Fiss. Even Foulkes's first two books were inspired by psychoanalysis and attempted its translation first into psychophysiology (*The Psychology of Sleep*, 1966) and later into the language of cognitive psychology (*A Grammar of Dreams*, 1978). The Jungian tradition has meanwhile produced important books by James Hillman (1979), Paul Kugler (1982), and James Hall (1977).

Second, the standard linear reading of our history misses the development of complex methods of empirical content analysis, contemporary with and even slightly preceding that of sleep laboratories. Calvin Hall and his associates Van de Castle, Domhoff, and Nordby elaborated and systematized Hall's pioneering collections of dream diaries from ordinary individuals not involved in long-term psychotherapy. While these and later content analysis systems (summarized in Winget and Kramer's *Dimensions of Dreams*, 1979) were seized upon as measures of the "dependent variable" in sleep lab studies, they were largely generated independently to test traditional clinical theories about spontaneous home dreaming, that fundamental phenomenon which in all times and societies has attracted such interest. Foulkes's more recent conclusion (1985) that REM state psychophysiology is irrelevant to the study of dreaming as a cognitive process leaves Hall's earlier program in place as a potentially appropriate means of evaluating the claims of Freud, Jung, and the eclectic traditions.

Third, the current cognitive science perspective tends to overlook a competing organismic-holistic cognitive psychology and its application to dreams and related states. Paul Schilder, Jean Piaget, Heinz Werner and Bernard Kaplan, and Calvin Hall all developed some aspect of the earlier cognitive revolution started by Gestalt psychology. Their base was in methods of natural observation, perhaps more attuned to the actual phenomena of dreams than laboratory experiments.

Finally, by limiting the history of "cognitive science" to the 1970s and 1980s, we miss the cognitive formulations of nineteenth-century dream psychology in all its diversity, and we miss part of the inner dynamic running through each era of dream psychology—the debate between rationalism and romanticism about the nature of the human mind. More specifically, we lose the elaborate, if implicit cognitive theories within the work of Freud and Jung and the way that these have been carried forward into current cognitive explanations of dreaming—first as something unitary rather than multiple and second as a process that is *either* narrative and linguistic in its roots *or* imagistic and aesthetic. Of course it might be both, and other things as well.

Freud, Jung, and Cognitive Psychologies

Freud's approach to dreams has three aspects: (1) dream interpretation, based on his technique of verbal free association to parts of the *manifest* dream; (2) dream formation, based on the four mechanisms of condensation, displacement, visual representation, and secondary revision; and (3) a causal process of dreaming, by which the latent dream thoughts, largely mnemic and verbal, are translated by means of the mechanisms of dream formation into the manifest dream, in such a way as to protect sleep by disguising and transforming all that might disrupt it. As Richard Jones (1970) suggests, Freud arrived at his four processes of dream formation by hypothetically reversing what happens when we free-associate. Freud reasoned that the largely verbal waking associations will follow the actual pathways of dream formation backward to one or more instigating wishes, based on both recent experience from the previous day (day residue) and more distant memories from early childhood. Freud's hypothesis is that if free association reverses everything that happens in dream formation, then the former can be used as a clue to the latter.

Just as our free associations tend to fan out from a dream segment, so in dream formation a process of condensation would have to occur in order to fuse these disparate memories and feelings into the final dream element. And just as free association may take us into personal areas surprisingly distant from the initial dream fragments, so the dream itself would begin in such emotionally relevant issues, which are in turn displaced and disguised as an ostensibly innocuous dream surface. Whereas the manifest dream generally has a more or less coherent storyline, free association breaks the dream into parts and follows each line of association separately into *latent* thoughts and memories that inevitably bear internal connections quite different from the connections in the original dream plot. Thus, any cohesiveness in the dream plot would result from a later "secondary revision." Finally, free association leaves the predominantly visual dream, with its supposed lack of critical reflection and rational use of language, and moves back into predominantly verbal memories and thoughts. Again, this is reversed in dream formation as a process of "visual representation" based on "considerations of representability." As arbitrary as Freud's linkage of postdream associations and predream formation has seemed to many over the years, it is essential to note that many dreams *do* contain specific examples of each of these mechanisms in their manifest surface, as we shall see. The question becomes their necessity and universality.

The cognitive psychology that lies within Freud's account is surprisingly close to the near-exclusive preoccupation of current cognitive science with language and memory. When interpreting dreams through free association, the largely verbal free associations leave the largely visual manifest dream and branch out into recent and distant personal memories whose cross-associations constitute the latent pathways by which the dream was supposedly formed. It is thus not accidental to this technique of interpretation that Freud believed *all* dreams are formed from a background of verbal-propositional cognitive processes. These are not permitted into direct awareness due to the limiting conditions of sleep (motor paralysis and the danger of premature arousal) and so must undergo a translation (via regression) into a more primitive visual mode of expression. For the psychoanalyst Marshall Edelson (1972), whose cognitive formalization of Freud's unconscious as the "deep structure" of language itself was a major influence on Foulkes's *Grammar of Dreams*, dreaming is a "surface array" visual paraphrase of narrative linguistic structure. Although in his more recent publications (1982 a, b, 1985) Foulkes rejects the idea that free associations reveal any single intrinsically symbolic core, he also sees dreams as originating in the processes of "inner speech," a kind of psycholinguistics ending not in speech production but in an alternative and secondary visual medium. The core of dream formation now becomes its narrative structure. The dream, for Foulkes, is syntax imposed on diffuse memory activations, but without any underlying intentional semantics. Although he has come to reject psychoanalytic formulations almost totally, Foulkes's model of dream formation is nonetheless a direct descendant of Freud's—rendered "cognitively scientific."

For Carl Jung, on the other hand, and more recently for the neo-Jungian James Hillman's revival of romantic imagination, dream interpretation does not unravel or reverse the pathways of formation but instead serves to *finish* the dream through a family of techniques usually called *amplification*. The supposedly visual core of dream formation is translated *into* language, starting with the finished polyvalent visual structure of the dream and ending by "saying" its multiple meanings in the sequential form necessarily lacking during dream formation. In other words, the dream is on its way toward a verbal mode but remains in whole or part outside language, perhaps owing to the limitations of sleep and the resulting strengths of a more immediate imagistic mode. In amplification the dream might be paraphrased in more general terms to bring out its embedded metaphoric structure; it might be connected to cross-culturally common *archetypal* themes of mythology; or, in Hillman's own approach, it might be transformed directly into a sort of expressive poetry by developing rhyme, wordplay, and etymology from the original dream account. The key to such interpretation lies in the view of visual imagery and metaphor as an abstract cognitive faculty in its own right.

Similarly, the heterodox organismic cognitive psychologies of Werner and Kaplan, Rudolph Arnheim, and Susanne Langer, centered on the presentational-expressive symbolism of aesthetics, locate the creative core of the human symbolic capacity in visual-spatial and physiognomically expressive imagination, with representational language regarded as its pragmatic medium of communication. On this view dream imagery and the closely related phenomena of altered states of consciousness are especially important because they offer uniquely direct access to the polyvalent and simultaneous superimpositions that constitute the "deep structure" of thought—or, at the very least, a line of intellectual symbolic development in its own right that comes to the fore in dreams and aesthetics. In this latter sense, visual-spatial imagery is "primitive" only with respect to its sequential articulation, since it already has the "reversability" that must be so gradually developed in Piaget's accounts of the distinct steps of logical-verbal thought. Visual imagery needs no increasingly rapid reversal of steps because it is based on the functionally simultaneous presentations of highly condensed expressive patterns. Its own development would rather consist in the difficult and gradual spelling out of meaning that characterizes aesthetics, literary criticism, and . . . dream interpretation.

The Symbolic Meaning of Dreams

The rationalist–romantic dichotomy in modern thought has had a still more fundamental impact, echoing throughout cognitive, psycho-physiological, and clinical perspectives on dreaming. To what extent can we claim at all that dreams have verifiable meanings? After all, whatever the method or model of dreaming, dream interpretation comes *after* the dream. Empirically it is superimposed upon an episode recalled on awakening. Whatever the subjective power of the dream as transmuted by its interpretation, and despite potential insights so novel and personally revealing that it feels ungracious to regard the dream as anything but an intentional communication of some sort, it nonetheless remains the case that the interpretation is *added to* the dream. This holds true even if the meaning spontaneously jumps out at one immediately upon awakening.

Most certainly, the dream can be *turned into* a symbol for fundamental life issues. The human metaphorical capacity allows us to see one thing in terms of another. Wittgenstein helps show how this "seeing as" allows us to relate anything to anything else along the various lines of pragmatic usage, no matter how initially distant the meanings of the two things. The thematic and structural similarity between a dream and one's waking life is not in principle any different from the potential similarity of any one segment of one's waking life to any other segment—once one is selected and framed as a potential symbol of the other.

The fundamental question for a cognitive psychology of dreams is whether there are demonstrable features *within* the very fabric of dream experience and open to empirical and experimental study that show the direct operation of symbolic processes—and if so, whether these processes are verbal-representational, visual-metaphorical, kinesthetic-affective, or some complex and shifting balance of all three. It is necessary to show that the dream is *formed in* such a way as to meet its interpretation at least part way, or that the interpretation actually *finishes* something that the dream *started*, and this *because* it is a dream. The opposing view, long fashionable among scientific dream researchers from the nineteenth century to the present, is that the dream only *seems to* afford meaning richer than average waking experience because it is a relatively disorganized and randomized form of that same experience. These theorists see the dream as a form of delirium that at best mimics the conditions of creative insight. Anything learned about oneself from this random mélange is not due to an intentionality of the dreaming process but is a secondary effect of waking thought. Truly we see here the need for a cognitive psychology of dreams to address their most basic source of historical interest— symbolic meaning and its genesis.

What evidence is there, for the scientifically minded, of symbolic activity in the very fabric of dreaming? Most attention has been given to those features of dreaming that show transformations of one's ordinary waking environment ("dream bizarreness") as the potential expression of metaphorical imagination. Yet for other investigators these are the very signs of the dream's delirium and primitivity—all that which led the nineteenth-century mechanist Robert, for example, to dismiss dreams as "froth" (Freud, 1900). Robert's most radical successors are Sir Francis Crick and Graeme Mitchison (the former, having attempted one of those risky shifts from a Nobel Prize for the discovery of DNA to computer simulations of the mind). These investigators see dreaming as a form of forgetting—a "neural dumping" that clears semantic memory stores of all excess information from the previous day (Crick and Mitchison, 1986). The dream remembered is dreaming gone wrong; and it is then the very height of nonsense to allow such material to influence one's waking life.

From their ten-year-long critique of Freudian dream theory, the neurophysiologists Allan Hobson and Robert McCarley (1977) similarly conclude that dream interpretation is wrong-headed and somehow dangerous. They are especially struck by findings of a relation between dream bizarreness and phasic bursts of neural activation (i.e., dense bursts of eye movements) triggered by intense firing of the same brain cells that initiate the REM state. This they interpret as a one-way causal process leading from a primitive and random brain stem discharge to dream bizarreness. Along these lines, they regard the vestibular arousal that is part of REM activation as a direct cause of dream sensations of flying, falling, and physical disorientation. Sudden intensification of the descending inhibitory neural activity that prevents physical movement during the paralysis of REM sleep would be associated with the sensations of inability to move or frustratingly slow motion in terrifying dreams, for example. Such sensory effects of the discharge of cells in the pontine formation of the brain stem could only *disrupt* the synthesizing capacity of the central nervous system that creates the dream sequence. These sensory expressions and forms of bizarreness are thus too rudimentary to be the metaphors of anything but their own origins in random neural firing.

Although David Foulkes (1982 a, b; 1985) sees a cognitive account of the dream process as independent of any specific psychophysiology of the REM state, he agrees with Hobson and McCarley that condensations, sudden displacements and scene changes, and fantastic sensory intrusions and transformations—the very stuff of dream symbolism from Freud to the present—are "peripherally induced aberrations in the central organization of dreaming" (Foulkes, 1983 a, p. 358). Again, the most striking "cognitive" feature of dreaming is its narrative cohesion; with the visual surface of the dream only a secondary expression of a deeper syntax. Thus, bizarreness in dreams is akin to slips of the tongue in speech. Following linguists like Fromkin rather than Freud's extensive comments on verbal parapraxes, Foulkes suggests that such errors demonstrate purely formal or deep-structure aspects of cognition and are without semantic significance.[1]

Agreeing with Hobson and McCarley, but substituting a central initiation for their peripheral brain stem activation, Foulkes argues that dreams are formed from a "diffuse mnemic activation" of multiple recent and long-term memory stores that occurs more or less randomly and without any semantic or communicative intent. The organization imposed on these diffusely and simultaneously activated memories is syntactic, not semantic. The result is the structured storyline of the dream, which includes whatever peripherally induced disorientations it could not fully subordinate. The dream lacks semantics and communicative intentionality because, unlike language, we cannot check the result against a preliminary plan or intention. Unlike language, dreams are simply imposed. Foulkes writes:

> The reason why dreamers can't understand what their dreams mean, and why we have such difficulty in constructing adequate accounts of what they might have meant, is that they didn't mean anything. That is, unlike the case in speech production, no unitary message is momentarily or sequentially encoded during dream production. The dream isn't, therefore, any kind of translation of such a message, and if we persist in searching for one, we're in the angel counting business. (Foulkes, 1985, pp. 165–66)

Since the question of the meaning of dreams, as we will see below, is explicit or implicit in all research on dreams, whatever the method or orientation, it is well to pause now to consider some actual lines of evidence suggesting (1) that dreams can be social and communicative, and (2) that dreaming is closely related to measures of creativity. It is important to a full understanding of Freud and his influence to realize that he regarded the dream as "completely asocial," and this in specific contrast to jokes that otherwise show many of the same tendencies to condensation and displacement. The dream, Freud writes, "has nothing to communicate to anyone else; it arises within the subject as a compromise between the mental forces struggling in him, it remains unintelligible to the subject himself and is for that reason totally uninteresting to other people" (Freud, 1905, pp. 95–96). Freud missed much here in not going further with the comparison to jokes (cf. Jones, 1980) and aesthetic activity in general (cf. Ricoeur, 1970).

There is considerable indication that dreams can be socially malleable and patterned—that dream formation can become part of an ongoing dialogic process. First, numerous anthropological studies have commented on the way most cultures specify set forms and contents for "important" dreams ("culture pattern dreams": see chaps. 5, 10). Such dreams can have considerable consequence, good and ill, for the individual dreamer and the social group. It seems to be an index of this importance that they are often told to the group regardless of the consequences. Of course, the specific content of these dreams differs greatly across societies. Similarly, many primitive and classical societies have practiced forms of dream incubation in which specific sorts of dreams are deliberately sought.

Contemporary studies show that both dream content and dream form can be modified by direct experimental suggestion (Tart, 1979) and even by simply directing the subject to attend to specific nontypical features of dreams. Thus, being told to attend especially to dream situations where one is alone will actually tend to increase such dreams (Belicki and Bowers, 1982). Richard Jones (1980) describes ongoing seminars in which students' dreams are interrogated as clues to the literary meanings of major novels being studied by the group. Over the semester their dreams show more and more indirect (metaphorical) and direct reference to the works in question. Similarly, several clinical researchers have described striking changes in clients' dreams over the course of intensive psychotherapy (Boss, 1958; Winnicott, 1971). The psychoanalysts Greenberg and Pearlman (1975) and Palombo (1978) have offered detailed descriptions of the progressive interplay between therapy sessions and preceding and subsequent dream content. Finally, the striking thematic parallels that can emerge in the dreams of family members and/or close friends have been noted (Taub-Bynum, 1986). Henry Reed (1978) attempted to formalize this process some years ago by successfully suggesting to large groups of subjects that they "meet" at the same dream locations on the same night.[2]

Several experimental studies link dream bizarreness and creative imagination. Most strikingly, Robert Watson (Watson, Butler, and Liebmann, 1982) found significant correlations between individual differences in the amount of phasic discharge, so central to Hobson's and McCarley's model of dreaming and related in several studies to dream bizarreness, and the movement response on the Rorschach inkblot test—widely used as a research and clinical measure of creative imagination. Other studies report specific associations between psychological tests of creativity and both dream bizarreness and dream recall (Sylvia, Clark, and Monroe, 1978; Belicki, 1987), as well as between dream bizarreness and the schizoid and paranoid scales of the Minnesota Multiphasic Personality Inventory (MMPI) (Cohen, 1979)—regarded as a measure of creative imagination *in normal samples* (Claridge, 1972). Subjects who experience many "flying dreams" (Brink, 1979) and nightmares (Hartmann, 1984; Belicki and Belicki, 1986) have also tested as unusually imaginative.

The needed direction here may come from two studies linking dream bizarreness to the creative arts. Adelson (1974) found that subjects with more fantastic dreams were significantly superior students in creative writing classes. Naomi Schecter and her colleagues (Schecter, Schmeidler, and Staal, 1965) found that university students in the creative arts recalled significantly more dreams and that their dreams were more vivid, bizarre, aggressive, and characterized by philosophical-religious themes than dreams of students enrolled in the sciences or engineering. Thus what has widely been taken as most "primitive" about dreaming, its "bizarreness," turns out to express capacities related to imagination and aesthetic ability. But perhaps this is not so surprising if we recall that what is "instinctive" and "biologically basic" in human beings is our symbolic capacity, as manifested cross-culturally in both language *and* the arts. If the primitive activation centers of the brain stem are necessarily linked to species-specific behaviors, they will also help to mediate human symbolic imagination and all its characteristic drivenness.

A strong connection between dreaming and the creative arts, in comparison to, say, mathematics, suggests a solution to the doubts of Foulkes and others that dreams can have any communicative semantic basis because, on his careful arguments (1) unlike speech, you can't check a dream against your original intention, and (2) all interpretive techniques lead to multiple meanings for the same dreams. Susanne Langer has introduced a distinction, almost totally neglected within experimental cognitive science, between *representational* symbolism, best illustrated by language and most formalized in mathematics, and the *presentational* forms of symbolism that predominate in the expressive arts and apparently (less formalized and finished, of course) in at least some dreams. In representational processes, the connection between symbolic vehicle (word, sign) and its referent is relatively fixed, arbitrary, and largely automatized, and the properties of the medium itself are generally ignored during ongoing communication. There is nothing in the sound of the word *book* that is connected to the object you now hold. Very different sounds in other cultures represent this same object.

In the presentational side of symbolism, however, meaning resides directly in the felt qualities and rhythm of the expressive medium—to the point where material in the visual arts, poetry, and music and certain imageries in altered states of consciousness, while clearly semantic and communicative, nonetheless resist any full or complete narrative formulation. Presentational meanings are obviously symbolic and as equally beyond the capacities of lower animals as is representational language. They depend on a full and even contemplative experiencing of the formal properties of the expressive medium in a way reminiscent of Arthur Deikman's (1982) characterization of a "receptive mode" involved in meditation and contrasting with the more actively and volitionally directed mode of ordinary language use.

Foulkes may dismiss dream semantics because the meanings of dreams are always multiple, but presentational meanings in the arts are also necessarily polyvalent and multiple. When William Gass (1976) describes the metaphorical significance in the arts and everyday life of "blueness," he fills out an essentially unrelated cluster of usages related to pornography, aristocracy, grief, and expansive freedom and release. The overall content of a dream or novel may determine which of its multiple possible meanings predominates, but the richness of such material often depends on the fact that the context evokes more than one such signification. It is just this multiple evocation and open spontaneous intentionality that we appreciate in the arts and that artists strive to achieve.

Indeed, an important characteristic of creative phases in artistic expression is the way spontaneous imagery and insight may actually change and redefine one's original intention—thus making Foulkes's method of checking whether a mental expression fulfills its intent as unworkable for dreams as it is for the arts. Unless we propose to remove aesthetics from a cognitive science of the human symbolic capacity (and risk psychology's becoming the handmaiden for a society so patterned as well), we should accept its parameters as part of our object of study—whether they appear in works of art or in dreams. Otherwise, the "liberation" of the human sciences afforded by the cognitive revolution will lose those multiple forms of human intelligence that should be its focus (see also Gardner, 1983).

In the more operational terms that a cognitive psychology may afford us, the notion of a presentational symbolic capacity helps make sense of the otherwise difficult insistence of such diverse figures as Freud, Jung, and Samuel Lowy that dreams occur in a different "place" or topography—the unconscious. If we apply the psychology of aesthetics offered by Langer, Werner and Kaplan, and Rudolph Arnheim, we may no longer need to speak of mysterious forces hidden from all awareness (confusing the latter with linguistically organized consciousness). We can speak instead of a different pattern and use of the same symbolic capacity that gives rise to ordinary language and mathematics but that here operates directly within sensorimotor media of expression.

Dreams are *unconscious* only if one obtusely restricts *consciousness* to what is voluntarily directed and singular in its semantic significance. Otherwise, to use Howard Gardner's felicitous phrase, dreams show, at least at times, an alternative imagistic "frame of mind." When a patient of Rycroft (1979), instead of dreaming of overt sexual activity at the point of a nocturnal emission, dreams of watching a train enter a dark tunnel, then whatever we may learn about his life unfolds in the same way and via the same patterning of our symbolic capacity that allows us to respond to Rousseau's *Sleeping Gypsy*. Both dream and painting show in their very fabric the work of an abstract, symbolic human intelligence.

Methodological Dilemmas in the Human Sciences and Their Relevance to Dream Research

Just as experimental researchers have questioned the scientific merit of the interpretive traditions, recent approaches to dreams as expressions of metaphor often question the relevance of cognitive and psychophysiological processes to a genuine psychology of dreams. Charles Rycroft states, "If dreams have meaning and can be interpreted, they must be creations of the person or agent who endows them with meaning, while if they are phenomena with causes, they must be explicable in terms of prior events without reference to an agent. One cannot really have it both ways, and the attempt to do so leads only to confusion" (Rycroft, 1979, p. 4).

However, the attempts to recast Freud's dream theory both as part of the hermeneutic-interpretive tradition (Ricoeur, Habermas, Guntrip) and as neurocognition (Pribram, Sulloway, Erdelyi) miss the point that the source of fascination in Freud, as with other paradigmatic psychologists like Luria, Piaget, and James, lies precisely in their curious and deliberate running together of the language of meaning and the language of causal process. The way Freud mixes in the same sentence references to Oedipus and mobile cathectic energies need not be taken as the expression of a fixed and final or even successful system to see that it captures a paradoxical duality at the very heart of the human sciences, and in human nature itself. This duality is carried to the extreme in the diversity of dream psychologies. Perhaps Rycroft's "confusion" is not the worst result in a era where scientific and interpretive dream psychologies engage each other at best with only a dismissive glance.

In psychology we attempt a *science* (its models of method and theory drawn ultimately from the physical sciences) of material that is classically *expressed* in mythology and the arts. Whether acknowledged or not, the social sciences aim to formalize theories and observations already embodied not only in great artistic achievements but within ordinary language as well. The human sciences differ from the physical sciences in that we are identical with our object of research. The major phenomena of psychology, neurocognition, sociology, and anthropology are already available to us intuitively in the course of our own life experience. Such intuitive understanding is, of course, far short of the formalization of theory and method that we call science, but it does confer on the social sciences a unique and problematic identity which can neither be fully utilized nor fully suppressed.

Indeed, most definitions of the human symbolic capacity stress this very reflexivity—the way our consciousness naturally turns around on itself. We encounter the dilemmas and possibilities of reflexivity—our appearance as both subject and object—much more promptly in the human sciences than even in the indeterminacies and complementarities of modern physics. This reflexivity has given rise to two very different yet conjoined reactions. One insists we must eschew all subjectivity and research only the human behaviors and capacities that can be studied using laboratory methodology (in dream research, proponents of this school include Hobson and McCarley, Foulkes, and Antrobus). The other is a humanistic insistence that the phenomenon as lived comes first and that methodology, which should consist first and foremost in careful observation, must be determined by the nature of the subject matter rather than the subject matter by the method (Freud, Jung, and the clinical-phenomenological tradition of dream studies hold this position).

My point, certainly not original, is that the enterprise of human science must entail and will always entail two complementary and constantly interacting "sciences." Each view attempts to eliminate or subsume the other but cannot succeed therein since their duality is inherent in the subject matter. All human reality can be taken twice over, in terms of meaning and cause, subject and object. The subject–object division itself and the postmodern realization of our inherent relativity and perspectivism guarantees that any foreseeable science of human beings will be perpetually two-sided.

Accordingly, we cannot follow the humanistic-phenomenological rejection of laboratory experimentation as somehow antithetical to our inner being and suitable only for the investigation of the nonhuman physical universe. For good or ill, the would-be control and manipulation of others are as much a part of everyday life in societies as are empathy and understanding. Indeed, some have suggested experimental and technological control of nature is an extension of that same social propensity to control others—an extension and projection of the motor capabilities of the human body into the nonhuman realm.

It may even be, as the philosopher Martin Heidegger has stated, that the very notion of an inward subjectivity as a central characteristic of modern humanity is a secondary consequence of the scientific and technological revolution. By locating a nonhuman objective order to be manipulated and controlled for our own purposes, we paradoxically render our relative and shifting motivations as the "measure of all things." Consciousness then becomes the hypothetical residual after all attempts to measure the physical universe, a residual which then warrants, finally, in the nineteenth and twentieth centuries, its own suitably "subjective" sciences (phenomenology, hermeneutics, structuralism, deconstructionism).

On the other hand, even the most toughminded and objective psychologists, when they approach dreams or any other manifestation of human living, cannot rid themselves of the tendency to organize their materials in terms of awareness, verbal description, and intuition. This is fortunate, whether explicitly acknowledged by these investigators or not, for there are no *human* facts that come for inspection apart from complex and largely tacit layers of cultural and personal meanings (Koch, 1985). This is perhaps most clear in the primacy of the great clinical neurologists in the scientific understanding of brain functioning—with their reliance on meticulous observation, classification, and the case study method (Luria, 1973). It is not just that pure laboratory experimentation suffers from the special indeterminacies of method created by experimental materials that are reflexive and respond humanly to the experimental situation and its "demand features" (Orne, 1969). Rather, the experimental tradition cannot get away with its widely heralded assumption that natural observation and case study methods are merely an adjunct to laboratory methodology, suitable only for the generation of hypotheses.

How can one of these methodological perspectives, experimentation or natural observation, be relative or secondary to the other when it takes just as long to become a good clinician and natural observer as to become a skilled experimentalist? Progress in any area in the social sciences at a given historical point may come from the shift either to the laboratory or to the field. Witness the development of Jane Goodall's research tradition of natural observation of apes in the wild, which *followed* years of laboratory work with these relatives of man. The scientific questions she asks cannot be answered, or often even asked, at the Yerkes laboratories.

We are perhaps very lucky that our own nature is not so easily subdued by either the scientific or the humanistic hegemony, but continues to admit of such multiple accountings—perhaps just because it is multiple and contradictory in its actual function. Our postmodern relativism is associated with the sense that any "truth" evaporates precisely as we approach for a closer look. Accordingly, what is now of real intellectual interest may be not just a new discovery confirming this or that theoretical model, but raising our hands precisely when we locate the next complementarity of theory or indeterminancy of method. This has something to do with that capacity to be aware of what we do *not* know, basic to so many discussions of creativity, but even more with the importance of staying open and pluralistic in our view of our own nature and avoiding all forms of theoretical totalitarianism. What is lacking in dream studies, as surely as in most current psychology, is the enforced dialogue of these curiously antagonistic fraternal twins of the social scientific method. For it is in their collisions, recombinations, and separations that our double nature stands forth and our knowledge of that nature progresses and even deepens.

Yet having sounded these noble sentiments of coexistence and dialogue between mutually exclusive perspectives in dream studies, one must still ask whether any psychology of dreaming must not be inherently skewed toward the subjective polarity. Can we even begin to study the dream without acknowledging it first and foremost as an immediately experienced subjective state—a lived story with rich imagistic properties and powerfully felt meanings? The accessibility of dreaming to science, however defined, depends entirely on the individual's later description of his or her subjective experience. Any currently optimal balance/antagonism between objectivity and subjectivity in psychologies of the dream is itself superimposed on a phenomenon that renders the latter unavoidably primary—which is of course why most academic psychologists give dreaming such a wide berth; even those who do call themselves dream researchers often end up sounding quite defensive in their scientism.

The key to this analysis comes from Paul Ricoeur's recent writings (1984–85) on history as a social scientific discipline. In the face of increasing quantification in historical research that utilizes the statistical methods of psychology, sociology, and economics, Ricoeur argues that however compelling such objectivity, history is characterized by a primacy of the narrative mode. Historians are telling a story and to that they must always return. Quantitative and causal studies of past societies are, for Ricoeur, important primarily because they help clear away impediments to more satisfying narrative formulations. All historians must ultimately see their data in terms of its potential to smooth or complicate the *story* of those times, places, and people.

Similarly, unless one concentrates exclusively on glucose metabolism in individual cells during sleep, and takes not even an implicit interest in concomitant experience, psychophysiological and experimental-cognitive research on dreams will always return at some point to the potential implications for meaning and interpretion—whether these implications be positive or negative mattering not a wit here. For it is the question of meaning that is fundamental to our interest in dreams: how am I to understand this thing that seems partly full of powerful meaning and partly nonsense?

The ubiquity of this return to meaning is most clear with psychoanalytic researchers like Charles Fisher, Richard Jones, and Greenberg and Pearlman, who suggest modifications in Freud's dream theory on the basis of laboratory findings. It is still clear when researchers like Hobson and McCarley suggest that we reject personal significance for dreams of paralysis, falling, flying, or sexual arousal, since these are the products of an impersonal physiological process. Whether these authors are wholly correct, partially correct, or dead wrong, meaning is still their preoccupation. It is even present when Crick and Mitchison or Foulkes advances the "scientific" view of dreams as semantic froth—for such repeated denials of meaning affirm just as inexorably that meaning must be the fundamental question. The issue of meaning and interpretation is *forced* on the observer by the very nature and variability of dreaming. It is a bit like atheists and God. Thus the issue of meaning is fundamental to dream studies whether or not one concludes that all dreaming is neural dumping or imposed syntax without semantics. These are just negative answers to that more fundamental question, which will continue to interest human society as long as people dream.

The primacy of the question of meaning has a number of consequences for dream research. Certainly it necessitates the development of a cognitive psychology of dreaming, since there is no other way to investigate whether the processes involved in dream formation entail symbolic operations. It also necessitates all possible variations on a method that might best be termed *descriptive phenomenology*, since research must always come back to empirical descriptions of dream experience. This in turn raises two fundamental methodological points that go to the heart of the concern about whether dream research can be "scientific" and whether there might be more than one way to understand that term in the human sciences.

1. Certainly the demand characteristics of sleep laboratories, including in-

terview techniques, can influence something as subjective and personal as the dream report. Recall for color and verbal dialogue in dreams seems to fall off rapidly (as in waking experience), so that the dreamer must be specifically questioned to ascertain their presence (Snyder, 1970). This surely communicates the experimenter's interest and changes what would otherwise have been a spontaneous dream report. Also, a dream first reported in the middle of the night, upon a subject's being awakened in the laboratory, will be recounted as a more cohesive story when it is described again in the morning (Antrobus, 1978). Which report is more "true" to the actual dream experience? The first report is modified by sleepiness, the second by economy of communication. In studies by Cartwright and Kaszniak (1978) and Greenberg and Pearlman (1975), subjects avoided reporting certain dreams—often sexual—to one interviewer while describing them more freely to another (depending, for instance, on the sex of the interviewer, or whether one was talking to a laboratory technician or one's own psychotherapist). These are typical examples, however, of the variability found in all psychological research.

More profound doubts about the validity of dream reports seem misplaced. Most people take their dream experiences very seriously and literally (for whatever reasons) and visibly struggle to find just the right words. This is in marked contrast to the subjective reports studied by Nisbett and Wilson (1977), where people fall back on commonsense beliefs about their own experience that may manifestly contradict their observed behavior. Although the dream is surprisingly dialogic, both individually and culturally, it is really not all that malleable. On the contrary, it is curiously isolated from the rest of one's life and from one's other dreams as well (Rechtschaffen, 1978). For instance, individuals interested in lucid dreams may struggle for months and years with widely available techniques for their induction and report total failure. (Others, whose cognitive and perceptual propensities favor dream lucidity, may report their first lucid dream the night after first reading about them—see chapter 8.) Similarly, we find the same variations in types of dreams across tribal, classical, and modern societies, suggesting a cross-cultural commonality among the basic *forms* of dream experience. Certainly there are a robustness and regularity within the variations of dreaming that render it open to systematic empirical study.

Accordingly, it is as true in dream research as in all other areas of psychology that—depending on the features of dreaming that are the focus of research—demand features, expectations, and "grammar" may or may not be a problem. These methodological effects are probably least present in studies of dream bizarreness, which is so salient and striking that it is spontaneously communicated by most subjects. The investigation of dreaming as a cognitive

process does not involve methodological barriers any greater than those elsewhere in modern psychology or science generally.

2. Most extensive studies of dreams, clinical and experimental, include
several illustrative dreams. This tacitly acknowledges the primacy of the dream
experience on all levels of research. When such examples are few or nonexistent, as in Cohen's otherwise admirable review of the experimental literature
(1978) or in Antrobus's current cognitive formulations of the dream process
(1987), the reader will feel that something is missing. Sample dreams are
necessary to comprehend the full implications and potential success or failure
of the model presented. The presence of the dream report at the center of this
research area makes dream psychology one of the places where the phenomenological and experimental paradigms of the human sciences will be necessarily and continuously juxtaposed—hopefully to creative effect.

Accordingly, this book includes dream reports from diverse subjects, including myself. Concerning reporting of my own dreams, I cite Lowy (1942)
on the utility of one's own dreams where one is concerned with the immediate sources of the dream and the cognitive properties of the dream experience.
The deeper psychodynamics of dream interpretation, on the other hand, may
well require that one's own insight be supplemented by the insights of others.
My primary concern is with the possibility of natural variations in dream
forms and dream cognition. Unlike Medard Boss, I have not had the opportunity to collect multiple dreams and complete background circumstances from
a sufficiently diverse group of people. I have, however, kept a continuous
dream diary for seventeen years, much of it long before I had any particular
theoretical axes to grind. In my own research on the varieties of dream bizarreness (Hunt et al., 1982), I found that while each subject has a predominant
style of dream experience, most subjects will on occasion range across the full
spectrum of potential dream forms. My own dreams offer just such a spectrum—so it seems reasonable to make some use of them.

Yet in so doing, I find myself on the dangerous grounds of self-display
that pioneers like Freud, Jung, and Lowy have somehow trod with far more
grace than recent contributors. Since attention to the cognitive fabric of
dream experience is paramount to this book, I plan to be even more circum-
spect than Freud himself (who interestingly enough offered no deep interpretations of his own dreams). If I proceed aright, my clinical readers may be
annoyed at the sketchy incompleteness of my personal commentaries on these
dreams, while my more academic colleagues will criticize my use of the full
range of anecdotal materials and observations available to me as part of the
empirical reality against which dream theories and experimental research must
be judged. Such usage is not substantially different from that in the field of

clinical neurology, except that where it links tests, behavior, and subjective reports to lesions in the brain, I link unusual variations in the dream process across individuals and special groups to underlying *cognitive* capacities.

Any true science of dreams requires close attention to the widest variety of specific dreams, described and classified as meticulously as humanly possible. It is in the juxtaposition of phenomenology and normative experimental research that illumination is to be sought.

CHAPTER 2

Further Antinomies of Dreams, Dreaming, and Dream Research

H AVING set out the superordinate dimensions of our analysis—
cognitive science versus organismic-holistic cognition, Freud versus Jung, representational versus presentational symbolism, and
causal process versus meaning—we complete our review of the literature by considering the more specific antinomies of current dream research.
Each side of these contrasting dimensions is supported by important research
findings and consistent theory. This in itself may illustrate the actual multiplicity of the processes of dreaming. It is equally important to locate whatever
syntheses are afforded by this material and to understand them as necessarily
provisional and temporary—both because of the open-ended and indeterminate
nature of psychology and because of the natural diversity of dreaming.

Some of this material is highly technical, but if the reader perseveres,
patterns and solutions will emerge. We begin by seeing just how problematic
and complex the easy generalizations from early REM-state research have now
become.

The Centrality versus Irrelevance of the REM State

The attempt to derive the phenomena of dreaming from the unique physiology of the REM state has fallen on hard times. Early findings from the 1950s

23

and 1960s of associations between more activated or phasic aspects of REM with more vivid, emotive dreaming have often failed to be replicated. Even the old standby of penile tumescence as an invariant feature of the REM state among men has given way to the finding that 50 percent of erections during sleep occur outside of REM (Wasserman et al., 1982). Despite Hobson and McCarley's efforts to account for the more striking forms of dream bizarreness in terms of REM physiology (1977), we are forced to note that the most intense hallucinations and altered states that occur during sleep appear in NREM phases, for example, the hypnagogic period of sleep onset, often likened to the effects of psychedelic drugs, and the contentless horror of night terrors (*pavor nocturnus*), massive startle reactions that occur during the deep sleep prior to REM periods.

Even sophisticated attempts such as that of Ernest Hartmann (son of Heinz Hartmann, the originator of psychoanalytic ego psychology) to explain dream phenomena via REM-specific changes in biogenic amines (1982) can be subjected to the same critique. Biogenic amines are chemicals that facilitate and inhibit synaptic transmission in the brain. Coordinating the research on biogenic amine production in waking, REM, and NREM sleep, Hartmann suggests that the depleted noradrenalin levels which initiate the REM state are associated with the deficits of reasoning and memory typical of dreaming. High REM-state levels of dopamine, generally associated in wakefulness with neural energization and drivenness, will lead to some of the primitive "instinctual" behaviors of dreams, and low serotonin would be associated with hallucinatory experience and propensity to startle. Hartmann concludes that the REM state mixes the depleted noradrenalin and serotonin levels typical of normal deep sleep with the high dopamine levels of alert wakefulness—making REM sleep as unique biochemically as it seems to be neuroanatomically (i.e., in REM sleep central nervous system arousal is combined with muscular paralysis). But those who study daydreams in laboratory settings (Foulkes and Fleischer, 1975; Hoyt and Singer, 1978; Antrobus, 1986) report that hallucinatory dreamlike narratives and occasional altered-state-like bizarreness occur in normal subjects ostensibly independently of any REM-specific biochemistry.

Whatever the dreaming process, it can unfold independently of REM physiology. Harry Fiss (1979) shows this most strikingly in a study where subjects awakened from nearly completed REM periods described far more vivid fantasies in response to pictures from the Thematic Apperception Test (TAT) than those awakened at the beginning of REM periods—when presumably the biochemical priming of any physiological need would be at its highest. In other words, the need to dream pursues its own course and seeks its own completion potentially independent of the underlying biochemistry of REM sleep.

Any mind–brain isomorphisms left after such research are diffuse and general. Dreamlike and altered-state experiences occur during periods of relatively high cortical activation, inattention to immediate surroundings, and lack of movement (West, 1962; Antrobus, 1986). This general condition characterizes not only the REM state, but sleep onset, much NREM dream experience, and most hallucinatory syndromes, not to mention periods of deep mental concentration during wakefulness.[1]

Consider the three major functions suggested for the mammalian REM state of "activated" or "paradoxical" sleep. At first glance they seem independent from the phenomenology of dreaming and its variously proposed functions. But perhaps the connections looked for have been too specific.

Evolutionary functions. There is considerable agreement that REM sleep, with its paradoxical activation of the central nervous system (CNS) and inhibition of major muscular activity, appears as a regular feature of sleep as the relative size and complexity of the brain increases. In general, the evolutionary development of brain size and complexity is directly associated with correspondingly longer and deeper periods of sleep recovery. Tortoises, for example, sleep periodically throughout a twenty-four-hour period, their sleep consisting in phases of inactivity not easily distinguishable from wakefulness on electrophysiological measures. In contrast, human slow-wave sleep (EEG stage 4), occurring first in the nightly sleep cycle and made up first after sleep deprivation, bears some electroencephalographic similarity to a light coma; it is strikingly distinct from the EEG of alert wakefulness. The lengthy and relatively deep sleep of higher mammals seems to function as a restitution necessitated by the complexity of their nervous systems, and there is evidence of decreased glucose synthesis within single neurons throughout NREM and REM sleep (Ramm and Frost, 1986).

On the other hand, whereas length and depth of sleep seem to be a function of the evolution of the nervous system, REM sleep seems to be a function of the amount of preceding slow-wave sleep (Horne, 1978, 1983). The length of each REM period increases as morning approaches and the deeper phases of sleep fall away. Prior to morning wakefulness, the brain, while still asleep, is in a condition of CNS arousal very close to that of alert wakefulness. This has led to the hypothesis that the REM state arouses and maintains a condition of cortical tonus to compensate for the lower tonus necessitated by the restitutive function of deep sleep. The REM state readies the organism for adaptive behaviors necessary on awakening (Ephron and Carrington, 1966). A piece of confirming evidence comes from the existence of the fitful REM-like bursts in some reptiles and a more definite if erratic REM sleep in birds—in which the motor coordination necessary for flying is associated with a highly developed cerebellum and so a larger and more complex nervous system than that found in most reptiles.

On the broadest level of analysis, this cortical homeostasis model of REM is consistent with all theories of dream function that emphasize adaptation to the problems and stress of everyday reality.

Fetal and neonatal functions. The REM state, in its most regular and organized form, is confined to mammals. It does not seem to be present in the evolutionarily transitional egg-laying monotremes (Winson, 1985). This has suggested a possible function of REM specific to fetal development, reinforced by the discovery that all mammals which experience REM show the highest percentage of REM sleep immediately after birth, sharply decreasing with maturity. In mid- to late gestation, the fetus spends most if not all its time in the REM state. In addition, the REM state in mature mammals (and man) is characterized by poikilothermy—the form of body temperature regulation in which temperature is controlled by the surrounding environment (typical for reptiles). In other words, the internal temperature regulation that characterizes waking and NREM sleep in mammals is specifically absent in the REM state. Thus we are unable to shiver while in the REM state. The fetal condition is also characterized by poikilothermy, presumably because body temperature is regulated by the mother.

It has been suggested (Roffwarg, Muzio, and Dement, 1966) that the REM state is a biologically efficient condition for the rapid maturation and high metabolism typical of fetal development. The REM state would also prevent the energized physical movements that otherwise might result from such a high arousal condition and that might endanger the fetus.

The continued predominance of REM sleep during the neonatal period (in human beings, especially for the first three months) also suggests that it plays some role in the endogenous maturation of brain structures (Roffwarg, Muzio, and Dement, 1966; Emde, Gaensbauer, and Harmon, 1976). Fetal-neonatal REM seems to constitute a critical period beginning six months after conception (when anomalous eye movement patterns can indicate major neurological abnormalities [Birnholz, 1981]) and ending six months after birth (when continuation of intense bursts of rapid eye movement, normative earlier, is associated with retardation [Becker and Thomas, 1981]). Research by Robert Emde (Emde, Gaensbauer, and Harmon, 1976) has shown that during the first three months of neonatal life a cluster of behaviors—smiles, fussiness, erections, and startle responses—appears mainly during the REM state. These behaviors seem homeostatically regulated as more or less equivalent processes of nervous discharge. Between three and six months, the first appearance of NREM restitutive sleep is associated with a shift from this organization of behaviors to a more active stimulus-seeking and the first appearance of social smiling. In other words, REM-state smiling ("smiling at the angels," as it is sometimes called) appears before the social smiling of wakefulness. Roffwarg adds complex emotional expressions of perplexity, amusement, and disdain to smiling as social behaviors that first appear in the REM state (Roffwarg, Muzio, and Dement, 1966). These behaviors seem to rehearse and anticipate capacities that appear in wakefulness only weeks later. Such findings have led Michel Jouvet (1967) to suggest that the REM state plays a crucial role in the maturation of a species-specific "instinctive" repertoire.[2]

On a suitably general level of analysis, it is interesting to note how consistent is this maturational role of REM sleep with theories of dream function that stress anticipation (Adler, Jung) and "playful" rehearsal of developing capacities (Maeder, Piaget, Jones).

✗ *Learning and memory.* The function of REM sleep most obviously linked to theories of dreaming is its suggested role in learning and memory consolidation—an issue that runs like a red thread through the following chapters, since it is widely claimed that memory models can explain all the psychological characteristics of dreaming.

Several animal researchers have demonstrated that REM deprivation immediately before or after the learning of complex tasks impairs that learning. Others have shown an enhancement of the amount and intensity of REM sleep following acquisition of such tasks—but not when the animal has been unable to learn successfully (Block, Hennevin, and Leconte, 1981; Fishbein and Gutwein, 1981; Smith, 1981). The suggestion that REM is crucial to memory consolidation is further strengthened by the discovery that projections from the pontine formation that mediate noradrenaline levels in the forebrain terminate there in the hippocampal and amygdala formations that are responsible for memory consolidation (Hartmann, 1981; Zornetzer, 1981). The removal of the hippocampus in human beings (as an experimental procedure to control epileptic seizures originating from the area) and in animals allows the retention of previously learned materials but destroys the capacity for new learning. Indeed, one of the major physiological features of the REM state is the presence of activated hippocampal theta rhythms, which are also characteristically present in wakefulness during exposure to emotionally arousing stimuli

(Winson, 1985). It has been suggested that learning and attentional processes in the forebrain deplete biogenic amines like noradrenalin and dopamine, which in turn triggers REM sleep in order to restore amine levels to an optimal level for memory consolidation (Hartmann, 1981; Stern, 1981).

But is this effect on memory consolidation specific to REM physiology or is it a secondary by-product of the extra consolidation time afforded by the CNS arousal that is part of REM sleep? For instance, in rats, electrical stimulation to the reticular formation (associated with brain arousal) after learning blocks the deleterious memory effects of previous REM deprivation and eliminates the immediate postlearning augmentation of REM sleep (Block, Hennevin, and Leconte, 1981). There are other indications that the periodic arousals created by the REM state can function as a means of lowering stress: REM deprivation, for example, leads to poorer emotional adaptation to a stressful stimulus like an upsetting movie (Greenberg, 1981). Perhaps REM sleep simply finishes *whatever* is pending from immediately previous experience, much as all psychological processes are intensified in periods of higher activation during wakefulness. In that way the "functions" of the REM period would be as multiple as the psychological phenomena that can be completed during it.

While there *is* much evidence along these lines, it does now seem that there is something specific to memory consolidation that is not just a by-product of REM. Over the past few years Carlyle Smith (1981) has studied the REM augmentation following learning in rats over several days and has found that these increases occur as regular "windows" that climb steadily over a six-day period (Smith and Lapp, 1984). Deprivation of REM during these specific windows of augmentation was at its most effective in disrupting prior learning between 48 and 60 hours after training (Smith and Kelly, 1986). A three-day period of maximum vulnerability is consistent with protein synthesis models of long-term memory consolidation (Drucker-Colin, 1981). So much for Crick and Mitchison on neural dumping, except in the limited sense that recall of some materials necessitates the forgetting of others. [3]

This lengthy preoccupation with the multiple functions of REM physiology would be perverse indeed in a dream book if the process of dreaming were truly independent of it. It is just here that recent work by Adrian Morrison (1983; Morrison and Reiner, 1985) comes to the rescue, demonstrating that REM physiology is actually a specialized version of a more general organismic function—the orientation response. On the present interpretation, Morrison provides us with a common underlying psychophysiology for the diverse settings associated with the full range of dreaming and dreamlike experiences.

Morrison replicated Jouvet's famous surgical procedure on cats, in which the descending neural fibers that inhibit movement during REM are cut. This procedure releases overt behaviors during REM sleep that have impressed many observers as acted-out cat dreams. Morrison noted some further effects. During wakefulness the cats were indiscriminately mobile in strange surroundings. They seemed to lack features of the orientation response to novel stimuli (Pavlov's "curiosity reflex"), which involves fixation of attention and concomitant cessation of movement. These damaged cats literally had the "curiosity that killed the cat"—without the freezing that would ordinarily save them. There are indeed striking similarities between the REM state and the orientation response. Both are initiated from the same giant pontine cells of the brain stem; both involve motoric paralysis, activated cortex, elevated brain temperature, hippocampal theta rhythms (associated with short-term memory processing and attention to novel stimuli), and even poikilothermy. Morrison thus suggests that the neural systems controlling REM sleep are the same as those responsible for the orientation response in wakefulness. The REM period thus becomes a special reuse (serving potentially multiple functions) of the orientation response. Glenn (1985) extends this model by linking the more specific and periodic phasic activations within the REM state to the organismic startle reaction—both are suddenly activated, and both involve intensified motor paralysis. Startle is an especially strong orientation response.

The implications of this reclassification of REM physiology are significant on several fronts. As Morrison points out, it is consistent with previous suggestions (see Vogel, 1978a) of a forebrain influence on REM sleep and perhaps even initiation of its brain stem activation, since the orientation-curiosity response clearly entails cortical responsiveness. Morrison revives earlier suggestions that there is a limbic-frontal center for REM sleep (Morrison and Reiner, 1985), supplementing Hobson and McCarley's (1977) exclusive emphasis on the brain stem. Indeed, experimental electrical stimulation of the cortical areas adjacent to the hippocampus and amygdala has been associated with vivid dreamlike states (Penfield and Perot, 1963; Mahl et al., 1964; Halgren et al., 1978). The orientation response model of the REM state also calls into question Hobson and McCarley's assumption that the activation of cells in the pontine formation constitutes a "random" input to the cortex, since the curiosity reflex depends on the cortical processing of information in order to recognize its novelty. This would entail complex feedback between the cortex and the brain stem.

The orientation response model also confirms nature's parsimony. Its specialized and regular recurrence in sleep as REM physiology would compensate for the low arousal levels of restitutive deep sleep, provide endogenous stimulation during the critical fetal-neonatal period of CNS maturation, and aid memory consolidation of novel situations, as determined also by the requirements of protein synthesis in long-term memory. In addition, all of the major functions proposed for the *dreaming* process—memory consolidation, stress adaptation, mood regulation, wish fulfillment, problem solving, anticipation, play—entail the orientation response as their organismic background. Such functions would not only be by-products of a state based on the orientation response, they could as easily and in turn have a causal effect upon it.

Finally, Morrison provides us with a common organismic background for dreaming and altered states of consciousness. These are often separated in recent treatments because they seem to occur in such physiologically distinct settings—REM sleep, the hypnagogic period (with its common startle responses), activated NREM sleep, fantastic forms of daydreaming, sensory deprivation, hypnosis, meditative states, and even night terrors, catatonia, and the early onset phases of schizophrenia. The last three phenomena are associated with *tonic immobility*, an intensified form of the orientation response found across the evolutionary spectrum as part of a response to intense stress (Gallup, 1974). Here, also, we have a brain-stem-controlled immobility in the form of a tonic paralysis, more energized and complete than the loss of major electrical activity in the muscles during REM. Tonic immobility is based on the simultaneous and total flexion of opposed muscles in the major muscle groups and is associated with the "waxy flexibility" of catatonia and all situations that involve "freezing in horror." Where it had been customary to separate night terrors (as massive EEG stage 4 startle responses) from anxiety dreams, with their common inability to move or cry for help during and immediately after the REM dream, we now see that they have a common physiological basis—differing primarily in degree of intensity.

We might note that in human beings, creatures for whom novelty is characteristically cognitive-symbolic, an endogenously driven orientation response becomes hard to separate conceptually from our general capacity for creative reverie and intellectual concentration. Are intellectuals and artists in their times of intensely aroused concentration—motionless, prone to startle on disruption, and subject to occasional sexual and aggressive activation—also incapable of shivering while so absorbed?

We have come full circle: dreaming and REM physiology, although capable of appearing as separate causal processes, also share a background organismic state. What is the significance, then, of recent pessimism about REM psychophysiology and the failure to replicate the mind–brain isomorphisms of the 1950s and 1960s? It would seem that the level of analysis has been wrong and the associations sought both too specific and too general.

1. A number of investigators have noted surprising individual differences in the somatic manifestations of emotion. For example, some people when

frightened may show heart-rate variability, breathing changes, muscular tension, flushing, and so on. Thus Hauri and Van de Castle (1973) suggested that failure to find general associations between variations in REM state physiology and dream content may reflect these differences in individual responsiveness. The same feature of REM physiology might be associated with very different dream content in different individuals.

2. Certainly, if we adopt a level of analysis better suited to the generality of the orientation response, there is ample evidence that the intensification characteristic of REM-state physiology is reliably associated with a correspondingly intensified or exaggerated dream experience. For instance, Hartmann (1982) gave subjects small amounts of L-Dopa, a precursor to brain dopamine that in much larger doses produces energization in chronic Parkinson's patients (Sacks, 1983). The amounts used by Hartmann were not enough to change waking behavior, but they did extend and intensify REM periods. The resulting dreams were correspondingly more vivid, emotionally intense, and even nightmarish and bizarre in form. Similarly, narcolepsy is a sleep disorder associated with the intensification of REM sleep and a propensity to enter the REM state immediately upon falling sleep. The REM states of narcoleptics are unusually long and especially intense physiologically, with a correspondingly intensified dreaming—often nightmarish and including vivid sensations of flying and falling (Vogel, 1976). If such experimental and natural intensifications of REM physiology can elicit similar intensifications of dreaming, then clearly the REM state still offers a selective window for the investigation of dreaming—whatever their potential for relative separation in other contexts.

Years ago the pioneer psychoanalyst and clinical neurologist Paul Schilder (1924), in rejecting any simple relation between brain and mind based on linear causality, pointed out that if we consider neurophysiology and experience from a practical methodological perspective they appear as separate causal series, potentially independent and yet capable of interaction, so that either can determine and direct the other. Alcohol or LSD may lead someone to act on or change a decision, but the physical effects of either substance can be all but completely put aside in order to cope with a sudden emergency that requires one's total attention and energy. Sometimes one can drown one's sorrows, sometimes not. Personality still shows through the dementia of general paresis. Schilder's term for this form of coexistence and potential interaction is the suggestion that these causal streams can "cogwheel" into each other, especially in conditions of high arousal. This helps to understand how at times the penile erections of REM, its vestibular activation, or its phasic startles are dramatically and directly reflected in dream content, while more typically they appear only tangentially, if at all.

The antinomy of the relevance *or* irrelevance of REM physiology to dream studies must be recast. Neither extreme is correct. Certainly no one should feel obligated by the simple-minded models of mind–brain isomorphisms imported into the early sleep lab studies. It is foolish indeed to base our dream research on any single "solution" to what many see as the ultimate unsolved scientific dilemma—the relation of consciousness and neural tissue. Mind–brain relationships will vary by level of analysis and specific features being studied. The only rule seems to be "catch as catch can."

The Centrality versus Irrelevance of Psychoanalytic Theory

Nothing has caused more controversy than the question of how Freud's complex model of dream formation and the dreaming process fares in light of the current psychophysiology of the REM state and cognitive science of dreaming.[4]

At one extreme we have the views of Charles Fisher (1965) and Richard Jones (1970), who, making allowance for what Freud could not know (i.e., the specifics of the REM state and its biochemically mediated periodicity), argue that Freud's theory of dreaming receives considerable confirmation. On the other hand, Hobson and McCarley and Foulkes reject psychoanalysis, claiming that it is based on misleading and archaic notions of neuronal hydraulics and "the instincts."

Since all twentieth-century dream theories are to some degree reactions to Freud's 1900 classic, full consideration of *The Interpretation of Dreams* is spread throughout this book. With respect to the more extreme rejections of Freud's dream theory, however, it is worth noting an irony: if the dreaming process is *potentially* independent of specific REM psychophysiology then two points become apparent. First, the latter cannot be used to refute Freud's model of dream formation—which itself involves elaborate submodels of memory, the relation between language and imagery, childhood development, the restorative functions of sleep, and the "instinctive" roots of the latent dream "wish." Second, making some allowance for recent physiological research and giving some room for necessary revisions of neurology since his 1895 *Project for a Scientific Psychology*, some of Freud's conclusions about dreaming as a causal process are suprisingly consistent with current knowledge of the REM state as orientation response. Here, as in much else, Freud is often "right" but for the wrong reasons, or on grounds of organismic principles far more general than the overspecificities of his theory.

Consider Freud's basic assertion that dreaming is the guardian of sleep. He elaborates this, somewhat baroquely, by claiming that memories of unresolved problems from the previous day (day residues) and/or extraneous so-matic stimuli impinging on and disrupting sleep arouse related associations from the more distant past of similarly unresolved developmental crises—all more or less verbally formulated as "latent dream thoughts" or, perhaps better, "worries." These are barred from direct expression by the motor inhibition of sleep, which they threaten to disrupt. The resulting dream is a compromise formation between the need for continued sleep and the latent psychological material aroused within sleep. This compromise is expressed in a more primi-tive visual form and is disguised, displaced, and reorganized so as not to overtly disrupt sleep.

Much of this model is overly elaborated and its assumptions are often questionable. But the evolutionary model discussed above similarly explains REM sleep as compensatory for and protective of the lengthy deep sleep neces-sary for large-brained creatures. Without the periodic cortical arousal of the REM state, that restitution either would be endangered or would itself endanger cortical homeostasis. On a more general level of analysis, therefore, Freud's compromise model of dream formation is partially confirmed—at least if we admit the possibility of some very general psychophysiological isomorphisms in dream theory.

What of Freud's infrequently cited comment that the suppression of affect is the second major function of dreamwork, after the disguise/displacement of latent content? Freud suggests that a sort of "affect metabolism" is central to dreaming. It clearly fails with anxiety dreams and nightmares but is typically successful as part of the motor inhibition entailed by sleep, since the close relation between affect and muscular expression will carry the former out with the latter. One is hard put not to think here of REM physiology, which simulta-neously energizes and paralyzes major muscle groups, leaving only small mus-cle twitches and eye movements to attest to the heightened activation of this condition. Along these lines, Nielsen and Kuiken (1986) have shown that emotional arousal (EMG) is relatively suppressed immediately after laboratory awakening while subjects describe and free-associate to REM dreams. Indeed, many readers will be familiar with the curious delay of full emotional reaction to dreams, not only within the dream but continuing on awakening. That REM dream affect often rolls in so late may help to explain how it is that through dreams we often encounter such deeply emotional and powerful themes, which otherwise we might not be able to withstand long enough to be fully depicted and experienced. This simultaneous energization and inhibi-tion is reflected also within REM and post-REM affect—a phenomenon first described by Freud and connected by Kuiken to Morrison's orientation response.

More tangential, but perhaps more striking, is Freud's view that dreaming revives the situation of the physically helpless neonate. Freud describes early infancy as a period in which accumulating pressures of physical need (e.g., hunger, cold) necessarily lead to "internal affective discharge" (crying, flailing). This primary principle of discharge is only gradually assuaged by the hallucinatorily vivid re-cathexis of memory images of previous situations where intervention by the mother prevented affective disaster. The root of dreaming thus involves a formal regression to a parallel sort of motor helplessness and a necessity for emotive release through the same hallucinatory expression. Now, of course, very few psychoanalysts or child psychologists still believe hallucination to be a normal phase of neonatal development. But once again Freud manages, however fortuitously, to put his finger on a crucial feature of the REM/dream state—its revival of an organismic condition preponderant in fetal-neonatal development. In other words, *something* about dreaming and its physiological background (endogenous orientation response) may well be formally and functionally related to earliest infancy— whatever we may care to make of it.

Finally, we come to the most apparently farfetched of Freud's dream hypotheses—that full and free association to one's dreams will ultimately lead the interpreter to a latent sexual wish, triggered as part of the latent dream thoughts. Such wishes may also appear more directly within the manifest dream as one or more standard sexual metaphors (telephone poles and weapons, caves and tunnels, staircases, etc.). Surely we can dispense with this questionable assertion in light of sleep lab findings—especially since most neo-Freudian dream theorists minimize its importance (despite the fact that most of Freud's examples of dream interpretation after 1900 rest entirely on this search for direct sexual metaphor). Even here, however, we find a partial confirmation. Consider first the evidence of peripheral sexual activation (male and female) in both REM and the more alert phases of NREM sleep and juxtapose this with numerous experimental studies showing the potential for periodic incorporation of extraneous somatic stimuli into ongoing dreams— (*especially* tactile and kinesthetic stimulation [Arkin and Antrobus, 1978].) Given additional evidence that long-term REM deprivation in cats produces waking syndromes of hypersexuality, it does not seem farfetched to suggest that peripheral sexual activation could potentially "cogwheel" into dream content. Accordingly, a potential sexual level of meaning in any dream becomes a meaningful hypothesis and not the arbitrary imposition that our enlightened era sees in so much of Freud's original thought.

Freud's linkage of sexuality, dreaming, and creative imagination is echoed almost to the point of parody in Charles Fisher's report of a patient overmedicated for severe narcolepsy (Fisher et al., 1972). The hapless individual lost almost all REM sleep, waking erectile potency, and normal levels of imaginative creativity on the Rorschach and TAT. This does not, however, require us to follow Freud explicitly in his theory of a sexual-aggressive instigation for all dreaming. It seems much more plausible to assume that what we see here are the potential and occasional side effects of a more general organismic arousal state—much as threatened bears are sometimes reported to have erections as part of the diffuse and nonspecific autonomic activation of territorial response. Such a diffuse activation would also be entailed as part of the orientation response of REM sleep, rather than in any sense being its cause. But still, something more than a snicker is required for Freud's sexual etiology of dream formation. Again he is focused on a fundamental issue, but on very different grounds than might be advanced today.

Our present interest in Freud rests chiefly on his explicit and implicit cognitive psychology of dreaming and his often one-sided and incomplete dream phenomenology. This requires some overview of the variously proposed revisions of psychoanalytic dream theory in the light of both cognitive and clinical evidence. We have already rejected Freud's notion that the dream is "completely asocial." It is the burden of part 2 to show how Freud's (and Foulkes's) claim for a universal model of dream formation actually rests on an unwitting restriction of evidence to a particular *type* of dream—one indeed based on processes of memory reorganization and largely controlled by a verbal-propositional deep structure. It remains for now to point out how questionable it has seemed, from Jung to Ricoeur and many contemporary psychoanalysts, to regard the dream's ostensible shift to "image" as a developmental regression. It has been widely suggested that Freud's "primary process" fantasy thinking is not necessarily more primitive or preliminary than secondary process ego functions but instead undergoes its own parallel developmental history that eventuates in imaginative creativity (Galin, 1974; Kohut, 1971) and in certain expressive states of consciousness (Hunt, 1985b).

Finally, contemporary psychoanalytic dream interpreters like Greenberg and Pearlman, Palombo, and Jones agree that Freud overemphasized the necessity of disguise as a feature of all dream formation, as mediated by the displacement of affective significance in the shift from a latent to a manifest structure. Only by positing a systematic disguising function could Freud maintain that the latent meaning of *all* dreams takes the form of a "wish" (that semantically elastic concept so wedded to Freud's instinct model). Greenberg and Pearlman (1978) argue that the semantic reference of most dreams is obvious once the day residues have been located, since most dreaming is a direct, undisguised, metaphorical rendering of the recent past. They further suggest that the disguised meaning of Freud's famous specimen dream of "Irma's injection"—in which Freud locates a latent wish that his approach to psychology not prove laughably wrong to his colleagues—stems, not as Masson (1984) would have it, from his deliberate dissembling of his share in Fliess's disastrous nasal surgery, but quite simply from the fact that this more obvious meaning did not occur to Freud. Indeed, it is a fascinating feature of dream interpretation that the *obvious* meaning occurs more readily to others than to oneself. In other words, Freud's strict insistence on the universality of disguise in dreams may come ultimately from the inherent limitations of any self-analysis. In this sense, Freud missed the more obvious directly metaphorical properties of most dreams.

Still, to be fair to Freud (and to further stress the social malleability of dream formation), we need to recall that, while Freud himself states that dreaming without displacement and based only on condensation and visual representation is possible, he also stresses that the dreams of patients in long-term psychoanalysis, centered as it is on dream interpretation, become more and more elaborately disguised and baroque. We need to remember Freud's historical-cultural context and his tendency to draw analogies between dream censorship (and repression) and political censorship in the press. European modes of expression, perhaps especially in the political turmoil of the nineteenth and early twentieth centuries, tended to be more indirect and allusive than the style of communication favoured in contemporary North America—the historical-cultural context of most of the attempted revisions of Freud's dream theory.[5]

Accordingly, we should not be *too* quick to turn away from Freud's elaborate notions of disguise in favor of "open window" metaphors. Persons and peoples may well dream much as they communicate with others. In that sense Freud's own fragmented and apparently disorganized dreams—once replaced by his disarming but carefully edited free associations—present us with both the formidably complex and intricate manners of fin de siècle Vienna and Freud's own astonishingly intense but carefully hidden political nature, as later manifested within the inner circles of psychoanalysis.

Dream as Perception; Dream as Imagination

A lengthy debate pits phenomenological against both clinical and cognitive science approaches to the core of the dreaming process. Does it rest on a direct reuse of perceptual schemata, open to all creatures with an activated brain during sleep? Or, as Foulkes has it, are the roots of dreaming found in the more abstract imagery processes involved in symbolic memory and thought, thereby excluding most other mammals and even very young children? On the latter model, dreaming is necessarily a form of imagination, since your eyes are closed and you still seem to be seeing things. If so, all dreaming would depend for its very existence on symbolic and self-referential capacities. Those who approach dreaming from the perspective of research on daydreams (Singer, 1978; Antrobus, 1986) and sleep onset (Foulkes and Fleischer, 1975) are more likely to take this view, since daydreaming seems to begin as an isolated counterpoint to ongoing verbal rumination. Then, with the fading of cognitive orientation to time and place that comes with intense daydreaming, these imaginal reveries turn into the ostensibly perceptual scenes of extended dreaming.

On the other hand, in the cognitive psychology of imagery developed by Shepard (1978), Finke (1980) and Kosslyn (1981), the capacity for mental imagery is understood as part of perception and so in itself does not require a true symbolic capacity. The development of the latter would then be indexed by the complex narrative structure and metaphorical bizarreness of some dreaming. For Medard Boss the fundamental descriptive feature of dreaming is that it comes to us in the same fashion as our waking being-in-the-world. We are *in* a total setting, within which we perceive, move, think, *and* image.[6] Similiarly, it can be argued that the activation of the central nervous system in a way that closely overlaps with waking functioning will reproduce the normal features of such activation—namely, the species-specific perceptual life-world of the creature so aroused. An important component of such an argument is the "scanning hypothesis" for rapid eye movements during REM sleep, the view that like waking saccades they scan the features of the dreamt environment. Vivid daydreaming, on the other hand, is generally associated with a relatively fixed gaze (Singer, 1978), and rapid eye movements do not normally accompany the more thoughtlike phases of sleep onset and NREM sleep.

Foulkes (1985) follows Zenon Pylyshyn's (1981) approach to imagery which stresses the separation of perception and imagery and the dependence of imagery on what we "know" rather than what we "see." "Literally, of course, conditions of sleep make it impossible for dreaming to be any kind of perception. Dreaming is a mental-imaginal process: It can be nothing else" (Foulkes, 1982b, p. 281). But this only follows on the narrowest "copy" model of perception. It makes no sense at all if we concede any constructive aspect to perceptual activity.

Nonetheless, several studies by Foulkes suggest that we dream as we know the world rather than as we perceive it. Kerr, Foulkes, and Jurkovic (1978) report on the dreams of a patient with Turner's syndrome, an hereditary condition in which girls and women show an almost total incapacity in spatial problem solving and kinematic imagination (tests of imagined figure rotation), while their direct perceptual functioning seems unaffected. They see perfectly well, but may have difficulty finding their way around the block. Kerr and colleagues reasoned that if dreaming is a process of propositional thought— only *peripherally* expressed in visual imagery—then their patient would dream as she thought, without imagery. In fact her reported dreams had some of the properties of the Würzburg introspectionist accounts of imageless thought at the turn of the century. Complex dream situations and narratives were just "known," with no perceived detail whatsoever. Surely this is striking evidence of a sort of "propositional" or "left hemisphere" dreaming, which is thus demonstrated to be possible and thereby to be a possible *component* of all adult dreaming.

However, the problem with this and two other cases in which radical disability in kinematic imagination was associated with purely narrative-propositional dreaming (Kerr and Foulkes, 1981) is that, given the apparently close functional ties between perception and imagery, we may see here some sort of defensive compensation rather than the core of all dreaming laid bare. Indeed, the Turner's syndrome patient lacked not only visual components to her dreams, but auditory and tactile ones as well, which suggests that in this subject there was a diffuse inhibition of the imagery-perception side of dreaming in all modalities. This goes well beyond the hypothesis that the patient would dream literally and only as she thought.

More to the point is Kerr, Foulkes and Schmidt's important study of partially blind subjects (1982). Their visually precise dreams of settings encountered only after their blindness shows that these subjects indeed dreamed not as they perceived the world, but as they imagined it to be on the basis of the blurs and blotches of light and dark that had become their visual world. Yet even here, it is difficult to reach firm conclusions about an underlying dreaming process—especially given the unresolved debate in current cognitive science as to the relations among perception, imagery, and thought (Gardner, 1985). If we accept the evidence of Kosslyn (1981), Finke (1980), and more recently Farah (1985) that dream imagery may at times directly reuse the processes of visual perception, then what Kerr and colleagues may have demonstrated in the dreams of the partially blind is a kind of gestalt completion effect. Thus scotoma patients, who have blind spots due to central cortical damage to the visual association areas, are often not aware of any visual deficit because perception automatically constructs or fills in the missing area. Similiarly, rapid exposures on the tachistoscope, too fast to be accurately seen, may produce fully detailed "percepts" where there is a strong cognitive set for what might be presented. These examples —more perception than imagery— show how imagery may be utilized to complete what perceptual processes have started.

The need for further clarification of the potential interrelations of perception, imagery, and imagination is underlined by a series of research studies that seem to demonstrate the opposite effect, that dreaming rests on perceptual processes which may then interact in complex ways with more cognitively based imagery. The most striking evidence here comes from Roffwarg and his colleagues (1978). Subjects who continuously wore red-tinted goggles when awake carried the perceptual effects into subsequent REM dreams, reporting more red and less of all other colors. This effect appeared first in the earliest REM periods of the night, extending gradually over the three-day study into later periods. The goggle effects were present from the beginning in all episodes of sleep onset at whatever time of night, but they penetrated the least into the more cognitive, daydreamlike reports of NREM sleep—suggesting that sleep onset and early REM periods have a large perceptual component. These subjects dreamed as they saw, not as they knew. But there were also complex interactions between perceptually based imagery and memory processes, in that some subjects reported a red tint in dreams of scenes originating long before the experiment.

A study of dreaming in recent amputees with phantom limbs (Shukla et al., 1982) demonstrates that some subjects dream as they "sense" and others as they remember and "know." Almost 50 percent of the subjects dreamed of an intact limb in normal use (70 percent of those whose left arm had been lost— presumably because they would not get as much immediate corrective feedback as those who had lost a right arm or either leg). Many of these subjects were openly skeptical within their dreams since they "knew" the limb was missing. Later dreams, in which the limb is increasingly experienced as missing in the dream, seem to be associated with full psychological acceptance of the loss (Burd, 1984).

The intricate tangle of research on the scanning hypothesis proves similarly indeterminate and/or equally supportive of both positions—truly an occasion for postmodern rejoicing. Early experiments reported largely anecdotal coordination between REM-state eye movement patterns and corresponding dream events, but these have proven immensely difficult to replicate. Herman, Roffwarg, and colleagues (Herman et al., 1984) have reported statistically significant relationships between inferred eye movement patterns from dream reports and electrooculographic recordings just before awakening, but

only for high confidence predictions by the judges. (It has been equally difficult to establish relationships between eye movements and imaginatively recalled scenes during wakefulness.)

Research with the congenitally blind is also problematic. Some subjects
seem not to have any rapid eye movements, although vestigal electrical im-
pulses may not be picked up by normal measures. Other congenitally blind
subjects do show rapid eye movements, which suggests that they have nothing
to do with dream scenes—except that these eye movement patterns are more
disorganized and infrequent than those of sighted subjects (Rechtschaffen,
1973). The major doubt about whether rapid eye movements scan perceptlike
dream surroundings comes from the continued presence of rapid eye movements bursts in decorticate cats and humans (although these REMs are also
more disorganized) and from Jeannerod's (1975) finding that kittens in total
darkness for up to ten months show normal rapid eye movements during REM
sleep. It is less than clear what these kittens might have been scanning. Still,
as Rechtschaffen states, there is nothing to prevent a scanning function from
being added to an energy discharge function during maturation.

Systematic differences between waking saccades and rapid eye movements
was a further problem until Herman, Barker, and Roffwarg's (1983) demonstration that the slowness and reduced amplitude of eye movements in REM sleep
were similar to waking scanning patterns in darkened surroundings.[7] However,
Aserinsky (1986; Aserinsky et al., 1985) has recently advanced the coun-
terclaim that REM-state eye movements are more abrupt (jerky) and slower
than waking saccades and maintain the same velocity regardless of amplitude—in contrast to the increased velocity of waking eye movements with
wider scanning. Aserinsky posits a central inhibition in the REM state that
mechanizes eye movements. His findings, although disputed by Herman,
make it seem less likely that dreaming could operate like waking perception.

However, any such differences between waking and REM-state eye movements are consistent with previous research by Pompeiano (1970, 1974) demonstrating activation of the vestibular nuclei of the brain stem responsible for
phasic eye movements, muscle twitches, and phasic motor inhibition. The
vestibular system—linking brain stem, cerebellum, and the balance system of
the inner ear to body *and* eye movement in normal wakefulness—can under
special circumstances exert effects on waking eye movement similar to those
that Aserinsky found in REM sleep. Destruction of these vestibular nuclei reduced the amplitude of horizontal eye movements in awake monkeys, and
electrical stimulation to this same area produced waking eye movements of
constant velocity (Cohen, 1974). Since in normal wakefulness compensatory
eye movements in response to head turning and physical movement are con-

trolled by the vestibular system, it seems likely that the same processes would occur during the massive motor activation/inhibition of REM sleep. Certainly it makes sense that the normal vestibular movement in all waking eye movements would predominate over their scanning function during the endogenous activation of the REM state (thus their presence in moving but functionally blind kittens). This does not rule out the possibility that scanning is superimposed on these vestibular restraints. Eye movements of the REM state might reverse the balance between scanning and vestibular relations in waking eye movements, but the same system would operate nonetheless. Such a shift in dominance would also help account for the difficulties of correlating dream reports and eye movements. Accordingly, eye movement physiology cannot rule out the idea that rapid eye movements during sleep—whatever their balance of vestibular activation and scanning—are primordially involved in organizing a perceived environment, much as in wakefulness.

Physiology then returns us to cognitive psychology, as it so often does, without the final clarification that many would expect, and to the dilemma that dreaming can operate both as mnemic imagery and as perception. Some clarification may be found in Ulric Neisser's (1976) discussion of the similarities and differences among perception, imagery, and creative imagination. At its most basic level imagery would be "a detachment" of perceptual schemata from perceptual-action cycles, as manifested in the capacities for anticipation and recall that are part of learning in lower animals. The roots of imagery rest in the anticipatory aspect of perception itself. Neisser, influenced by Frederich Bartlett (1932), distinguishes this rudimentary form of imagery, as detached *perceptual* schemata, from "schematic rearrangements," which are necessary for the higher mental processes involved in self-reference, creative imagination, and language. To prove that dreaming—in whole or part, on all developmental levels or only in adult humans—is a form of thinking and not just a process resting on reproductive-anticipatory imagery detachments, we must look for evidence in the dream of creative reorganizations of previous experience. Insisting that dreaming is "imagery" does not tell us anything here because we must distinguish between imagery as detached perception—essentially part of perceptual functioning—and imagery as rearrangement, which merges with symbolic cognition.[8]

Especially if we follow out the view that all thinking ultimately reuses perceptual schemata, locating the core processes of perception versus memory versus imagination will be impossible. We are left with the more organismic-holistic traditions of cognitive psychology and their insistence that symbolic intelligence ultimately rests on and reorganizes the senses. We are back at the point of having to regard flying in dreams as both a sensory expression of vestibular activation and an imaginative metaphor. Dreaming thus becomes *the* focus for any study of the functional continuity and interrelations of percept and image.

Dreams in Young Children, Neonates, and Animals

If, as David Foulkes would have it, dreaming is a psycholinguistic skill, controlled by the abstract processes of inner speech and only secondarily generating a visual surface array, some fascinating and controversial consequences emerge. Any view that the core of the dreaming process is necessarily symbolic entails that very young children and animals would not dream, for they lack the necessary linguistic and/or self-referential capacities to construct imaginative scenarios. Their REM periods would be "empty" (Foulkes, 1982, p. 289) with respect to subjective experience. Note that this position instantly resolves (or, better, absolves us of—perhaps too quickly) the two chronic dilemmas of REM psychophysiology: first, what to make of the predominance of the REM state, associated in adults with dream recall, in late fetal and early neonatal periods (what could a fetus dream about?); and, second, how to conceptualize Jouvet's and Morrison's cats, operated on to remove the motoric inhibitions of REM physiology, who stalk, pounce, fight, and groom, oblivious to their actual surroundings, during their ambulatory REM periods. On Foulkes's model, neonatal and animal REM periods manifest only reflex motor discharge; there is no dreaming as subjective state and cognitive skill. Given the importance of its consequences for our understanding of dreaming, any evidence pertaining to the possibility of dreaming in young children and animals must receive a special scrutiny.

Children and Neonates

In the only longitudinal sleep lab studies ever done with young children, Foulkes (1982b, 1983b, 1985) found that three- to five-year-olds described content from only 27 percent of REM awakenings. Most of their REM periods indeed seemed "empty." Their reports were strikingly simple and short: single static images without narrative transformation or perceived physical movement, and without significant affect or an actively responding self figure. In form, these dreams were based on passive observation and their predominant content was of animals (38 percent of recall episodes) and themes of fatigue or sleep (25 percent of dream reports). Dreams described included a bird singing, chickens eating corn, and being "asleep and in the bathtub." Between the ages of five and seven, only 31 percent of REM awakenings produced recall, and although children almost never mentioned an active self figure, the snapshot quality of their dreams had given way to some physical movement and the appearance of very simple storylines. The stories were centered less on animals and more on social interactions—with the first mention of dream "strangers" (persons unknown to the child from waking experience). Between ages seven and nine (48 percent REM recall) we find the first major indications of an active participatory self figure. But strong affect, dream bizarreness, and complex narration only appear after age nine (79 percent recall).

Foulkes rightly calls attention to the way these dream stages parallel the waking development of cognitive skills as studied by Piaget, including the slow development of cognitive representation of self and children's difficulty with tasks that require kinematic imagery, such as imagined figure rotations of even the most elementary sort. Nonetheless, it should also be noted that developmental tests for kinematic imagery are based on instructions to image moving objects *voluntarily*—potentially quite separate from the spontaneous, nonvolitional imagery of dreams (or play). Piaget was testing the volitional and imitative reuse of perceptual schemata. The more basic question here is whether more elementary forms of imagery (e.g., spontaneous, eidetic), which in all probability are present, are recoverable at these early ages. Still, the earliest reporting of these first simple dreams *and* their rate of progression toward narrative complexity were correlated not with measures of recall but instead with tests of visual-spatial reorganization and abstraction, like the embedded figures test and block designs. It is of real interest then that Foulkes' own evidence suggests that dreaming originates in visual-spatial cognition rather than in linguistic-propositional thinking, which seems to be added later as dreaming becomes more complex. (A recent study by Butler and Watson [1985] demonstrates visual-spatial skills to be a major predictor of dream recall in adults as well.)

Foulkes's results are impressive and his methodology is careful. He is undoubtedly picking up a sequence of development only available through the sleep laboratory. However, as we will see, the laboratory method, like the spontaneous home recall about which Foulkes is so caustic, *also* entails its own indeterminacy and artificiality. We must still address the many anecdotal and clinical reports of narratively complex and bizarre dreams in children two and three years old, parents' reports of telltale confusion in awakening children that may indicate dreaming in the first and second years, and the powerful nightmares and anxiety dreams of very young children. An inclusive science of dreaming cannot afford Foulkes's outright rejection of such nonlaboratory observational data or his strange dismissal of nightmares as "abnormal" (and so the province of psychiatry and not cognitive psychology).

The dreams Foulkes's subjects recalled would, in all likelihood, have been forgotten without laboratory intervention, whereas it is the anecdotal dreams that actively intrude on children and their parents, thereby creating a major source of evidence concerning the inner life of young children. The developmental timing and formal quality of these dreams are strikingly different from those collected by Foulkes.

Whatever we ultimately make of them, some mention should be made of the earliest observational indications of dreaming. Of many possible examples, let us begin with Milton Erickson's (1941) report of an eight-month-old girl whose activity and laughter during sleep, while her father was away, resembled her customary behavior with the father. John Mack (1965) reported on a thirteen-month-old boy's terrified sleep cries of "boom! boom!" after the child had so shouted in response to the vacuum cleaner on the preceding day. In more detail, here are the dreams of a three-year-old boy immediately preceding and following the birth of a younger sibling and carefully recorded by his mother for her former therapist (Niederland, 1957). They cast doubt on Foulkes's assertion of a developmentally necessary absence at this age of kinematic motion, strong affect, self-representation, narrative sequence, active self-participation, and the presence of strangers.

> [He] woke up in the morning at his usual time and reported excitedly: "I had a special kind of sleep. It was raining and there was water jumping up and down, up and down. There were cars coming in the street, many cars." While relating this with great excitement, he started jumping up and down on the floor himself in an effort to explain how the water had been moving and jumping in his dream, and then added that it had been raining hard (no rain had fallen during all these days and nights).
>
> "There is a parakeet in the bed. He will bite you!" He then explained in vivid detail that "the parakeet flew out of the tunnel zoo from the cage where the sea lions are. The parakeet flew first to my house. He did not find me in my house, because I slept in grandma's house. The parakeet then flew all the way to grandma's house into my bed and bit me in my hand. He came in through the window."
>
> "Tonight I was a pigeon and I was flying."
>
> "I had another daddy." As an afterthought the dreamer then said again turning to his father: "The daddy was taller than you." (Niederland, 1957, pp. 194, 196, 199, 200)

Spontaneously reported dreams such as these are so vivid that children often insist that they really happened, as in the following early nightmares—from a boy of three years, nine months, with strong waking ambivalence toward his father, and from another boy, five and a half, aggressive toward his older sister and upset by direct exposure to his mother's affairs:

> The mother found him cowering at the side of his crib, his eyes white with fear. He was not consoled by her turning on the lights and comforting him. Through his sobs he said he was trying to get away from "the thing." This he described as big, black and like a man with an angry face with some red on it. He said it wanted to hurt him and had already hurt his hand, arm, and leg with one of the father's radio wires. He slept no more that night and for several nights feared going to bed and kept his parents up looking for "the thing" which he insisted was still under the pillow or in his room.

> "In the dream I was with a girl. The girl was on top of me and I was very scared. I threw her out of the window. I was very frightened I would be killed. God was upstairs. I went with the girl down to the cellar to get a Coke. God was angry and was going to kill us. He saw us running out of the cellar. I was scared and woke up." The only additional information he supplied concerning the dream was that the girl was four years older and that God was black and in heaven. He then protested, "It's too much. Let's not talk about it any more." (Mack, 1965, pp. 413, 418)

Some dreams of early childhood stay with the individual for a lifetime, and this is part of what calls our attention to the study of dreaming in the full context of "ecological validity" (Neisser, 1976). The long-term retention of such "big dreams" has been demonstrated by Kluger (1975), in his development of a classification system for "archetypal" dreams (especially imaginative and vividly bizarre, often with religious-mythological content: see chapter 9). Jung's own dream of an underground "phallus" on a throne, estimated to have occurred at age four, is well known; he explained it in his autobiography *Memories, Dreams, Reflections* as partially determining his inward preoccupations as a child and his later psychology. Another informant, born and raised in Italy, described the following dreams as occurring on three successive and uniquely memorable nights at age seven. He remembers a deep and continuing ambivalence about attending Mass even before these dreams. (On Foulkes's account these should not be possible):

1. In church. God tells him that his grandmother has died because he did not attend church. He walks toward the coffin swinging a crucifix menacingly and insisting that she must become alive again or he will kill God. Suddenly she sits up in her coffin.
2. The devil is by the water fountain in the town square attempting to carry away his cousin. He attacks the devil and strangles him, holding him under the flowing fountain water.

3. He is in church. The statue of Saint Anthony is holding the baby Jesus. Saint Anthony offers Jesus to the dreamer to hold, who says, "But I don't even go to church." Still Saint Anthony smilingly offers Jesus until the boy awakes, in the cold sweat that ended each of these dreams and imprinted them as critical life experiences.

Along these same lines, I have encountered several adult informants who report flying dreams, lucid dreams, and/or out-of-body experiences dating from ages four and five (see also Stephen LaBerge's own published memories [1985]). Lucid dreams and out-of-body experiences would appear to involve just the forms of abstract self-reference that Foulkes claims to be impossible at these ages. One of these subjects describes dreams from mid-childhood rather like the elaborate and semilucid dream adventures of *Little Nemo in Slumberland*, without any knowledge of that turn-of-the-century newspaper cartoon.

It will not do to dismiss lucid dreams and nightmares as somehow aberrant or pathological. In adults they correlate with most of the psychological tests that predict dream recall and dream vividness in normative samples—embedded figures, imaginal rotations, and capacity for imaginative absorption (see chapter 8). In other words they are intensified forms of the same dreaming whose laboratory development Foulkes traces so carefully. Most child psychiatrists seem to agree that although early traumata can contribute to nightmares, these dreams are so universal that they attest to conflicts inherent in all childhood development. The psychoanalyst John Mack (1965) even asserts that nightmares as often inaugurate a developmental advance as indicate emotional disturbance.

Reconciling this insistent case study material (see also Ablon and Mack, 1980) with Foulkes's laboratory norms raises questions about the exclusive use of the laboratory method (to be pursued in the next section). Perhaps dream recall itself is like pulling out an embedded figure (the rapidly receding dream) from the complex array of the child's actual situation on awakening. Certainly if very young children (or animals) dream, their recall would depend on the abstract self-referential capacity that allows us to reflect on our own experience, unless something in the dream (as in nightmares) pushes it on the child's waking experience. On the other hand, Foulkes, as perhaps Piaget, may be underestimating the symbolic-imaginative capacities of the very young child—as attested by mirroring games played by neonates almost from birth, out of which develops the symbolic capacity (Werner and Kaplan, 1963; Winnicott, 1971; Kohut, 1971) and by nonverbal waking fantasies about being eaten or sucked down the drain that are directly inferable from the behavior of children under the age of two. (On this point see the account of Susan

Issacs in Klein et al. [1952] of the one-and-a-half year-old child who was so terrified by the broken and flapping sole of her mother's shoe that it had to be hidden—she was able to say fifteen months later on seeing it again, "Once I thought that could eat me right up.")

Foulkes may be missing the existence of a perceptual imagery core of dreaming, roughly reproducing the forms of waking experience and necessarily lost to recall in the young child. His experiments would then be tracing the progressive symbolic transformations of that methodologically inaccessible dream core, gradually made more accessible by the child's growing capacity for the abstract self-reference necessary for such recall *and* by a progressive transformation of dream formation by abstract visual-spatial intelligence.

Certainly the "first dreams" described by Foulkes of being in bed and/or watching anthropomorphic animals show just the emerging self-reference or autosymbolism that would be expected to eventually ride through state-specific and developmental barriers to recall. Possibly along these lines, Purcell and colleagues (1986), using a classification system of degrees of self-awareness in adult dreamers (ranging from brief scenes with no active self, to a dream self that can both act and reflect on the dream experience, to full lucidity), have found that habitually low dream recallers also report dreams that show lower levels of self-reflectiveness. What best favors dream recall is the presence of abstract self-reference informing the actual processes of dream formation. The childhood development of a self-referential capacity would at first be most naturally attuned to the recall of forms of dreaming also transformed by the same capacity, but eventually it would allow even realistic, true-to-daily-life dreams through the recall barrier—a barrier that even the most direct laboratory intrusions can never completely eliminate.

Lower Animals

If dreaming depends on a cognitive symbolic capacity, even should we extend that back into its species-specific origin in the mirroring ("self"-creating) games of infants, then we must also conclude that creatures incapable of symbolic thought cannot dream—and this despite the occurrence of complex incipient behavioral sequences in REM sleep. Jouvet's oneiric cats would accordingly be demonstrating only patterns of motor discharge, nonexperiential and nonsentient. On the other hand, if we concede any constructivist aspect to perception and if reproductive-anticipatory imagery is closer to perception-action cycles than to the capacity for imaginative reorganization, then the arousal of the central nervous system during the REM period should lead to a similar arousal of the species-specific life-world, be it dog, cat, or human. After all, if the REM state did not exist we would have to hold (since there would be no conceivable exceptions) that a fully activated and intact central nervous system operates inseparably from its life-world—these being two sides of the same phenomenon. An activated brain incarnates a species-specific world. If lower animals do dream on this basis (as the inner side of their capacities for recall and anticipation), then they would lack the abstract attitude needed to recall their dreams.

Of course, we can never know for certain whether animals dream. The question would be merely tilting at conceptual windmills were it not so heuristic as a sort of litmus test for competing theories of dreaming and their cognitive implications. It helps us to think through the complex relations between perception, image, and imagination on the one hand and more general debates about the nature of consciousness on the other.

Most recent discussions of human consciousness (Natsoulas, 1981) and animal awareness (Griffin, 1976) have tried to distinguish at least three levels: immediate sentience, as indexed by patterned and sequential motor responsiveness; the capacity to image in the absence of concurrent stimulation, indexed by response delays in anticipation and by various forms of learning; and the self-referential capacity, uniquely developed in man, potentially present in higher primates and dolphins, indexed by novel recombinations of past experience or what Neisser terms *schematic rearrangement*. The first two levels would allow animal dreaming. If such dreaming in lower animals and infants reactivates perceptual activity, there is no reason to believe they are conscious of that as *experience* in anything like the introspective fashion that opens out with the full development of human intelligence.

On Foulkes's model, only organisms with the capacity to turn around on their own perceptual and affective processes—what George Herbert Mead called "taking the role of the other"—could dream. For Foulkes, defining consciousness in terms of organismic responsiveness is ultimately uninteresting; conscious awareness must entail multiple levels of information processing, what he defines as *internal self-reference* or the ability to "process the fact that we are processing." Foulkes, like many other psychologists, follows the view that the unconscious comes first phylogenetically and ontogenetically; consciousness only emerges out of it in human ontogenesis (and perhaps in higher primates). This is in marked contrast to other suggestions that all motile organisms are necessarily conscious (sentient) and that the unconscious is a secondary result, initially of the automatization of repeated behavior and, on the human level, of the potential split in mental organization created by the capacity to take the role of the other toward one's own experience.

We have all been taught to wield Occam's razor on the issue of animal awareness, but there are more and more dissenting voices. We need to consider the corresponding dilemma of theoretical parsimony in trying to explain how creatures with an activated cortex, organized sequences of outwardly inhibited behavior (which can be surgically disinhibited), and scanning eye movements are not experiencing anything. All of us with pets have noted the twitches, groans, vocalizations, sexual, aggressive, and appetitive behaviors, and rapid paw movements of ostensible walking and running that occur during the animals' sleep. Parsimony calls this dreaming. And so we are returned to the notion of levels of dreaming (and imagery)—from the imagistic functions of memory reproduction and anticipation closest to the perceptual schemata, to the complex stages of schematic rearrangement and imaginative recombination.

Yet there is a further practical consideration. Although it is clearly most parsimonious in a theoretical sense to posit a primitive form of dreaming in nonsymbolizing creatures, it is also the case that only when human dreams manifest self-reference and recombination do they become truly interesting as psychological phenomena in their own right—offering us an alternative avenue for developing a cognitive psychology of mind. Foulkes's stages of dream development, suitably amended by good anecdotal observation, may not show the first dreams but they are the first dreams that offer clues to the nature of our symbolic capacity.[9]

A Methodological Indeterminism of Dream Studies: Home Recall versus Laboratory Intervention

Since the advent of the sleep lab, researchers have wondered about the possible effects of such an active intervention on the dreaming process itself. Sleeping in strange surroundings, subject to unpredictable disruption and interrogation: the physiological and emotional impact of participating in these studies is considerable. Researchers have long been cognizant of the "first night effect"—a randomizing of the otherwise highly regular periods of sleep in new subjects. The result can be little clearly identifiable REM or EEG stage 4 sleep and the subjective sense of a broken, troubled sleep. A few subjects never adapt to sleeping in the laboratory. Similarly, and attesting to the continued impact of laboratory conditions after initial adaptation, the content of laboratory-collected dreams often centers on the experimental situation itself. So insistent is this dreaming about the laboratory situation that several researchers investigating the incorporation of experimental stimuli into ongoing REM dreams have had to note that their deliberate intrusions were less often incorporated than the unintended stimulation provided by the laboratory situation itself.

There has been much less agreement on whether laboratory dreams are rendered "artificial" by the experimental conditions. In contrast to the spontaneous home recall that forms the sample of dreaming common to all clinical traditions, normative laboratory research has shown dreaming to be far more mundane and true to daily life in theme, emotion, and cognitive form than the self-reports of Freud or Jung or some of the dream diaries collected by Calvin Hall led us to expect. [10]

Explicit attempts to assess the impact of the laboratory have not produced any consensus among researchers other than what is expectable: Hall, Van de Castle, and their colleagues cite the significantly greater sexuality, aggression, and emotional intensity in home dreams and the relative absence of nightmares in the laboratory—even in nightmare sufferers. They stress the ecological validity of spontaneous home dreams. The new cognitivists (Foulkes, 1985) point to the lack of significant differences in the form of dream experience. Indeed, my colleagues and I found few differences in the bizarreness of dreams reported in home diaries and after laboratory awakenings (Hunt et al., 1982). Whether we can conclude that nothing essential is lost in laboratory dreams depends on the focus of research, but surely much is gained from methods allowing controlled sampling, immediate recall, and directed questioning.

An obvious solution would be to conclude that both methods are necessary and valuable. But such methodological eclecticism should not obscure evidence, on the clinical-phenomenological side, that the spontaneous recall of a dream is a psychological event in its own right—one that at times may be based on a very different form of dreaming than is involved in the otherwise obliterated dreams rescued by the laboratory. Even if subjectively powerful home recall dreams are rare, they influence people's lives and are the source of what people value in dreaming. Further, it is always possible that laboratory dreams may be transformed in ways not yet fully identifiable by content systems that break dreams down into separately rated dimensions like aggression, bizarreness, number of characters, and so on.

Heynick (cited in Foulkes, 1985) found mundane dreams no different from laboratory awakenings but distinct from spontaneous home recall when he phoned subjects at home during the night to collect dream reports. Thus Foulkes concludes that laboratory reports provide a more representative sample of dreaming than spontaneous home recall. Yet such studies are also consistent with the possibility that in a self-referential organism, it is systematic intrusion on dreaming, rather than the laboratory setting per se, that changes dreaming from the vivid dramatic phenomenon studied by psychoanalysts and anthropologists to the mundane form of dreaming that emerges from the sleep laboratory. What grounds are there to suggest that any well-controlled experimental approach to the dreaming process inevitably creates its own specific level of "psychological vigilance" in human subjects? Changes in cortical arousal and personal defensiveness triggered by the experimental situation could (1) *eliminate* or curtail forms of dreaming associated with the enhanced self-reference and symbolic elaboration that normally leads to spontaneous recall, and/or (2) actually *create* forms of dreaming and sleep mentation where none would otherwise be. We have not eliminated the possibility that the mentation laid bare in experimental laboratory studies is essentially reactive and even defensive in nature.

Samuel Lowy (1942) was the first to suggest possible systematic differences between cognitive processes involved in spontaneously recalled dreams and those in "forgotten dreams"—those awakenings in which we are convinced we have dreamed but recall either nothing or at most a vague feeling state. Lowy suggested that such feeling, a precursor of Eugene Gendlin's "felt meaning," might reflect the actual form of dream experience minus the "something more" added to some dreams that permits recall by waking consciousness. Subsequent sleep lab research has confirmed his intuition that the vast majority of dreams are naturally forgotten, while Purcell's (1986) research on self-reflectiveness suggests something of the transformation process which could be added in spontaneously recalled dreams. In addition, laboratory dreams from subjects with naturally low dream recall tend to be less organized, less vivid, and less easily recalled when presented to other subjects (Goodenough, 1978).

Clinicians working with schizoid or withdrawn individuals have called attention to an incapacity to dream. This must refer to something more than just an incapacity for recall, because when spontaneous dreaming begins in the context of their therapy, the dreams of these individuals show specific patterns of progression over time. Medard Boss (1958) provides one such example: the patient's first dreams involved only machines, then for weeks simple creatures like worms and snails, then reptiles, then mammals, until finally the patient's first dreams of human interaction began. We might regard these machines and animals as incipient metaphorical representations of self, based on visual elaborations of a changing body image. Similarly, the British object relations analysts D. W. Winnicott and Masud R. Khan speak of a gradually developing capacity to dream in such patients, which first centers on the possibility of withstanding the *experience* of dreaming, before those dreams can come to reflect multiple *meanings*. Patients (and first-night laboratory subjects) who are unable to dream often experience highly repetitive thoughts instead, which might be termed REM *rumination*.

There seem to be some laboratory reflections of this incapacity to undergo the dramatic, polyvalent, condensed experience of dreaming. Goodenough (1959) and Lehmann (1981) have independently called attention to laboratory REM recall that seems more like thinking than episodic dreams; it is associated with increased levels of EEG alpha rhythm, normally found with sleep onset and resting wakefulness. At the other extreme, REM periods of a stormy variability and intensification of phasic measures are associated in some subjects with complete absence of recall (Hauri, 1975; Lavie, Metz, and Hefetz, 1983), possibly reflecting an incapacity to experience the dream—given the way that the intensification of REM physiology normally entails an intensified dreaming. Lavie and colleagues (1983) studied traumatic nightmare sufferers who had come to him complaining of disturbing dreams and difficulty falling asleep. These subjects' unusually stormy REM physiology was accompanied by little or no *laboratory* recall. Perhaps similarly, Foulkes reports that some of his child subjects were worried beforehand that they might have nightmares in the laboratory, but none did. Here we may not have so much a modification of recall but an elimination of forms of dream experience through the extra psychological vigilance created by experimental participation. We have to face the possibility that laboratory intervention affects the full dreaming process by some mixture of mundanization, disruption (where dreaming tends toward its more intense forms), and the actual generation of full dream episodes (where home experiences would leave only diffuse feelings on arousal).

That the laboratory situation actually creates forms of mentation that would otherwise not occur is also a possible implication of findings of thoughtlike and dreamlike reports from NREM sleep stages—chiefly from the relatively activated EEG stage 2. There is no question that the thoughtlike NREM mentation (first described by Foulkes) exists, albeit with widespread individual differences. It was overlooked in earlier research because awakened subjects were asked only what they had "dreamed" and not "what had been going through their minds." Such thoughtlike experience fades much more rapidly on awakening than dream episodes. The possibility that such NREM thinking is an automatic defense against the stresses of laboratory participation has rarely been addressed. Indeed, when experienced senior researchers well used to the laboratory environment used themselves as subjects, levels of NREM thinking fell from the 70 percent found by most studies to 20 percent (Kales et al., 1967). A telling anecdote comes from William Dement, one of the psychophysiological pioneers (1975). He was erroneously awakened by a laboratory technician only during NREM periods, whereas Dement expected only REM awakenings. Throughout the study he could at best recall "vague feelings" with no specific content whatsoever, despite his anxiety and embarrassment about being such a poor subject. While some subjects report vivid dreaming from NREM awakenings (especially those with high scores on the MMPI schizophrenia scale, which can be associated with pathology and/or creativity in normal samples), other subjects report "thinking," while still others experience nothing at all. There is some laboratory and clinical evidence that the last may be the functional norm, while the first two are defensive reactions created by an artificial psychological vigilance carried into normally restitutive sleep.

Zimmerman (1970) found that very light sleepers (with lower thresholds of auditory awakening) were significantly more likely to report vivid dreamlike experience from EEG stage 2 NREM sleep than deep sleepers (71–21 percent of awakenings). In this study, all subjects reported some mentation on awakening, but in a more recent report by Harsh and Burton (1986), subjects trained to turn off a beeping tone by deliberate rapid breathing responded on 80 percent of the NREM trials where no parallel mental activity was reported on subsequent awakening, but on only 47 percent of trials in the presence of such reports. (They were also significantly more likely to respond with rapid breathing when the stimulus was not incorporated into their mentation than when it was.)[11] Of course there is no way to prove whether experience was occurring when none was reported, but these results suggest that different levels of cognitive transformation may be involved when subjects awakened from NREM sleep describe dreaming, thinking, vague feeling, or nothing. It also appears likely that level of cortical arousal, not a variable directly indexed by any one physiological measure, has something to do with these transformations.

That NREM mentation may actually be dysfunctional and defensive is suggested by a telling observation from the psychiatrist Harry Stack Sullivan (1953). He calls attention to the quality of sleep when our waking problems press in on us and/or we expect an imminent but unpredictable awakening. These situations produce a form of sleep experience that seems to be a spontaneously recalled version of NREM thinking. This state is very unpleasant and associated with sleep that is not subjectively restful. One awakens with the sense that one has been "thinking all night." Some laboratory support for such an interpretation of NREM thinking comes from Brown and Cartwright (1978). They successfully trained subjects to activate an electrical signal when experiencing sleep mentation. In the case of a single high NREM responder, the number of signals per night was directly correlated with self-ratings of depression and poor mood before falling asleep. The British psychoanalsyt W. R.

Bion (1962) similarly describes patients—disturbed by nightmares and fearful of falling asleep—who cannot fully allow themselves to fall asleep, dream vividly, or to be fully alert and attuned to the waking world.

I suggest that NREM mentation, which seems so counterintuitive to our subjective sense of fully restful (contentless) sleep, is in fact a defensive activation—a sort of learned skill. It would appear spontaneously in subjects who are facing unexpected pressures, or who fear nightmares or falling asleep itself (as a deathlike "disappearance"), *and* it appears in a majority of experimental subjects as a defensive accommodation to the pressure and incipient distress of laboratory participation. Mentation in the NREM stages of sleep maintains a residual ruminating awareness lest we be caught off guard. It is not that the extra cortical vigilance of sleep lab participants simply *creates* NREM thinking and dreaming, but it would necessarily enhance any normally residual mental activity associated with lighter or dysphoric sleep and make it appear normative.

We can now return briefly to the laboratory dreams of young children as studied by Foulkes—which stand in such perplexing contrast to their more infrequent but spontaneously recalled dreams in the natural context of reporting to parents. Did the experimental intrusion involved in such systematic research inhibit more spontaneous forms of childhood dreaming and/or create a low-level dreaming that otherwise would have lacked the cortical vigilance required for its organization (and subsequent recall)? Foulkes rightly correlates such dreaming with waking cognitive development, but we have seen in the more anecdotal literature just how often the features he restricts to later development also appear in the vivid dreams of very young children—especially kinesthetic embodiment, an active participating self, physical movement, and strong affect. Freud, Melanie Klein, and Winnicott view the young child's imagination as potentially overwhelming; so much so that it can undergo automatic defensive inhibition. It seems possible that Foulkes has located both a sequence of dream development *and* something like Freud's repression of potentially overwhelming experience. Such repression would operate precisely by withholding the processes of cognitive self-reference, which indeed can be more developed in spontaneous anecdotal reports than in laboratory dreams at the same ages. Thus, very young children would at first not recall dreams because of their primitive cognitive development (awake and dreaming); later, they would not recall them because of a defensive inhibition or dissociation of that same cognitive development, when it threatens anxiety and stress beyond what can be safely "bound." The systematic intrusion of laboratory awakenings may create a compromise dreaming, intermediate between nightmare and suppression, whose unfolding Foulkes carefully traces.

Much of this discussion is conjectural. That such questions have not been more extensively pursued probably reflects the mutual antipathy between clinical and experimental dream researchers. Each group has overlooked the important fact that it is only their mutual juxtaposition and interaction that can make a science out of dream psychology—since each provides the only available context by which to evaluate the findings of the other. Laboratory work is valuable only when, while still utilizing its precision, we face its potential and probably inherent artificialities. Despite the limitations of observational and anecdotal methods, we must not overlook the striking developments and transformations of dreaming permitted by spontaneous home recall—the setting through which dreams originally presented themselves as worthy of study. Nowhere is the dilemma of being truly "scientific" in the human sciences more forcefully or paradoxically exposed.

CHAPTER 3

Pax Memoria: Memory versus Imagination in the Psychology of Dreaming

I T is fascinating how often ostensibly empirical debates in the human sciences actually rest on largely unarticulated philosophical antinomies. So it is that within cognitive approaches to dreaming we find intimations of a hidden and very old agenda. Does an empirically based account of dreaming require a theory of constructive imagination—with its roots in the idealist/romanticist tradition of Western thought? Or rather does it afford yet another opportunity to demonstrate that all imagination is really just a complex form of memory and learning—an extension of the rationalist and reductionist attempt, now computerized, to understand the complex in terms of its simpler elements? Contemporary dream researchers tend to choose either a language of imagination and thinking or one of remembering, forgetting, and learning. Perhaps dreaming could be both, in different dreams and in different aspects of dreaming—but in Western thought this sort of conflict has generally proven irreconcilable.

The claim of memory models on dreaming is clear enough: because daily life is so fundamental, it is easy to miss just how "state-specific" each day really is. The events and details of the day are all too much with us as we go to bed, but by the next morning they are gone. On the rare occasions when the morning does not bring some minimal sense of starting afresh, we feel somehow cheated of sleep's most restitutive gift. More specifically, the dreams we may recall on awakening are striking in the way they can at once show a special enhancement of long-lost memories *and* multiple indications of memory deficit. These deficits are both within the dream, as we fail to recall the most elementary facts of our waking lives, and about the dream, since so much of it is hazy and lost. So we feel compelled to agree that in some basic sense dreaming "involves" memory.

Let us consider first the positive manifestations of memory processes within dreams. Observers from Freud to Palombo, Greenberg and Pearlman, and Foulkes have been struck by the way dreams so often include some reference to very recent events—the day residue, generally not recognized as such during the dream itself. Some years ago, Ernest Hartmann (1968) reported that approximately half of his own dreams contained references to the immediate past and that 94 percent of these were to the day before the dream. More recently, Arthur Epstein (1985), in what may be a striking confirmation of Carlyle Smith's demonstration of REM augmentation "windows" following learning, found that 46 percent of his dreams contained references to events that occurred two or three days previous, while Nielsen and Powell (1988) report the highest rates of dream incorporation at one and six days after emotional events. Stanley Palombo (1984) confirmed the observations of Freud and several nineteenth-century dream investigators that dreams reactivate early life memories. Questioning his own patients, Palombo found that 68 percent of their dreams contained central features directly reminiscent of childhood experience. The earliest datable events were to age two, with a median age of ten years.[1]

Most striking is the way dream episodes "condense" (Freud) or "superimpose" (Palombo) past experiences—possibly in terms of categories from long-term semantic memory. Bartlett (1932) and more recently Endel Tulving (1983) see such condensation or "synergy" as illustrating the constructive nature of personal memories. Condensation in dreams helps support Foulkes's conclusion that dream formation must involve a diffuse mnemic activation, that is, a parallel memory processing that mixes and fuses past material from very different semantic "files." Foulkes suggests that some of the signs of memory deficit (discussed below) could result from an excessive "loading" of memory capacity associated with the REM state, which fits well with findings that emotional, novel, and "unprepared" learning enhance the special orientation response of REM at intervals suggesting the biochemical functions of memory consolidation.[2]

We may easily miss the many indications of memory impairment in dreaming precisely because they are so common. Yet once located and framed for inspection, they suggest a similarity between dreaming and neurological syndromes associated with severe deficits in waking memory. Consider the amnesic aspects of dreaming: not only do we commonly forget most or all of the dream after awakening, but within the dream we are amnesic for the events of previous waking experience. We do no recall that the last thing we did before the dream events was to go to bed and we do not even recognize the memories that can occur in our dreams *as* memories. That usually requires waking reflection and often free-association. The impression of dreaming as an amnesic syndrome—so reminiscent of diffuse conditions like Korsakoff's psychosis (alcohol-induced memory deficiencies) or some kinds of damage to hippocampal areas—is further supported by the tendency to active confabulation within the dream. On occasion, elaborate memories are constructed within the dream that turn out to be totally false on awakening. More common is an ad hoc attempt to make sense of ongoing dream events via confabulated and utterly inadequate "explanations." Finally, of course, repetitive dreams, both traumatic and mundane, indicate a more or less direct miscarriage of memory function. The unique aim of memory to repeat the past is literally fulfilled and the same dream recurs over and over. "Memory" fails because it only parrots its idealized function, giving us exactly the same again and so lacking the flexibility of recasting past in terms of present that constitutes the adaptive function of ordinary remembering.

In fact there are parallels between the phenomenology and the physiology of dreams and neurological research on the role of the hippocampus in remembering. The REM state and the orientation response of wakefulness involve the very regions of the limbic system—the hippocampus and amygdala—that are associated with the registration and memory consolidation of novel stimuli via the association of sensory patterns from the different sensory modalities with each other and with corresponding affect (Murray and Mishkin, 1985; Winson, 1985).[3] Direct electrical stimulation to temporal areas adjacent to the hippocampus in humans (pioneered by Penfield in surgery for severe epilepsy—see Penfield and Perot [1963]) produces a state that has been termed dreamlike—with considerable confusion or clouding of critical faculties and dreamlike flashes that Penfield initially misinterpreted as repetitive memories. Later research has shown that the repetitive stereotyped quality of these electrical stimulations is far less than Penfield's original reports implied (Mahl et al., 1964; Horowitz, 1970)—the episodes are constructed more like dreams than like ordinary memories (Mahl et al., 1964; Halgren et al., 1978). In other words, the "flashback" is actually a fusion of hypothetical past experiences and ongoing mentation based on immediate subjective reactions to the surgical procedures. Electrically induced hallucinations are an imaginative or primary process fusion of a day residue (the laboratory) with past experience; they are often described by patients as "dreaming." It seems more than coincidental that epileptic patients with seizure activity located in the temporal lobe may sometimes report unpleasantly repetitive night dreams (often with a disturbed accompanying EEG) (Epstein, 1979). Natural trauma in these areas (and in the prefrontal regions projecting to the hippocampus) is also associated with severe deficits of memory, confabulations, and delirious dreamlike experience (Luria, 1973).

However tempting this linkage of hippocampal activity with the diffuse mnemic activation of REM sleep and the amnesic-confabulatory dimensions of dreaming, we face the same dilemma here that we encountered in earlier attempts to *equate* the neurophysiology of REM with the psychology of dreaming. It explains at once too much and too little—at least in the absence of evidence of similar hippocampal activity during vivid daydreaming, sleep onset, and hypnotic dreaming. Certainly the memory consolidation function of REM sleep located by Carlyle Smith and others is too diffuse and general to have any clear implications for dream content. Indeed, the neurophysiology and biochemistry of memory consolidation in REM may have no discernible relation to the phenomenal fusions of past and present in dreaming. If in the morning we could only recall material from the previous day about which we had dreamed (whether the dreams were remembered or forgotten), we would be in serious trouble—and we would be infinitely more state-specific (and day-specific) than we actually are. Hippocampal activation during REM sleep presumably helps in the parallel consolidation of diverse recent learning, automatically primed by the state-specific "curiosity reflex." But such consolidation is more general and on a level of analysis different from the memory aspects of *dreams* as located by Foulkes, Greenberg and Pearlman, and Palombo. In other words, if Carlyle Smith's trained rats dream during their learning-primed, enhanced-REM periods, their dreams need not be *about* their experimental training for their dreams to be memories and for their REM states to consolidate prior learning. Features of the REM state will not establish for us whether dreaming is a variant of remembering. Only phenomenology and experimentation on a molar psychological level can do that. And there we must not just evaluate evidence showing how dreaming might be "for" memory (and vice versa)—we also need to ask what memory models may be "for" within cognitive theory.

The two most detailed attempts to show how the major phenomenal features of dreaming could be produced by relatively simple memory processes come from the psychoanalyst Stanley Palombo and the experimental neuropsychologist John Antrobus. Both present their models as more parsimonious alternatives to the creative imagination and problem-solving theories of dreaming.

Palombo (1978) bases his approach on the major positive indications of memory activity within dreams—the tendency for their generally true-to-daily-life settings to be intruded upon by persons or events plausible in waking experience but not in the dream setting. He sees this "superimposition" of material—one setting often with associations to the distant past, the other more contemporary—as illustrating the essence of constructive memory. These imagistic fusions assimilate past and present, transferring short-term into long-term memory. Dreams may present fresh insights into current problems, or in ongoing psychotherapy an interpreted dream may be "answered" by a "correction" dream, but this is all a secondary by-product of relatively crude processes of memory consolidation. Palombo posits a "repetitive mechanism which produces an adaptive result by distorting and degrading the representations of experience" (1978, p. 9). He echoes Freud in questioning the necessity of attributing the sort of creative problem solving posited by French and Fromm, Jones, and Jung to something as "cognitively crude" (p. 8) as the dream, when it is far better done with the conceptual tools of wakefulness *in response to* the thought-provoking fusions of past and present that directly reveal the memory function of dreaming.

Antrobus (1977, 1978) similarly argues that everything we know about dream metaphor can be accounted for by the principles of mnemic (and perceptual) assimilation. Opting for a model of long-term semantic memory based on abstracted features or attributes (rather than prototypes), he suggests that the creativity of dreams comes from their fusion of separate events on the basis of partially overlapping features. As an example he uses the dream of a logger prior to an aneurectomy to remove a vascular blockage. The logger dreams he is trying to clear sand and rust from the inside of a railroad switch. The dream is thus based on the abstraction of attributes related to tubes, blockage, and repair common to both medicine and logging. Since these attributes have a longer personal history for the dreamer in the logging context, that is the setting to which the new and frightening operation is assimilated. This creates a metaphor for the medical operation that is useful and illuminating for waking consciousness. Yet the processes involved are no different from those that led Antrobus to return from his dining room with a stapler when he went in search of the salt shaker. Both objects were metallic, grey, and on the table and so were assimilated to each other in Antrobus's distracted state of mind. One can account for the similar assimilation of present and past in the dream by assuming that the sleeping mind generates only a partial set of mnemic attributes, the unintentional basis of dream metaphor.

Antrobus revives a species of nineteenth-century associationism (found for instance in Saint-Denys, see chapter 5) to account for progressions within the dream. The only context available for memory nodes during sleep is the on-going dream setting itself. Thus the dream situation activates memories that share overlapping but incomplete features. These then appear as the next dream setting, but correspondingly transformed by their assimilation to the first setting, and so on. Antrobus has attempted an experimental illustration of this process by conditioning attribute lists to different tones and presenting the tones during REM sleep. In one anecdotal demonstration a tone associated with *cutting* and *tree* was presented to two subjects who both happened to be dreaming of kitchens at the moment of stimulation. Both subjects dropped the *tree* attribute; one then dreamt of *cutting* a pie, the other of *chopping* vegetables.

Foulkes (1985), in his development of a still more specific "cognitive science of dreaming," suggests that dream formation involves some of the same processes that Endel Tulving has termed *episodic memory*, which Foulkes, in turn, uses to support his conclusion that very young children do not dream. Tulving (1983, 1984, 1985) differentiates episodic memory from *semantic* or *conceptual memory* on grounds of physiology, function, and phenomenology. Episodic memory involves some experiential sense, however vague, of an actual episode or event as the source of one's recollection. It *feels* like remembering, reflecting that state-specific context dependency raised to its ultimate expression by Marcel Proust. It is severely impaired or even destroyed with damage to the hippocampal and forebrain areas. Semantic memory, on the other hand, is more abstract and nonexperiential—a "just knowing" that something is the case, without recollecting where and when it was learned. It requires that areas of the neocortex be intact. Episodic memory is clearly related to dream condensation and superimpositions in that it is based on what Tulving calls *synergy*—a lack of mutual inhibition between the source memory and the current situation by which it is activated. This creates the fusions of past and present that characterize all remembering.[4]

Foulkes applies Tulving's approach to his cognitive-psychological model of dreaming by citing the special susceptibility of episodic memory to amnesia (in contrast, semantic memory may be largely preserved in even the most serious amnesic syndromes). The patient may not remember who he or she is, where he or she was born, or that he or she is a trained electrician, but placed in the work setting he or she "knows" what to do. Tulving (1983,

1984, 1985) studied several patients with severe antereograde amnesia associated with hippocampal damage. At times they could recall items from a list taught to them a few minutes before, but without recalling anything of the circumstances in which the list was presented or even that they had seen the list before. Such patients also lack the capacity to imaginatively project an anticipated future. They can no more say what they might be doing in an hour than they can recall where they were an hour before. This iron restriction to the mode of the present is of course strikingly reminiscent of dream phenomenology (see chapter 4), although in dreams it remains unclear whether it reflects a specific deficit of episodic memory during dream formation, whether it is a general decrement in cortical tone associated with sleep, or whether it is a secondary consequence of absorption in imaginative activities.

Still, and this is Foulkes's basic point, the vulnerability of episodic but not semantic recall is reminiscent of the memories of young children—who are deservedly notorious (like some academics) for "knowing what they know" but not remembering the situation in which they just learned it. In some parts of his 1983 book (but contradicted in others), Tulving suggests that episodic memory develops later in childhood, differentiating out of the more firmly established semantic capacity. Foulkes (1985) concludes that this lack of symbolic self-reference in early memory (i.e., a lack of the autobiographical memory sense that constitutes episodic recall) can account for children's and animals' failure to experience dreams. Here, episodic memory and dreaming would equally depend on "turning around on the schemata" or "taking the role of the other"; neither could begin until Piaget's phase of concrete operations. [5]

However, the support Tulving's episodic memory can offer to Foulkes's model of dreaming is quite slender. Tulving (1983, 1984) and Olton (1984) have presented evidence suggesting that episodic recall develops relatively independent of semantic encoding and that something like the episodic-experiential versus semantic distinction is experimentally demonstrable in animals as well. Tulving (pers. comm., 1986) agreed with my suggestion that a non-self-referential but experiential-eidetic stage could precede the appearance of the genuinely autobiographical episodic memory of later childhood—that self-reference might be added at some point to an earlier experiential form of recall. With respect to animal behavior, Olton (1984) has suggested an analogous distinction between an immediate "working" memory and a more generic "reference" memory in the rat. The former is manifested in spontaneous alternation of choice behaviors associated with curiosity, foraging, and learning to avoid nonrewarded maze passages (all requiring some recall of where the animal has previously gone in order to avoid repetition). These capacities, but not more general learning, also disappear in amnesic conditions produced by experimental hippocampal damage, and they require the developmental maturation of hippocampal functioning.

Given the shift in human REM physiology and the increase in infants' spontaneous exploratory behavior after six months, Tulving and Olton may be pointing to the cognitive-mnemic basis for dream experience, as well as an explanation why subjective experiential episodes might not be associated with the intensified REM periods of fetal and early neonatal development. We have seen that these early maturational phases of REM sleep and related behaviors are controlled in terms of energy release and may be associated with the exercise of motoric capacities prior to their full experiential engagement. Later in development, coincident with the maturation of the hippocampus, dreaming in human beings and other animals could function on the same basis as does the primitive form of episodic recall in animals—that is, as reproductive-anticipatory imagery unmodified by any self-referential symbolic capacity. As self-reference develops we would also have the development of both autobiographical episodic memory and symbolically transformed dreaming.[6]

If we are applying Tulving's episodic/semantic distinction to dreaming, there are indications of both operations in dream phenomenology. Apart from the experience of "just knowing" (whether true or confabulatory) within ongoing dream experience, there is the striking presence of what Tulving courageously labels *free radicals* in ordinary and amnesic recall—states of mind which are clearly mnemic but not so identified by the subject, experienced instead as "thoughts just passing through my mind." Tulving sees these as transitional between episodic and semantic functioning, attesting to the rich interactions of the two systems. We have already seen that dreams are full of free radicals, as in all those events, scenes, and people that turn out on waking reflection to be recent and/or distant memories but that are rarely felt as "remembering" within the dream. In Tulving's language, dreaming is one of those rare situations in which recall is superior to recognition.

Whatever the intricacies in current memory theory as applied to dreaming, there is agreement among a wide range of dream researchers—Freud, Greenberg and Pearlman, Palombo, Antrobus, Foulkes, and Hartmann—that dreaming involves the processes of memory. Dreaming is a *kind* of remembering, rendered confabulatory and confused by the special conditions of sleep. Although these figures represent a wide range of disciplines and levels of analysis, they all operate within a single epistemological point of view. As a way to account for the essence of dreaming, memory models can be criticized on both empirical and philosophical grounds. Surely the cognitive processes involved in remembering are part of all dreams, and they may be the entirety of some dreams. Since dreams are internally generated life-worlds, they must reflect prior experience and its schematization in both semantic and episodic memory. Because the influence of prior experience is so great in our experience generally, it must be even more salient in dream construction. But it will be the burden of much of this book to show that memory cannot entirely account for dreaming as a cognitive process.

For instance, it is hard to see how the cognitive psychology of memory can account for dreams of flying, extreme and often perverse sexuality and aggression, or the fact that our most blissful and terrifying life experiences may occur in dreams.[7] If we attempt to explain such dreams via memory, we must embrace the overly elaborate psychoanalytic theories of experience in early infancy that the cognitivists are at such pains to reject—for example, flying as a memory of being carried as an infant. While the more common forms of hallucinatory intrusion within the fabric of dreaming can be interpreted as mnemic superimposition and condensation effects, it is much harder to account in this way for many nightmares, lucid dreams, problem-solving dreams, dreams expressing somatic disorders, and what Jung termed *archetypal* dreams—dreams that involve mythological and spiritual themes often associated with a numinous-uncanny emotion that goes beyond all prior waking experience. Both common sense and the notion that there are multiple frames or faculties within the human symbolic capacity urge us toward the concept of a creative constructive imagination and its role in some forms of dreaming. It helps to recall that the degree of bizarreness in dreams is empirically correlated with waking measures of imaginative creativity and that the development of dreaming in childhood is linked to spatial abilities and not mnemic ones. The occasional association of sleep onset and REM dreaming with major breakthroughs in the arts, sciences, and technology suggests that if these are to be entirely accounted for as mnemic condensations, we will need a new vocabulary for distinct levels of memory functioning, one that comes far more naturally from the cognitive psychology of thinking and imagination anyway.

This problem of vocabulary is seen, for instance, in Antrobus's model of dream metaphor as an automatic fusion of partial feature lists from different semantic domains. He fails to distinguish condensations that are properly mnemic (and akin to effects demonstrated by Bartlett and Tulving) from those that constitute constructive and novel solutions to a current impasse—unless creative thought is to be accounted for as an incidental by-product of incomplete memory. Thinking would then become a form of memory consolidation, leaving us wondering how animals capable of mnemic reorganization and possibly primitive episodic memory nonetheless don't "think" in the sense of creatively recombining features of their world. What is gained by substituting *self-referential episodic memory* for *imagining?*

We are back at the often covert philosophical debate at the heart of psychology between reproductive associationism and creative constructionism. In light of these concerns, surely we do well to shun solutions to the problem of dream formation that come in the form "all X is really Y"—substituting in whatever order thought, affect, memory, perception, imagination. Each of these concepts is still regarded as a "something" in its own right by various keepers of our ordinary and psychological lexicons. As Oliver Sacks (1987) suggests about memory confabulation in Korsakoff's psychosis, there comes a point when the energy and creative frenzy of such patients suggests a special enhancement of imagination rather than memory, precisely because memory is so severely impaired that *another* function must fill its void. These patients could then be said to "remember *instead* with their imaginations," as could many dreamers.

The real danger in assimilating all dreaming (or its essence) to memory is false reductionism—specifically to a form of epistemological realism and elementarism. Here, mainstream cognitive science, with its computer simulations of memory storage and access, seems to have become hostage to academic psychology's earlier concentration on animal learning. Memory and learning seem safer topics for North American psychologists than imagination and creative thinking, and so the temptation arises to see the latter in terms of the former—if they are seen at all. Ironically, cognitive memory models actually perpetuate the valuative side of psychoanalysis most criticized by figures as diverse as Jung, Erikson, and current life-span approaches, namely its tendency to understand the present and future as exclusively determined by the past—and this in a creature apparently unique on this earth for its imaginative openness to an indeterminant and unknown future. The only way that the psychology of memory can account for all aspects of dreaming and for all dream types is by expanding its vocabulary and assumptions beyond the point where empirical distinctions can be made. Ultimately, this leads to Platonic demonstrations that all knowing is *really* remembering.[8]

In the pax memoria of current cognitive approaches to dreams, *memory* has too often been stretched beyond its natural range of convenience. I will leave it to someone who does not take Wittgenstein's cautionary admonitions as seriously as I do to find the underlying single truth about dreams. As we look at the full range of dreaming and its potential developments, such an essence seems elusive—except perhaps at the price of that relativism, covertly and heedlessly embraced by many a hard-nosed researcher, in which anything can be turned into anything else in the service of one's own special hypothesis. Rather, I will stay close to the descriptive phenomenology of dream experience, which will require distinctions between different cognitive symbolic faculties or "frames of mind" in order to address the natural range and variations of dreaming.

PART II

Forms of Dreaming

[Freud] wanted to find some one explanation which would show what dreaming is. He wanted to find the *essence* of dreaming. And he would have rejected any suggestion that he might be partly right but not altogether so. . . . It is probable that there are many sorts of dreams, and that there is no single line of explanation for all of them. . . . There is no one reason why people talk. A small child babbles often just for the pleasure of making noises. This is also one reason why adults talk. And there are countless others.

—Wittgenstein, *Lectures and Conversations*

Fluidity, relativity, elasticity is a most distinctive aspect of the type concept. Types are unlike Platonic ideas. . . . They are constructed by intensifying, exaggerating, and purifying single traits. . . . They exist in no single instance, and are thus unnatural—which is precisely their value for seeing through the natural. The act which forms an ideal type is . . . an insight into essence, and not a statistical averaging.

—Hillman, *Egalitarian Typologies Versus the Perception of the Unique*

CHAPTER 4

Problems in the Definition of Dreaming

S INCE Hughlings-Jackson, neurologists and psychiatrists have attempted to distinguish between *positive symptoms*—anomalous behavior and experience that seem to define a syndrome or condition—and the more fundamental *negative* or *loss of capacity symptoms*. The latter constitute the core dissolution, for which the positive and more obvious signs compensate as the essentially normal capacities still left intact. Freud (1911, 1919a) was influenced by this tradition: he understood hallucinations and delusions as spontaneous attempts to recover interest in the world in the face of a more primary narcissistic withdrawal. Generally it is assumed that the negative core is harder to identify. After all, it must be intuited as a "void" defined only by what comes to fill and partially mask it.

By contrast, and curiously, there is far more agreement about what is lacking or missing in most dreams than on what defines them in a positive sense. Perhaps this suggests that dreaming is an utterly unique and elusive amalgam of remembering, perceiving, thinking, feeling, and imagining. More likely, as we will see below, the dream is a relatively true-to-life reconstruction of our human being-in-the-world. Accordingly, like daily life, once parsed into separate dimensions it will not readily go back together again. If our reflexive intelligence cannot get fully around itself to illuminate the nature of our waking life, we may not get much more by moonlight.

What is missing from dreams? Does what they lack constitute the unique nature of dreaming, or is it merely an exaggeration of what is lacking in all of us awake, or is it a combination of both? Rechtschaffen (1978), in an especially influential article, has pointed to the "single-mindedness" of dreams, their isolation from each other (i.e., their lack of continuity in contrast to waking experience), and the isolation of dreaming from our full waking reflective capacities. Specifically, not only is there an absence of alternative lines of thought within dreams, in contrast to the way we are distracted when awake by multiple competing concerns, but dreams seem to lack that self-reflectiveness which in wakefulness leads us to awareness of our overall context. In dreaming such reflection would lead to the realization that one is in fact asleep and having a dream. In effect, the opposite of single-mindedness would result in that relatively infrequent type of dream referred to as *lucid*. To paraphrase Binswanger's phenomenology of "dream existence," we find in ordinary dreaming multiple mirrorings of "I do not know what is happening to me."

Ernest Hartmann (1982), echoing Freud, has emphasized the lack of actively directed volition or will in dreams, along with the absence of ongoing reflective judgment. Medard Boss (1958, 1977) has likewise called attention to the narrowing of the dream to the mode of the immediate present—a phenomenological analysis that may subsume Rechtschaffen and that is also reflected in Freud: "Dreams make use of the present tense" (1900, p. 573); the "it is" of dreamwork (1905, p. 162). Boss, while insisting that dreaming manifests all the existential potentialities of waking, concludes that it necessarily narrows the openness and freedom of waking life. The dream, after all, is uniquely characterized by that expansion of consciousness we call "waking up," implying that the preceding awareness is somehow contracted. It is only this opening up allowed by full waking consciousness that permits the immediacy of the dream to begin its shift toward potential metaphor.

Boss also shows that such characterizations are necessarily relative. Multiple (if infrequent) dreams will violate them while still possessing something dreamlike. Boss reports a woman's dream showing enhanced cognitive reflection and a decisive volitional behavior:

> It is a moonlit night. I am in a courtyard in the middle of which there is a stable. . . . I descend the steps from the stable to the courtyard where I have a rendezvous with some man. I know it is a man who looks coarse and strong and Russian. I don't actually like anything about him but he attracts me irresistibly and magically. While I descend the steps . . . I think: "Perhaps my husband is right when he says there is no freedom of will. Everything is fate; one is forced to act in a certain way and that way only, even if it is against one's will." Then I ask myself

if I am perhaps like this because my own will and my own resolution were broken during early childhood by my willful mother. By collecting all my physical strength I suddenly pull myself together and exert my will to turn back and to leave this man to his fate.   (Boss, 1958, p. 131)

Perhaps we could still say that some hypothetically "full" reflectiveness would have led her to realize that this was a dream and so to expand the arena of her struggle against passivity by deliberately waking up and facing the more difficult dilemmas of her everyday life—although such increased "realism" might also be a serious loss.

Similarly, the very existence of lucid dreams (whether or not most people can be trained to have them) seems to show just that expansion of awareness, increased self-reflectiveness, and directed volition that is supposedly impossible in dreaming. On the other hand, even the most experienced lucid dreamers attest to their inability to think fully and completely through the consequences of being in a dream: they verge on taking aspects of their experience literally again or forget their well-rehearsed plans to experiment within the dream. There is, however, a further problem in defining passivity and nonreflectiveness as the gap that dream experience must fill in a way essentially different from wakefulness. Perhaps the true waking parallel to the "I am dreaming" of lucid dreams is "I am alive" or "this is a life and someday it will end." Everyday life is also characterized by a similar inability to see the full consequences of our ongoing experience. Most of us realize that we oscillate between overcontrol and excessive passivity in the face of complex social, personal, and physical forces that are always in some measure "beyond us." Accordingly, we can miss the overall context of our waking experience as surely as can the dreamer.

My own empirical approach, based on a content analysis of the anomalies and transformations of experience that occur in dreams (Hunt et al., 1982), similarly identified a diffuse cognitive slippage as the underlying characteristic of dreaming. But it was also relative and entailed rating as "dreamlike confusions" simple mistakes that also occur in the midst of waking life. In this system, whenever anything occurred in the dream that would not be expected in alert everyday wakefulness, it was rated in terms of the transformations of perception (hallucination), thought, memory, emotion, and interpersonal relations that also characterize the wide range of waking altered states of consciousness. No effect occurred in dreams that was not also prominent in some such waking alteration.

Typically, dreaming showed a delirium profile, the sort of diffuse and often subtle decrement characteristic of alcohol- and fever-induced states, rather than anything resembling schizophrenia, meditation, or psychedelic states (see appendix, table 1, column 1). There were sudden breaks or gaps in experience (occurring in 20% of home recall dreams), confusions in thinking and irrational intuitions (41%), problems in sustained attention within the dream (5%), and deficiencies in memory both within (15%) and about (30%) the dream. Even when subjects were asked for their most realistic and true-to-life recent dream, 51 percent of these contained some such clouding of consciousness, although often very minor. These effects seem to be reflections within the dream of the lack of self-reference and passivity that some have taken to be the negative core of dreaming, but that can only be intuited from these more overt discontinuities. But these discontinuities cannot represent the essence of dreaming, since they do not occur in all dreams.

There is other evidence that a clouding of consciousness runs through dreaming. Subjects describe their experience with delirium-producing agents (Cartwright, 1966) as "like dreaming" or as "having dreams," and the EEG of clinical delirium shows the same superimposition of fast and slow waves that characterizes the EEG of the REM state (Itil, 1970). Yet the clouding of consciousness that largely defines delirious and confusional states is itself a continuum. At best we can say that it starts to characterize our experience short of its full mental acuity and alertness. Confusion and lack of recall are very much part of the "psychopathology of everyday life," as attested by many people's subjective sense that somehow they should think more clearly or have better recall—as if the implicit standard was a computer or a god.

We can also approach the potential cognitive lacunae of dreams more deductively, by asking what sort of neurological syndrome would produce the "negatives" of dreaming. Luria (1973) has identified what he terms *tertiary* areas of the neocortex as those regions where the secondary association areas, each centered on elaborating the information from a separate sensory modality, are synthesized and integrated. These neurological areas are the slowest to mature (up to age seven) and constitute those capacities more or less specific to human beings. It seems likely that deficits in the tertiary regions would produce the negative signs of dream experience. Neural damage to the frontal lobes, the tertiary area for the limbic (hippocampal) and motor regions, is associated with waking deficiencies in planning and volition; damage to the left parietal lobe leads to decrements in complex relational thought; and damage to the right parietal region, loss of kinesthetic self-awareness (such individuals are remarkably unaware of major losses in functioning, whereas left-hemisphere-damaged patients generally understand their losses). Yet even this neurological perspective leaves dreaming on a continuum with normal waking and fails to establish a genuine discontinuity. People tend to feel that the capacities supported by each of the tertiary areas are also somehow "unfinished," both in themselves and in humanity in general. As the psychoanalyst W. R. Bion has stated, "the capacity to think is rudimentary in all of us" (1962, p. 14). It is doubtless a species-specific contribution of the right parietal tertiary zone that we sometimes experience this curiously unfinished quality in our own faculties.

Although all characterizations of what is lacking in dreaming merge into the norms of waking life and admit of no exclusive dream essence, still very different observers agree on these lacunae. It has been much more difficult to arrive at a positive definition of dreaming. If dreaming is not exactly remembering, perceiving, or imagining, neither is it exactly hallucinating—despite the widespread and problematic use in the literature of the word *hallucination* to describe the fact that while the dream goes on, we generally take it as real. But dreaming, in the REM state or awake, is very unlike clinically defined hallucinations, which only rarely recreate a total environmental context alternative to that of consensual reality (as dreams do). *Hallucinations of setting* (visions, out-of-body experiences) do occasionally occur, but unlike ordinary dreaming, they tend to involve exotic scenes (astral planes, flying saucer scenarios) or, if mundane, they are reconstructed from an unusual angle of regard—like out-of-body experiences and autoscopic hallucinations. Most clinical hallucinations involve an intrusion of something incongruous or alien into an otherwise plausible environment.

Indeed, dreaming is so like the structure of waking experience that the major positive forms of dream bizarreness in my rating system (see table 1 in the appendix) were just such *hallucinatory intrusions*, varying in degrees of probability and appearing within dream settings that were themselves more or less plausible in the person's waking life. In other words, dreaming is so much like waking that something very like clinical hallucinations can occur within it. Most of these improbable intrusions were visual (47% of home recall dreams). It is difficult to determine whether the striking predominance of visual content intrusions over somatic (10%) and auditory (14%) hallucinations stems from a natural bias toward the more simultaneous imagistic modality of vision, occasioned perhaps by the relative clouding of dream consciousness, or from modality differences in recall similar to waking experience. More striking "psychedelic" transformations of dream consciousness —LSD-type transformations in the formal properties of visual perception (13%) and somatic perception, including flying (4%), numinous-uncanny emotion (4%), mythological thinking (3%), encounters with strange or bizarre figures (4%), and changes in identity of the dreamer or other characters (3%)—are rare in normative dreams.

All these dream transformations also occur in one or more standard altered states of consciousness, but it is clear that most dreams are relatively true to daily life and not like clinical hallucinations or psychedelic drug states. The corresponding temptation to regard clinical hallucinations as the waking eruptions of a dreaming process seems equally implausible. If that were the case then hallucination would usually involve sudden replacement of one's here-and-now environment with an alternative setting that is more or less true to the other settings of one's daily life. This indeed does occur during highly absorbed daydreaming (Foulkes and Fleisher, 1975; Hoyt and Singer, 1978). But note also that this similarity between relatively mundane dreams and daydreaming, both being capable of fantastic transformations as well, does not explain either activity. It leaves the same gap between clinical hallucinations and dreaming. Our lack of a positive definition of dreaming as such, surprisingly, has not been addressed by dream researchers, perhaps because it bypasses the more specific functions and types of dreaming that have attracted the attention of investigators, perhaps because dreaming is already uncomfortably close to the life-world of wakefulness.

Only Celia Green, in the course of her pioneering investigations and classifications of lucid dreams, out-of-body experience, and related states, has attempted an inclusive positive definition of dreaming. In light of the above difficulties, it is not surprising that she proceeds by coining a new term, *metachoric experience* for situations in which "the subject's normal environment is completely replaced by a hallucinatory one. The most obvious examples of such experiences are dreams and lucid dreams. It should be noticed that although the subject's environment is temporarily completely hallucinatory, it may provide an exact or nearly exact replica of his real one, as in a false awakening or an out-of-body experience" (Green, 1976, p. 176). Thus a dream is the experience of a total situation that is different from what one would infer from the individual's behavioral stance alone—because the subject is either asleep or awake but experiencing a regenerated version of his actual setting in a *manner* distinct from ordinary perception. Although most dreams are not set in one's bedroom and one typically forgets that one is in bed asleep during a dream, this need not be the case. In out-of-body experience (see chapter 8), the perceived setting is generally a constructed version of the individual's actual environment but imaged from a different angle of regard.

This definition, although careful and inclusive, still does not tell us anything about the cognitive processes involved, whether perceptual, mnemic, and/or imaginative, nonsymbolic and/or symbolic. Only by comparing and contrasting the specific types of experience included in such a definition (e.g., lucid dreams, out-of-body experience, some daydreams, and ordinary REM dreams) and tracing their overlap and differences with such related phenomena as altered states, ordinary waking fantasies, and the waking life-world, can we hope to learn something of the cognitive bases of a dreaming process. For now, we have only the relatively unhelpful notion of a tendency to reconstitute an encompassing life-world whenever there is a loss of awareness of the actual environment (whether from sleep, disinterest, or directed hypnotic suggestion) and a sufficient activation of the central nervous system to permit whatever processes (perceptual, mnemic, imaginative) that can so "enworld."

Is it feasible or even useful to look for a single essence of dreaming? Wittgenstein (1966), in one of the most intelligent and fair-minded critiques of Freud's dream psychology ever attempted, asks why we would ever expect, as Freud and now Foulkes and Antrobus do, that there is an essential nature to the dream. Like the endlessly permeable consciousness of wakefulness, dreaming may have no set or fixed nature. Dreaming may simply have no essence. Is there an essence to talking or walking? For Wittgenstein, dreaming involves contexts of usage so different that any suggested essence of dream formation is either falsified by the actual varieties of dreaming or stretched to the point that it becomes a useless truism. Freud's notion of dreaming as wish fulfillment, for example, quickly becomes "disguised wish fulfillment" in the face of the diversity of the manifest dream. *Wish* becomes so elastic semantically that it includes literally all organismic functioning. As Wittgenstein points out, if all colors were shades of "red" the term would become curiously useless. Or else we must take Freud more literally and trace the ubiquity of *wish* to his concept of instinctive drive. Here, having finally entered the realm of the potentially falsifiable, we find wide agreement inside and outside psychoanalysis that the concept of drive discharge is much too narrow to explain all human capabilities.

Or consider Freud's view that day residue is the nidus of all dreaming—the model of the dream as "completing unfinished business." Several empirical studies seem to support such a view, as we have seen, but this concept is also far too general to tell us about dreaming. Klinger (1978) found that day residue is predominant in waking fantasies, which are nonetheless quite different from vivid dreaming. Something like a tendency for gestalt completion (the power of the unresolved) runs through all organismic behavior, so it cannot define dreaming. Finally, what of the Jungian view that dreams compensate for personal tendencies that are not lived out within daily life? To the extent that dreaming involves novelty and cognitive recombination then its distinctiveness from daily life becomes true by definition, and notions of compensation also become truistic. Only if some dreaming is identifiable as *not* wish fulfillment (which Freud [1919a] finally acknowledged), *not* based on unfinished business, and *non*compensatory do these principles become useful for identifying specific lines of dream development.

Medard Boss (1958, 1977) has gone further than any modern investigator in demonstrating, by copious example, the various possible forms of dream experience. If, as Boss states, all the experiential modalities of human existence potentially exist in dreaming, there are indeed many lines of variation to trace through dreaming, not just one. There may not be a fundamental *function* of dreaming, any more than we can find a function for human existence generally. A self-referential, self-transforming system like the human mind will evolve its uses as creatively and open-endedly as it evolved its structures.

There do seem to be relatively distinct types of dreaming, each with its own line of development and potentially one-sided exaggeration—as permitted or perhaps demanded by the subductive clouding or single-mindedness of dreaming. There are relatively mundane dreams that seem to be based on mnemic consolidations and reorganizations; Freud-type relatively fantastic, pressure-discharge dreams, often based on complex rebuslike wordplay; dreams based on somatic states and illness; dreams based on aesthetically rich metaphor; dreams based on problem-solving and deep intuition (perhaps extrasensory?); lucid-control dreams; the varieties of nightmare; and a Jung-type archetypal-mythological form of dreaming. These forms potentially overlap, and all may have in common some background mnemic reorganization, but each also has its prototypical exemplars. It may be because dreaming has no fixed function that it is open to so many different uses. Not only do these potentialities of the dream—while asleep, falling asleep, or awake—argue against any one deep structure for dreaming, they are also fully consistent with the recent view of Gardner and others that there is no single deep structure for symbolic cognition generally. Rather we find multiple and potentially independent symbolic faculties—each developing a reflexive recombinatory capacity in its own fashion.

If, as most authors believed before psychoanalysis and the laboratory era, there *are* relatively distinct types of dreams, then only by means of their juxtaposition and comparison can we shed light on a dreaming process—whether we conclude that such a process is ultimately unitary or as diverse as the forms it generates. Both classical and tribal peoples (as well as most Western phenomenological observers) describe the same types or forms of dream experience. We shall see how this cross-culturally redundant multiplicity of dreaming may now offer more to cognitive science than the other way around—by helping to locate the real multiplicity in symbolic cognition that is all too easily missed in a mass society and in the psychology it generates.

CHAPTER 5

The Multiplicity of Dreaming in Anthropology, the Ancient World, and the Nineteenth Century

Nineteenth-Century Gentlemen Dreamers

N INETEENTH-century dream studies, prior to Freud, continue to fascinate, in part because they are based on careful observations by single individuals (and their like-minded friends) of their own often distinctive and unusually developed dreams. Precisely because long, sustained self-reflection on dreams seemed to change their dreams in mulitple but characteristic directions, these writers also cast a unique light on normative dreaming (at least within our own tradition). William James, Sigmund Freud, and A. R. Luria all held that only the selective exaggeration of the average allows us to see its normally masked dimensions and processes. On this approach exaggeration, excess, and pathology are the natural microscope of the mind.

The often reclusive pioneers of modern dream research were first-rate observers. The failure to assimilate their work first into psychoanalysis and now into experimental dream research highlights our "modern" tendency in the human sciences to leapfrog the stages of observation and classification, so central to the development of classical science, in favor of the "certainties" of the laboratory. The shared emphasis of these pioneers on the cognitive psychology of the day helps to underscore our earlier discussion of the circularity that may be inherent in theoretical preoccupations in psychology. These early observers generally agreed with Plato (see *The Republic*) that the cognitive faculties predominating in dreams could vary, in marked contrast to the exclusive memory models of Antrobus and Palombo (and Aristotle). The early dream researchers also generally agree that dreaming entails a core delirium or dissolution that constitutes not the cause but the potential occasion (much as with later models of the action of LSD-25) for the release or "exaltation" of specific faculties—most commonly memory, but often creative imagination, intuition, and spiritual experience as well.[1]

Hervey de Saint-Denys's *Dreams and How to Guide Them* (1867) is the best example of the predominant rationalist tradition of dream studies. Saint-Denys understood dream formation, as did Maury in 1861, as a direct, one-way translation of verbal thought into visual imagery. The dream could be entirely accounted for by associationist principles of memory. We shall see below that Saint-Denys also initiated the study of lucid-control dreams, but primarily as an observational tool for investigating his own dreams.

If we make some allowance for the changes in our psychological language for cognitive processes, Saint-Denys's account of dream formation sounds remarkably like that of Antrobus or Foulkes:

> We see that the mere evocation of the images stored in the human memory is sufficient to produce what are apparently the most astonishing dreams, because of the different ways in which they are brought forth and combined. . . . I believe that there is nothing in natural dreaming so bizarre or complex that it cannot be attributed to one or other of the following two phenomena, or to both phenomena acting in concert: (1) The natural and spontaneous unfolding of a continuous chain of memories; and (2) the sudden intervention of an idea from outside the chain due to some accidental physical cause.   (Saint-Denys, 1867, p. 39)

Indeed, like these authors he explicitly reduces creative imagination to memory: "We see nothing in dreams that we have not seen before. . . . What after all is human creativity, what is invention in painting, in literature, in poetry? Surely it is the new combination . . . whose elements our memory—in other words our memory-images—supply" (p. 27).

Yet it appears that some of Saint-Denys's own examples fit better with the romantic tradition that sees in some dreaming a special enhancement of creative imagination. For Von Schubert in 1814, dreaming was an autonomous "picture language" based on a system of visual "hieroglyphics" common to all peoples and polysemantic in that it fused multiple concepts into single images—"a higher kind of algebra" (Ellenberger, p. 205). Von Shubert, Carl DuPrel (1889), and to some extent Scherner, writing in 1861, anticipate Jung and James Hillman in their portrayal of imagistic processes as largely independent of language, yet self-referential (symbolic) and with their own line of development.

Saint-Denys's account of the "double" dream of a mathematician is an interesting example of what Jung later termed archetypal dreaming:

> I dreamed I was transported to a sort of temple—dark, immense and silent. I was drawn by an irresistible curiosity towards an altar of ancient design which was the sole lighted object in this solitary and mysterious spot. An inexpressible emotion warned me that I was about to witness something unheard of. Then I saw a kind of embryo, half-black and half-white, struggling in a semi-transparent envelope which had the shape of an egg. I put my hand on this moving membrane. A child emerged. It was a parable, I thought. I felt inspired and my lips began to move of their own accord . . . pronouncing a whole series of axioms and sayings in verse which filled me with surprise and excitement; for I was convinced that some important meaning was to be found in them. . . . A being whose nature and face I could scarcely make out, began to repeat word for word . . . everything that I had just said, so that I recognized every word. Unfortunately, despite all my efforts, my memory of his words faded into blackness as soon as he had spoken. The fact caused me untold torment. . . . While his body was hidden in amorphous shadow, his head was luminous and of colossal proportions, and curiously enough seemed like a reproduction of my own face, reflected by some fantastic mirror. "Who are you," I repeated. . . . For a moment he was silent. Then he said "yourself!", and . . . I immediately had the conviction that what he said was true, that he was the part *that was not blind* to the duality which I could not understand but whose secret was enclosed in the parable of the half-white, half-black child. "If you are myself," I retorted, "why am I afraid of you." . . . He only continued to fix me with his penetrating gaze, while I realized that I was dreaming and began to wake up.   (Saint-Denys, 1867, pp. 94–95)

Of course it is always possible to trace the elements of such a dream back to previous life experiences (including reading and religious education), but if *imagination* refers to anything, it refers to such an experience—at least if we remain cognizant of the dangers of "universal redness."

To complete the lines of nineteenth-century dream studies synthesized by Freud in his own masterful but monotheistic fashion, we add the somatic models of dream formation. Going back to Plato, Aristotle, and Hippocrates, we find the notion that sleep, in eliminating external stimulation, allows a greater sensitivity to what we would now call background coenesthesis and entoptic sensation, which can then undergo translation into the visual surface of dreams. Such dreams thus can potentially diagnose the early stages of hitherto unnoticed medical problems. For Aristotle and later Bergson, these internal sensations could appear within the dream by picking up similarly patterned memories, but Scherner (in 1861) and Volkelt (in 1875) saw them as the immediate source material for creative metaphor—echoing views from Vico to Solomon Asch and even B. F. Skinner that metaphors are ultimately based on physical sensation.

Scherner also linked characteristic dream imagery to specific bodily organs in the diagnostic fashion begun by Hippocrates and also reflected in tribal shamanism. Dreams of flying were based on the lungs; heavy traffic, on circulatory conditions; knives and towers on the male genitalia; caves and staircases, on the female. The dream image of a house or building corresponded to the human body in general. One of my own dreams illustrates this striking process in which an unusual somatic sensation is translated into the visual structure of the dream:

> Feeling feverish and light-headed shortly after a flu shot and aware of an exhaustion in my limbs associated with a rapid, involuntary tremor, I lay on the floor, fell asleep, and found myself in my study facing a rattlesnake. Its uplifted head was oscillating rapidly (at what I realized on awakening was the same rate and quality of my shaking leg muscles). Sinking to the floor, overcome by terror, I crept backward before its steady advance. Finally, I pushed a chair against it. To my surprise, the rattlesnake stopped its advance, and I awoke with the brief fever gone.

Such an experience would be based on a tactile-to-visual synesthetic translation that may well be the core of metaphor. On a structurally complex level, such synesthesis seems unique to human beings.[2]

Finally, we need an overview of the phenomenological literature on lucid-control dreaming, begun in the nineteenth century and extending from Saint-Denys to Van Eeden (1913), Arnold-Forster (1921), Ouspensky (1961), Whiteman (1961), Fox (1975), and Green's (1968) careful phenomenology and classification. As with recent research on psychedelic drugs, we find two very distinct accounts of lucid dreaming: Saint-Denys's and Arnold-Forster's approaches are reminiscent of Heinrich Kluver's use of mescaline for the painstaking observation of the formal properties of visual imagery. Saint-Denys and Arnold-Forster used lucid dreams primarily as an investigative tool to trace the processes of verbal to visual translation that characterized their own dreams—as in the following account by Mary Arnold-Forster:

> We were walking in a country unknown to me. We had crossed some grasslands and came to a roughly made stile of wooden bars over which I helped my mother to climb. The path which we followed led down the side of a grassy slope which formed the side of a shallow winding valley. . . . Looking down the valley we were descending into, I saw that the path lay across it like white ribbon and then turned off to the right towards the distant village. "It looks just like a road marked out upon a map," I

thought, "or like a railway map." As I looked again I saw that there was running down the length of the valley a railroad track which I had not seen before and which crossed the path that we were following. We came nearer and I saw that no gates guarded the crossing of the roads. . . . "There would be no warning whatever of a train coming from behind the hills except the sound of it." I listened and then I began to hear, far away, the roar of a train; it came round the hill and round a sudden sharp curve at the foot of the valley rushing towards us very fast. . . . "What a fine thing it is to see the oncoming of a great train—it is like the description of a stampede of wild cattle on the western plains." . . . Again the suggested thought realized itself at once. From far down the valley there came the sound of many hooves beating the earth all together with a deep sound, and there came tearing up it a vast body of splendid wild cattle. (Arnold-Forster, 1921, pp. 132–33)

In contrast to the disinterest of Saint-Denys and Arnold-Forster in any special "sensation" from the experience of lucidity in dreams, Van Eeden concentrated on the *experience* of lucid dreaming, seeing it as a state of mind to be cultivated in its own right. We will see later how such dreams bear a kinship to the nonverbal self-reflectiveness involved in meditation. Here is one of Van Eeden's own observations:

I dreamt that I was lying in the garden before the windows of my study and saw the eyes of my dog through the glass pane. I was lying on my chest and observing the dog very keenly. At the same time, however, I knew with perfect certainty that I was dreaming and lying on my back in my bed. And then I resolved to wake up slowly and carefully and observe how my sensations of lying on my chest would change into the sensations of lying on my back. And so I did, slowly and deliberately, and the transition—which I have since undergone many times—is most wonderful. It is like the feeling of slipping from one body into another and there is distinctly a *double* recollection of the two bodies. I remembered what I felt in my dream, lying on my chest; but returning into the day-life, I remembered also that my physical body had been quietly lying on its back all the while. This observation of a double memory I have had many times since. It is so indubitable that it leads almost unavoidably to the conception of *a dream-body*. (Van Eeden, 1913, p. 151)

This more detached experiential approach, so similar in principle to the psychedelic drug research tradition of Grof, Masters and Houston, and Timothy Leary, is also characteristic of Fox, Whiteman, Green, and more recently Sparrow (1976) and Gillespie (1987).

Dream Types in Anthropology

Most tribal societies, especially the hunter-gatherer traditions, distinguish multiple types of dream, with a corresponding complementarity in their theories and methods of dream interpretation. Traditional cultures have generally understood dreaming as a wandering of the soul—some tribes distinguish among several such souls, each with its own special purpose in waking, dreaming, and death. Edward Tylor (1871), J. S. Lincoln (1935), and the contemporary anthropologists in Barbara Tedlock's collection (1987) have all stressed the importance of dreaming to cultural maintenance and innovation in these peoples (see chapter 10). Susanne Langer (1972) has even hypothesized that dreaming was the point of departure for the development of the human symbolic capacity. In contrast to Tylor's early speculations about "primitive" mentality, it now seems erroneous to assume traditional peoples cannot tell the difference between waking and dreaming. Rather, they value the dream as more real or more important in a spiritual sense.[3]

Most contemporary anthropological accounts of tribal dreaming (Dentan, 1987; Tedlock, 1987) explicitly or by implication show that natives identify the following dream types.

(1) "Personal" dreams, based on "remembering" or "things you think about during the day" or "wishes of the soul," regarded as both most common and least important.
(2) Medical-somatic dreams, often merged with the categories to follow; they are important in the shamanistic diagnosis of physical illness and/or spiritual loss of soul.
(3) Dreams that are prophetic and/or that present omens which may come true. In many tribes such dream omens can be negated by telling the dream to one's immediate group, as opposed to keeping silent and so preserving the omen's effectiveness.
(4) Archetypal-spiritual dreams, vivid, and subjectively powerful "big" dreams based on visitations by gods or spirits, encounters with one's guardian spirit in rites of identity and initiation, or travels of the soul to the supernatural underworld or heavens. Such dreams are often a special province of the shaman, who develops them for power and knowledge as well as healing. J. S. Lincoln termed them *culture pattern dreams* and saw them as a unique penetration of dreaming consciousness by social-cultural reality, while Jung regarded them as archetypal expressions of a cross-culturally common, autonomous imagination (see chapter 10).

In addition to the cross-cultural occurrence of nightmares or anxiety dreams in children and adults, there is considerable evidence that archetypal-spiritual dreams, especially as developed within shamanism, involve a lucid-control dimension (Guss, 1980; Dentan, 1987.) The shaman is often said to be "awake" during his or her dream, entering it either from sleep (via prior dream incubation and concurrent lucidity) or deliberately from waking trance. Such dreams are generally considered especially dangerous because the shaman uses dream control to enter realms in which mythic forces and beings can cause loss of soul (certain physical illnesses or madness). These dreams are especially intense, with a subjective sense of the *numinous*, a term coined by Rudolf Otto (1923) to refer to the sense of awe, fascination, wonder, and bliss/dread that is the spontaneous experiential core of religion.

For instance, Jivaro men in search of shamanistic power seek dream contact with "ancient warrior souls" (*ajutap*):

> *Ajutap* dreams typically have two parts: An initial vision of a terrifying beast or comet-like blast of light that the dreamer must confront and touch, followed by a second dream (sometimes separated from the first by a day or more) in which the *ajutap* presents himself to the dreamer in human form and tells him of his future victory in battle. A man who receives such a vision is called "owner of a dream" or "one who has had a vision." His outward manner becomes forceful and self-assured since he knows that his enemies cannot kill him.   (Brown, 1987, pp. 304–05)

A lucidity dimension is also implied within culture pattern/archetypal dreaming, as in Merrill's account of shamanistic dreams among the Raramuri of northern Mexico, in which God approaches and offers special power:

> In this dream, God offers the individual three (or four if the dreamer is female) light-coloured pieces of paper. If one takes the paper, then God provides the knowledge to cure and will assist in future curing endeavors. Sometimes the Devil stands beside God in such dreams holding three (or four) dark-coloured papers. The person then can choose to become a doctor, a sorcerer, or both, or neither, according to the colours of the papers he or she grabs. The role of Doctor is the only position in the society that requires legitimization through a dream.
>
> Every night, the souls of Doctors join God and his assistants in watching over the other members of the community, preventing the Devil and his cohorts from hurting them. . . . If soul loss is indicated, the Doctor concentrates his attention on locating the soul in his dreams on that or subsequent nights. The task is considered potentially quite arduous, requiring lengthy journeys through little known or often dangerous territories; as one man put it, it is like searching for a thief whose location is unknown.   (Merrill, 1987, pp. 331–32)

One senses here, as with Tibetan Buddhism (see chapter 8), that the attainment of lucid-control dreaming opens one to powerful visionary experiences.

The development of dreaming in its own right does seem to lead to a progressive unfolding of powerful visual-kinesthetic metaphors combined with lucid self-reflection—as seen in the cross-cultural potential to develop whatever is involved in becoming a mystic or shaman directly as a result of and sometimes mainly in certain culture pattern dreams. This special development of dreams has been noted by all classic civilizations and tribal cultures. It provides a more impersonal terminus for the variations of dream experience that emerge out of personal-mnemic reorganizations. If the latter are based on linguistic and memory processes that have become the center of current cognitive science, the former may represent an abstract self-referential capacity based on visual-presentational cognition, about which contemporary psychology has had little to say.[4]

Like dreams in the ancient classical civilizations, the major form of dream interpretation in tribal peoples could be termed "prophetic," but it involves a more specifically "performative" or "world-creating" sense. Their dreams are widely understood not simply to anticipate or foretell the future but actually to bring it about. The dream, thus, is understood as directly *causal*. We could refer to this as a "ritual" dimension of dreaming in that after awakening the dreamer is often required to act or interact in some specific way as the result of certain dreams. Whether to tell the dream is often a major decision. In many tribes the dream must also be publicly acted out to forestall its consequences. Sometimes the dream must be told to all the people who appear in it (the very antithesis of the private and asocial dreaming portrayed by Freud). Thus a Seneca Indian dreamed:

> A certain young women was alone in a canoe, in the middle of a stream, without a paddle. The dreamer invited the young lady to a dream-guessing ceremony at his home. Various people gathered and tried to guess what the dream was. Finally the dream was guessed. A miniature canoe with a paddle was thereupon presented to the girl. This ceremony was expected to forestall the dream disaster from happening in real life.   (Wallace, 1958, p. 240)

Perhaps most striking in this regard was the Iroquois midwinter dream festival: Small groups of men and women invaded dwellings, overturning utensils and creating chaos, while miming the content of especially significant dreams. They did not leave until the "soul wish" of the dream had been guessed and either ritually enacted by the occupants and/or assuaged by a suitable gift. No wonder some anthropologists label primitive societies, at least in contrast to modern and even classical societies, "dream-centered."

If merely writing out and interpreting one's dreams over time can change them (Ellenberger, 1970), how much more might dreaming be transformed in such societies, as the public mirror of personal and social concerns? Indeed, much of the function of modern psychotherapy might thereby be achieved. Correspondingly, native informants comment on the shift in dreaming patterns that comes with Westernization. Many native peoples complain that few "big" dreams are reported any more and that young shaman initiates no longer have socially significant dreams (Lincoln, 1935; Tedlock, 1987). A contemporary Huichol shaman states:

If a person doesn't believe in his dreams, he might say, "It's only a dream; it's not real; the gods aren't really talking to me." Little by little everything will become less clear. . . . If one doesn't do what a dream has directed him to do, one won't be able to dream well any more. That's why so many people don't know how to dream. . . . If a person . . . believes in the dream and follows the directions once the (shaman) explains it. . . the gods will then send more dreams of this type because the person has now proven that he believes in the gods and obeys what he is told.   (Valadez, 1986, p. 19)

The continuing centrality of dreams for North American Indians is indicated by a questionnaire study by Kuiken (1987). Not only did a group of Cree Indians from Alberta recall significantly more dreams and feel more alert on awakening than did non-Indian control subjects, but they made more attempts to understand and analyze their dreams. They were also significantly more likely to contact the people who appeared in their dreams—thus maintaining the traditional performative utilization of dreams.[5]

Dream interpretation is immensely variable and complex among extant tribal peoples (Tedlock, 1987)—ranging from reading the manifest dream for direct or literal meanings to elaborate systems of symbolic meaning, often based on reducing all dreams to the structure of one or more dream types. Many tribes include a "prophetic" significance (based on the translation of all content into its operational significance for major areas of daily life like hunting, sex, or illness), along with a purely personal (and inconsequential) interpretation in terms of recent past experience, and a culture pattern significance for those with shamanistic training or potential. Thus among the Quiche Maya, according to Barbara Tedlock (1981), who became an apprentice shaman with them, a dream of being chased by a large domestic animal (like a bull) is interpreted as portending death for the average person but if the dreamer is a shaman it refers to the importance of maintaining a shrine for one's ancestors.[6]

In terms of the cognitive processes demonstrated in their techniques of dream interpretation (and hence at least potentially in dream formation), the Jivaro (Gregor, 1981) make use of meanings reminiscent of Western distinctions between metaphor (connections based on imagistic and spatial similarities that ultimately transcend syntax and language) and metonymy (connections based on linear linguistic combinations). Thus even with no knowledge of Jivaro language or custom, we can see the metaphorical basis of their interpreting a dream of fire as portending a fever, of an erect penis as a snake (since, reversing Freud, the area of ultimate significance for them is success in hunting), or a turtle's neck as portending the penis in sexual intercourse, and of dangerous animals as the souls of witches. Yet other linkages between the dream and their waking response to it require special knowledge of language and/or custom. We can only understand how a dream of one's bow cord breaking could mean that one's wife may die if we know that the wife of the hunter always makes his bow string. Interpretations that are metonymic but that also include a potential metaphorical basis include dreams of fruit as referring to sexual organs (because the Jivaro word for fruit means "plant's genitals") or dreams of manioc porridge as referring to semen (because they believe semen comes from drinking manioc). Metonymy is necessarily predominant when Bob Dylan sings, "The sun's not yellow, it's chicken"— unintelligible without knowledge of English usage.[7] The distinction between metaphor and metonymy (and their constant intertwining) is a major clue to cognitive processes involved in different types of dream formation. Indeed it will help to distinguish between the dreams (and dream theories) of Jung and Freud.

Modern anthropology emphasizes cultural relativity, but the literature on dreams in tribal people demonstrates that dream types are highly similar across cultures *and* that these types are held together by an implicit spatial model— one that, with a crucial reversal in value, is with us still. I refer to the notion that dreams are based on the actual night travels of the soul(s). The soul stays closest when it conveys the condition of the body (the source of all dream imagery for Scherner), travels slightly farther when it reexperiences personal concerns from the present and recent past (Freud), still farther as it portrays the personal and social future (Adler and theories of dream telepathy), and moves farthest from one's sleeping form when it enters the realms of the gods or the underworld (Jung). Visitation and apparition dreams reverse this passage, in that spirits and deities travel to the actual sleep setting—thus preserving the spatial metaphor.

The metaphor is still with us, but there has been a characteristically modern shift in value. What was most significant to primitives is for most contemporary dream researchers merely "far out," and what was least significant is now most "real," that is, most easily researched. Today we seem to handle best the personal and physiological-somatic sources of dream content. Nightmares, empirical evidence to the contrary, tend to be dismissed as clinical problems; intuitive-telepathic dreams, lucidity, and archetypal dreams are uneasily assigned to the "fringe"—which would be fine had the phenomena themselves ceased with their loss of social sanction. We will see, however, that the full range of dream types continues to occur in Western society. We are left to ponder the significance of the creation of a dream psychology (psychoanalytic and/or laboratory-based) focused on a form of dreaming regarded as "trivial" by societies whose cultures were centered around and even originated in their dreams. Perhaps it is *our* dreams that have *become* single-minded, private theaters of personal memory.

Classical Civilizations: Between Tribal and Modern Dream Typologies

The civilizations of Greece, Rome, and the ancient Near East (Brelich, 1966; Meier, 1966; Oppenheim, 1966), as well as the Indian tradition, as examined in O'Flaherty's *Dreams, Illusion and Other Realities* (1984), preserve the dream forms we located among tribal peoples. Beginning in later Greek thought, however, we find a shift toward naturalism and secularism in its valuation of dreams.

Personal dreams, understood as relatively trivial and reflecting recent memories and wishes, eventually moved to a central position in the writings of Aristotle. Diagnostic dreams, once formalized by Hippocrates (and later Aristotle), were understood naturalistically rather than prophetically as reflecting somatic processes too subtle to be registered during wakefulness. Hippocrates saw dreams that reproduced recent experience without distortion as a mark of health. Physical ill health was indicated when the soul no longer "abides by the purposes of the day." Accordingly, what we now term dream bizarreness was necessarily centered on "some struggle or triumph" in somatic function[8]—with the fantastic transformation of various phenomena in nature (e.g., sun, wind, streaming water) associated with disturbances in specific organs in much the fashion revived by Scherner.

The central emphasis in all classical civilizations was of course on prophetic dreams and interpretations. There was a widespread tendency in Greece, Rome, and ancient Near East to regard dreams as omens of one's personal future. The connection was held to be immediately obvious and direct in some dreams but identifiable in all dreams by means of elaborate interpretive systems. Widely used dream books, of which the *Oneirocritica* of Artemidorus is the only survivor, were preoccupied with whether the dream omen should be read literally and directly or indirectly via complex rules for decoding specific elements of the dream according to metaphoric and metonymic associations. (The standard meanings were sometimes reversed according to the waking circumstances of the dream.) Visitational dreams, in which the dreamer is approached by a god, spirit, or ancestor, are prominent in Homer. They were later institutionalized as part of the mystery cults. Their significance was variously interpreted as spiritual, prophetic, or medically diagnostic and curative, but by Hellenistic times the accent of value had shifted away from dreams as divine revelation.[9]

By now it should not be surprising that the ancients were also cognizant of both nightmares and lucid dreams. Roscher (1900, republished 1972 with commentary by James Hillman) reviewed ancient Greek and Roman classifications of the nature spirits and demons that caused nightmare attacks. Similarly, the lucid-control dimension is implied by temple dream incubation in the mystery and healing cults, in which cure depended upon the dreamed god's touching the dreamer. More specifically, what we now call lucid dreaming is mentioned by Aristotle: "Often when a man is asleep something in his soul tells him that what appears to him is a dream." (*On Dreams*, p. 367). A variant of what Green calls pre-lucid dreaming (see chapter 8) is found in Plato: " . . . thinking in a dream that we are telling other dreams" (*Theaetetus*, p. 863).

A dilemma runs through all Greek and Roman writings on dreams: is the dream direct and trustworthy or is it "enigmatic," potentially deceptive, and requiring elaborate and careful deciphering? The first and most poignant mention of this distinction is found in *The Odyssey*, as Penelope tells her as-yet-unrecognized husband of her dream and her fear that it be chimerical:

> PENELOPE: From a water's edge twenty fat geese have come to feed on grain beside my house. And I delight to see them. But now a mountain eagle with great wings and crooked beak storms in to break their necks and strew the bodies here. Away he soars into the bright sky; and I cry aloud. . . . Then down out of the sky he drops to a cornice beam with mortal voice telling me not to weep. "Be glad," says he . . . "Here is no dream but something real as day, something about to happen. All those geese were suitors and the bird was I. See now, I am no eagle but your lord come back to bring inglorious death upon them all!" As he said this, my honeyed slumber left me. Peering through half-shut eyes, I saw the geese in hall, still feeding at the self same trough.
> ODYSSEUS: My dear, how can you choose to read the dream differently? Has not Odysseus himself shown you what is to come? Death to the suitors, sure death, too. Not one escapes his doom.
> PENELOPE: Friend, many and many a dream is mere confusion, a cobweb of no consequence at all. Two gates for ghostly dreams there are: One gateway of honest horn, and one of ivory. Issuing by the ivory gate are dreams of glimmering illusion, fantasies, but those that come through solid polished horn may be borne out, if mortals only know them. I doubt it came by horn, my fearful dream—too good to be true.   (Homer, *The Odyssey*, trans., R. Fitzgerald, pp. 370–71)

In addition to its being metachoric, in the more narrow sense of occurring in the actual physical setting of the sleeper, and pre-lucid ("Here is no dream"), Penelope's dream is clear and direct—made of allegorical horn. We need nothing of Greek language, etymology, or history to render it intelligible. Even apart from the story of *The Odyssey*, it is already metaphoric of any predatory situation.

Contrast this with the "enigmatic" dream of Alexander the Great as cited from Artemidorus by Freud (1900). Impatient and uncertain in the midst of his long siege of Tyre, Alexander dreams of a satyr dancing on a shield. Aristander, his astrologer and dream interpreter, suggested persevering in the attack (which was successful) on the basis that the Greek *Tyr Sa* means "Tyre is yours." Here we have Freud's dream as rebus—the visual structure of the dream leaping into convincing intelligibility when the right pun, phonetic rhyme, or linguistic reversal is located.

While it is true that dream types in tribal society and in the ancient world are strikingly consonant, a shift in valuation in classical times foreshadows the final narrowing of dreaming in the twentieth century to one type, the least important of the earlier types. Apart from special "mystical" groups—including the mystery cults, Stoics, and Neoplatonists—divine dreams were increasingly deemphasized.[10] "Since some of the lower animals also dream, dreams cannot be sent by God," says Aristotle (*On Prophecy in Sleep*, p. 379). Accordingly, he offers a naturalistic model of ostensibly prophetic dreams. They will variously anticipate or directly or indirectly influence the future, or match it by coincidence. Indeed, Aristotle's approach to dreams of divine origin manages to be definitive unless we raise or renew a more phenomenological question: what sort of cognitive faculty might be involved in dreams that are in a descriptive sense archetypal? Even when we avoid any resort to supernatural explanation, still they must differ cognitively from dreams lacking these features. This form of questioning could only arise with the romantic celebration of imagination and its development into Jungian and transpersonal psychologies—which still lack a formal cognitive psychology.

The accent of importance in the classical world fell on prophetic (and medical) dreams. But, in contrast with tribal peoples, there was a change in the understanding of prophetic/oracular dreams, first pointed out by Oppenheim (1966) with respect to dreambook fragments from the ancient Near East. In contrast to the "world-creating" and "performative" use of dreams in tribal cultures (where dreams are often understood as a secondary participation in the original creation of the world, dreamed into being by the gods), the new and endlessly elaborate "science" of dream omens was entirely subservient to the prediction and control of one's personal destiny. In that sense it was for the first time *genuinely* superstitious—since one sought to control fate by special knowledge of one's own future as revealed by dream soothsayers. In this sense, however, the dreambooks also represented the incipient dawning of a rational and empirical attitude, since they were based on a careful categorization of all possible dream events and their varying significance for one's future conduct. The dream no longer causes the world. In-

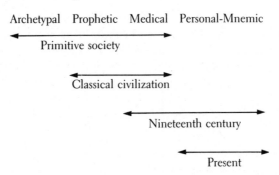

FIGURE 1: *Variation in Most-Valued Dream Types through Time*

stead it is a private sign to be read for personal fortune and avoidance of disaster, at the potential expense of one's neighbor. Indeed, the desacralization of the numinous-sacred phase of major cultures often seems to be associated with a magical and essentially paranoid attitude that differs profoundly in its emphasis on purely personal fortune from the so-called superstitious beliefs of tribal peoples (O'Keefe, 1982).

We find in each historical era and phase of culture a shift in relative importance across a common spectrum of dream typologies (figure 1). But despite these shifts in the predominant definition and theory of dreaming, despite the contrasting ontological assumptions of these cultures, there is evidence that the same forms of dream experience continue to recur. Although what was once the most objective and real (divine) of all dream forms may now seem the most subjective and inward (i.e., proceeding from a deep "primitive" unconscious) or just the "farthest out," the same natural order of dreaming obtains. Despite cultural and historical diversity and our own scientific urge toward parsimony, there is a natural order of dream forms. This is our most significant finding. Its implications for a cognitive psychology of dreaming have hitherto not been addressed—let alone its implications for a cognitive science.

Multiple Types versus Single Process

The modern narrowing of dreaming to a single paradigmatic type begins with Freud. Certainly we can appreciate the elegance and intellectual force of Freud's synthesis of the antinomies of the nineteenth-century dream literature. As James Hillman (1979) traces this achievement, Freud agreed with the rationalist tradition that the manifest dream is nonsensical, but he added a dimension of latent dream thoughts that he found correspondingly and ultimately rational. Freud rejected the romantic emphasis on creative imagination as a driving force of the dreaming process, but he included it within "dreamwork" proper—the processes or "mechanisms" by which the latent, predominantly verbal dream thoughts are translated into the visual elements of the dream experience. Thus imaginative condensation and symbolic metaphor are central to dream formation but subordinate to the necessity of disguise. Finally, the somaticist stream is central to the dream process but modified in terms of the "drives" of sexuality and, later, aggression.

Freud is acutely aware of the range of dream forms posited by the nineteenth-century phenomenologies, but he rejects it in favor of his well-known essentialist approach to the science of mind, modeled on Darwin and Galileo. In repudiating the idea that dreaming might "exalt" special mental faculties beyond their ordinary wakeful capabilities, he comes closest to recognizing our dilemma:

> Is it that some of our authorities have overlooked the non-sensical dreams and others the profound and subtle ones? And if dreams of both kinds occur, dreams that justify both estimates, may it not be a waste of time to look for any distinguishing psychological features of dreams? Will it not be enough to say that in dreams *anything* is possible—from the deepest degradation of mental life to an exaltation of it which is rare in waking hours? However convenient a solution of this kind might be, what lies against it is the fact that all of the efforts at research into the problem of dreams seem to be based on a conviction that some distinguishing feature *does* exist, which is universally valid in its essential outline and which would clear these apparent contradictions out of the way. (Freud, 1900, p. 96)

So, since everyone else looks for an essence, however one-sided their ultimate position, so shall Freud—the ultimate scientific conquistador! Freud paid a price for that decision and the price continues to be exacted in the continuation of this attitude in most laboratory and experimental dream research.

Freud fixes on what we can now see as one type of dreaming, making it the norm and core of his theory. These dreams are based on mnemic reorganizations of previous interpersonal and emotional experience, with evidence of associative linguistic processes operative beneath the surface of the dream. Freud's descriptive characterization of dreaming fits his own dreams, those of his patients, and normative dreams in laboratory and at home, but Jung, for example, dreamed very differently (see appendix, table 1; chapters 6, 9, 10). What other investigators and eras have seen as variations of the dreaming process Freud with characteristic bluntness declared "not really dreams."

The core of dream formation for Freud rests exclusively in visual representation, condensation, and displacement. Any dream lacking these, that is, formed differently, would "hardly deserve the name." Thus, dreams that Jung would report as coherent, well-formed expressions of archetypal imagination Freud sees not as dreams at all but as "phantasies" based on a defensive substitution of motifs recalled from fairy tales (Freud, 1913). Lucidity in dreams is relatively superficial and defensive, an aspect of secondary revision and thus pitted against the more affectively charged latent dream thoughts. "I am dreaming" masks the defensive "this is *only* a dream" (even though it is correct!). Freud's position is most explicit and even stark in his rejection of telepathic dreaming:

> The telepathic message—if we are justified in recognizing its existence—can thus make no alteration in the structure of the dream; telepathy has nothing to do with the essential nature of dreams. . . . The essential nature of dreams consists in the peculiar processes of the "dream-work." . . . Supposing, then, that we are brought face to face with a pure telepathic "dream," let us call it instead a telepathic experience in a state of sleep. A dream without condensation, distortion, dramatization, and above all, without wish-fulfillment, surely hardly deserves the name. (Freud, 1922, pp. 420–21)

(Note that we need not assert an extrasensory reality to such dreams, only that dreams may function at times in an outwardly directed, strikingly intuitive fashion). In this passage it is remarkable how Freud attempts to make his theory work by simply eliminating part of its rightful subject matter.

The price we pay for this restriction to Freud's own style of dream experience (even if it is statistically more common) and for the preemptory redefinition of other dream forms as "experiences in sleep" is an artificial impoverishment of our subject matter that continues to cripple laboratory-experimental research, with its concentration on "normative" dreams and its mostly college-undergraduate subjects. The dreams of special groups and individuals, which might best show the potentialities of the dreaming process, are dismissed as "the exception that proves the rule" (Foulkes, 1985, p. 44). This attitude is all the more disturbing since laboratory dreams are generally fairly boring, while it is precisely the more infrequent variations that call attention to dreams in the first place and make them uniquely worthy of study.

The challenge for a psychology of the natural diversity of dreaming is to avoid sliding into the empty eclecticism that Freud at least managed to avoid. On the contrary, perhaps only the study of multiple forms of dreaming will allow us insight into a deeper unity of dream formation that will continue to elude us if we restrict ourselves to normative dreams of mnemic reorganization.

CHAPTER 6

Basic Dimensions of the Dream Diamond

Methodology

The origins of the following system of classification are of interest in light of the historical and contemporary antinomies of dream research. At a recent conference of the Association for the Study of Dreams, Robert Monroe, a former television executive who has described his elaborate altered-state experiences in *Journeys Out of Body* and *Far Journeys* and is head of a private foundation for the study of out-of-body experience, gave an invited address. The laboratory-oriented members of ASD were somewhat uncomfortable with Monroe, but the crowded auditorium was in marked contrast to the sparse attendance at earlier research sessions. Monroe, in his folksy manner, was explaining that if we likened dreaming to television, then—and of course we professionals would already know this—there were two basic types of dream: those that were based on messages broadcast over different channels and those that reflected the properties of the set itself. Although Jung and Herbert Silberer had made distinctions that could be interpreted in this fashion, I suddenly realized that (1) of course we did *not* all know this, and (2) here was the initial key to a systematic ordering of dream forms.

Dreams based on the consolidation and reorganization of personal mem-

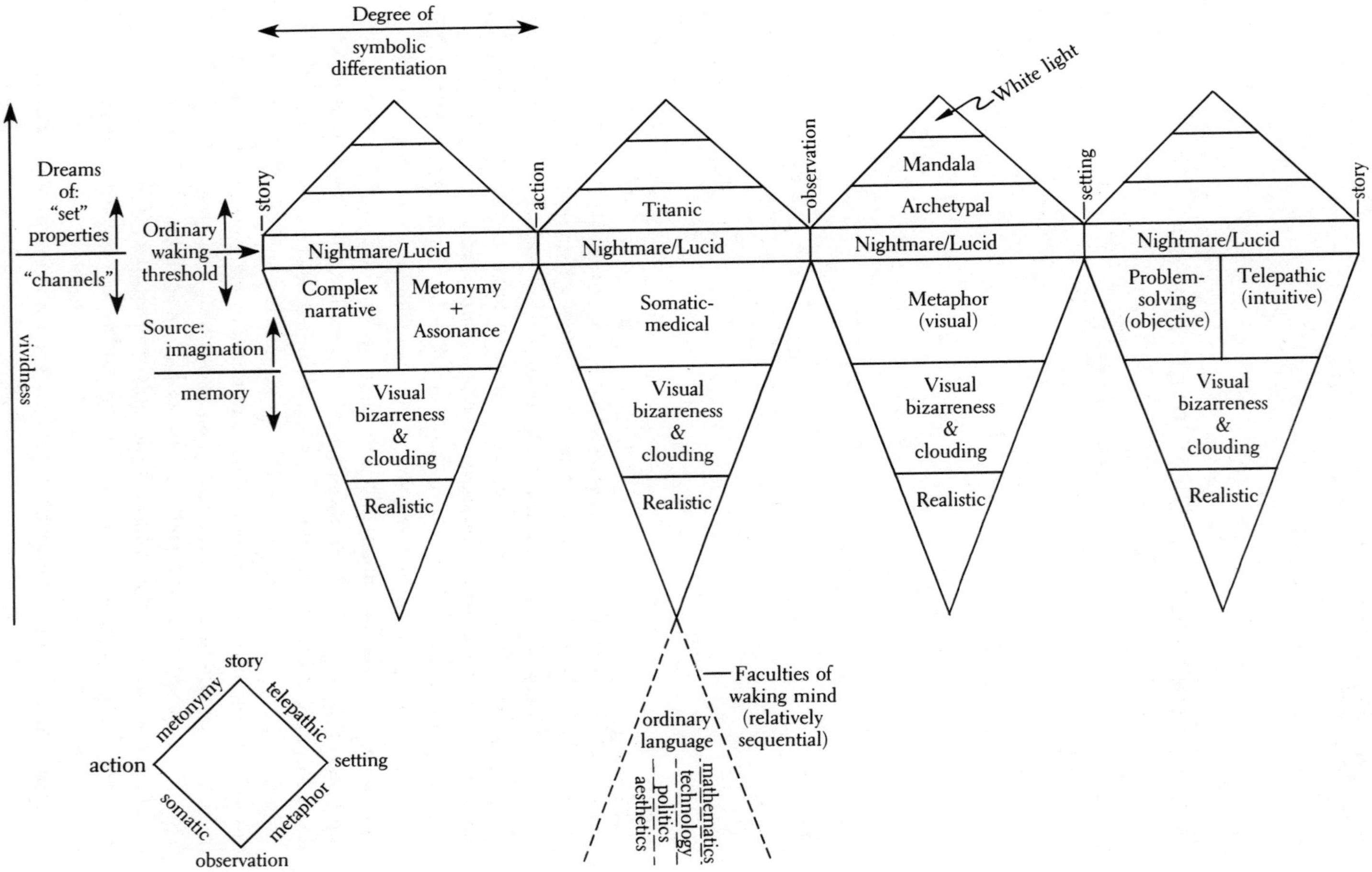

FIGURE 2: *Varieties of Dreaming*

ory, on visual metaphor, verbal metonymy (Freud's rebus), somatic-medical expression, and intuitive creative problem solving, under this system, would represent the "channels" to which the dreaming process could be tuned (these "channels" being more or less independent frames of mind). Archetypal dreaming, closely related to forms of experience associated with psychedelic drugs, deep meditation, and some hypnagogic experience, would express the *forms* of human cognition, relatively independent of specific content—the formal properties of the "set." Nightmares and lucidity could then be taken not only as transitional to the ordinary threshold of wakefulness but as transitional between "channels" and "set," in that essentially any other form of dreaming *can* become nightmarish and/or lucid (although differing orders of probability might well exist).

This system has turned into a three-dimensional diamond representing basic dream forms and their interrelations (figure 2).[1] The vertical dimension depicts vividness or intensification of the dreaming process. Dreams based on specific frames of symbolic intelligence crystalize out of a background of mnemic activation as a partial function of intensity. Archetypal dreams of formal self-reference appear at a point of dream vividness that would ordinarily awaken the dreamer. In other words, archetypal dreams, lucid dreams, and some nightmares occur in a twilight or transitional ("trance") state of consciousness highly similar to that associated with psychedelic drugs, sensory deprivation, and deep meditation. At the lower end of the intensity dimension, dreaming tends toward an inherently forgettable clouding and delirium, while its relatively rare manifestations at the upper end have a clarity and power that can stay with an individual for years. The horizontal dimension of the diagram indicates increasing degrees of symbolic differentiation (the unfolding of multiple frames of mind) versus symbolic integration (the relative subsuming of symbolic activity under one cognitive mode). Thus, with Foulkes and ultimately Freud, at the bottom of the diamond dreams of mnemic activation are largely controlled by the deep structures of ordinary language, while archetypal dreams are based on an overall integration of the human symbolic capacity in terms of an imagistic visual-kinesthetic intelligence.

Other features include a line along the vividness/intensity dimension beyond which the cognitive psychology of memory can no longer account for the variations of dreaming without seriously overextending its conceptual range of convenience. Here processes of creative imagination are posited as essential to dream formation. In addition, the closely related transitional forms of nightmares and lucidity can appear within any dream type, at least down to some hypothetical limit of vividness within the clouding of ordinary dreaming.

Finally, a two-dimensional depth diagram is integrated with and in turn orders the dream types. It is based on the notion that all dream episodes, like all waking situations, vary in terms of the complexity of the story narrative (sequential structure) and complexity of setting (simultaneous or spatial structure). To this structural dimension is added the interpersonal dimension of "role"—varying from actively initiated participation to observation and, ultimately, detached receptivity. Thus dreams of creative visual metaphor and archetypal imagination center themselves along a dimension shared by receptivity and relative simultaneity. Somatic-medical expressions develop in terms of a fundamental kinesthetic dimension ranging between action and observation. Dreams involving elaborate wordplay and narrative complexity (Freud and Foulkes, respectively) range along a dimension of active motor participation and sequential narrative structure (i.e., they essentially involve the left hemisphere). And dreams that are intuitively attuned to conditions and dilemmas of the external world (i.e., dreams that can mediate creative scientific breakthroughs) maximally synthesize simultaneous and sequential symbolic capabilities.[2]

It is important to note that all dimensions of the diamond reflect formal properties of dream experience; they tell us nothing about the relative frequency of these dream types. Any attempt to represent frequency within this diagram would entail either complex distortions in its surface areas (for example, 80 percent of a highly irregular polygon would be taken up by mnemic dreaming); or else we would have to give up the more important depiction of formal dimensions and draw a simple pyramid whose vertical and horizontal dimensions would represent only frequency. These alternatives would render the design either non-Euclidean or uninformative concerning cognitive process. It seems more useful to make each dimension depict formal cognitive processes potentially involved in all dreaming and simply state that normative frequency declines as vividness increases; that is, most dreams are low in intensity and, taken as a whole, do not reflect the release of semi-independent frames of symbolic creativity or formal self-reference.

Since classifications and typologies are rare now in psychology outside the areas of psychiatry and neurology, it is important to mention the problems this typology raises and the way it challenges the assumptions of content analysis studies of dreaming. Hillman says that in the humanities and social sciences "types" are best represented (and justified) by relatively exaggerated prototypes. Any given dream will fall under more than one heading—one hopes because the system is based on dimensions that vary continuously across all dream formation. Only if this is more or less true is the effort justified. When scoring dream aggression using standard content rating methods that for instance include references to death, how is one to decide whether the dream involves medical-somatic elements rather than simply the interpersonal reality assumed by Freud and most laboratory researchers to be the source of all dreaming? (see Smith, 1986). Measurement alone does not locate existent typologies. They are found only by the exercise of careful observation and judgment, such as were required in early classification work in biology and botany. Must we know the context of the dream in the individual's life before we can decide its type? In some instances yes, although it is not clear why that is any different from the importance (generally implicitly assumed) of knowing the ecological niche of a creature in order to understand its body shape, size, and characteristic movements. Perhaps current dream psychology can be likened to puzzling over the physical features of a duck in an immaculate laboratory, when only in its natural setting can the duck demonstrate their function. More generally, however—possibly because the system is based on dimensions common to all dreaming—it will often be possible to find dream features that identify metaphoric, metonymic, somatic, lucid, and/or archetypal forms.

Dream psychology, in haste for its own Darwin, has bypassed the necessary foundations of a Linnaeus. The various available systems of quantitative content analysis are complex and reliable (Winget and Kramer, 1979), and they correlate to a degree with cognitive, physiological, and personality variables, but they are still reminiscent of attempting to classify the natural order of species by first, ever so precisely, measuring length of limb, size of tooth, body weight, and so on—disregarding whether the animal is a reptile, fish, bird, or mammal. Dream researchers should rely instead on the initial basis of science: observation, judgment, and classification. We should expect that ratings of sexuality, aggression, friendliness, number of characters, emotion, and so on will have very different significance as we pass from multiple· indicators of one type to another. It is remarkable to me that dream psychology, like cognitive psychology generally, has largely avoided the fundamental observation and ordering of its materials in their natural context.

Normative Dreaming as Mnemic Activation and Reorganization

Thirty years of assessing laboratory and home dreams by means of systematic content analysis and more recent attempts to categorize the formal cognitive and affective transformations that define dream bizarreness provide a consistent picture of normative dreaming, centered on mnemic activation and reorganization and relatively plausible and true to daily life. It indeed appears that the classical clinically derived dream theories were based on more novel, somewhat atypical dreams, doubtless to their credit.

All observers seem to agree that normative dreaming is, to a remarkable degree, organized around long-term personal preoccupations and life themes. Recent events (day residues) figure prominently in dream content, although these are often relatively trivial impressions that were not fully processed or resolved during the day. Calvin Hall (1953) was struck by the fact that current life crises typically do not intrude into these endless variations on more personal themes. (Nightmares, of course, can be important exceptions to this tendency.) Jung stressed that "objective interpretations" (taking the dream as actually depicting external situations or people) were only occasionally justified, in contrast to the near ubiquity of subjective interpretation. Piaget similarly cites the predominance of assimilation over accommodation; Samuel Lowy sees dreaming as a representation of the immediate and total state of the ego (organic state, mood, and the way in which external events affect the self); and Freud finds a narcissistic core of dreams based on the withdrawal and disinterest of sleep itself.

The relative infrequency of the more striking categories of bizarreness in dreams (appendix, table 1) is surprising—especially if we take such formal variations as potential indicators of symbolic imagination. In content studies based on ratings of interpersonal relations (Hall and Van de Castle, 1966; Van de Castle, 1971), dreams tend to continue features of waking personality, except that the dreamer is more passive and more subject to the aggression of others. (This may indicate a latent tendency to experience the organismic orientation response of dreaming as something of an onslaught, which in a sense it is.) In terms of the more formal properties of dream experience, several research studies show that genuine novelty and qualitative recombination of past experience are relatively infrequent. Dorus, Dorus, and Rechtschaffen (1971) found 45 percent of their laboratory dreams to have occurred in largely identical or at least similar form in waking; another 20 percent were technically novel but fully plausible in the context of the individual's daily life. Only 9 percent were rated intrinsically bizarre and impossible in everyday life. Snyder (1970) found that 76 percent of longer laboratory dreams from good recallers showed high narrative coherence, and 68 percent were rated as highly believable; 60 percent had no bizarreness and only 5 percent were scored as highly bizarre. Of these accounts, 90 percent described speech content and 60 percent could quote it directly. Adaptive, reflective thought was present in 70 percent of the dreams. Heynick (1981) reported similarly high levels of recall for dream speech and stressed its linguistic competence and adequacy to the dream context.

Not only does this relatively successful reproduction of waking experience argue for mnemic models of dream formation, but it strongly argues against

any universality for the hypothesis of Freud (and Foulkes) that verbal propositional thought is necessarily "impaired"—"loaded" by the processes of translation from language into visual imagery and so excluded from the manifest
dream. It demolishes Freud's insistence that speech and thought truly original
to the dream setting are impossible (i.e., that all dream speech is a replay of
previous conversation). Certainly the presence of largely adequate reflective
thought and speech in dreams refutes the idea that dreaming in its totality is a
visual paraphrase of background verbal thoughts that are thereby eclipsed in
the process. Yet neither do these findings fit with the view that the entire
dream is a visual thought truncated prior to translation into language (Jung).
Of course both hypotheses remain possible for non-normative varieties of
dreaming.

Taking a more fine-grained approach, we find some agreement on the
typical kinds of formal cognitive anomalies and transformations in the dream.
We have already reviewed the tendency of normative home and laboratory
dreaming toward delirium—with intrusions of visual content implausible for
the dream setting and numerous indications of cognitive confusion and clouding (Hunt et al., 1982; see appendix, table 1). Hobson and colleagues' (1987)
category system for dream anomalies strikingly confirms these findings. They
also found approximately 40 percent of a dream sample showing what I would
term confusional thinking ("incongruous and vague" in Hobson's words) and
just under 50 percent with implausible, mainly visual, intrusions of content
("mismatching features"). Many of the cognitive confusions were in direct
reaction to the visual intrusions.

It has seemed most parsimonious to many observers to interpret these typical
features of dream bizarreness as expressions of the assimilation and reorganization of recent emotional memories in terms of the "interpersonal" categories of
long-term memory storage. Palombo (1978) calls attention to the condensation
or superimposition of past material in the dream as typically mnemic. So it is that
the mnemic activation postulated by Foulkes could be termed "diffuse"; that is, it
fuses material from different settings in terms of their significance in semantic
memory. Literal condensations in the fabric of the dream—direct reflections of
Freud's mechanism of condensation—are present in fewer than 10 percent of
laboratory and home recall dreams (Hunt et al., 1982). But if we consider "hallucinatory intrusions" (events, characters, and objects unlikely or impossible to the
dream setting) as evidence of mnemic superimposition, then these would occur
in up to 50 percent of such dreams. Of course if we apply free-association to
normative dreams we could say that essentially all such dreams, on reflection,
can lead back into one's recent and distant past. Although that in itself need have
no necessary relationship to dream formation, it is also the case that in class

exercises over the past ten years, in which students free-associate both to their dreams *and* to accounts of their everyday lives, it was almost universal that the associations to dreams were richer and led to more diverse memories than to episodes from waking life.

A brief illustration of mnemic superimposition (or diffuse mnemic activation) comes from Freud's dream of his uncle as literally condensed with his friend R, who had been refused academic advancement, in all probability because of anti-Semitism. This example is all the more interesting for being entirely without any background dream setting to be intruded upon—it is pure condensation:

> I. My friend R was my uncle—I had a great feeling of affection for him.
> II. I saw before me his face, somewhat changed. It was as though it had been drawn out lengthways. A yellow beard that surrounded it stood out especially clearly.   (Freud, 1900, p. 171)

R., with his yellowish-grey beard, was a good friend. Freud's uncle, who had an elongated face and a fair beard, had had legal problems and was regarded by Freud's father as a simpleton. Freud interprets their unlikely fusion as wishfully assuaging his fear about his own pending academic promotion by assimilating his friend's character to that of his uncle.

Not only does this dream show the condensation so central to the cognitive psychologies of memory in Bartlett and Tulving, it also suggests that the ostensible hodgepodge of some dream content can be unraveled by free association into a coherent expression of background, verbally mediated, recollections and reflections upon them. Accordingly, at least some visual intrusions/ superimpositions may illustrate the model of Freud and Foulkes that the manifest dream is a visual paraphrase of underlying verbal-semantic processes. Freud's fusion of uncle and friend is only fully intelligible as a sort of visual rebus for a complex if-then statement—"if he were a fool like my uncle then anti-Semitism was not the cause of his denial and I may be alright."

Of course mnemic superimposition need not be the only explanation for "visual intrusions," especially those leading immediately to reflections that clearly go beyond previous verbal understanding. Thus dreams associated with creative discoveries in science, art, and personal dilemmas express an autonomous capacity for visual metaphor that becomes "insight" only when finally articulated. The shock of discovery when that accompanies first verbalization of these visual structures suggests that such imagistic thinking can be relatively independent of preceding verbal formulations. Here we approach those multiple points where, if memory is to remain a useful explanatory concept for much of dreaming, parsimony equally decrees that other cognitive faculties or frames related to imagistic intelligence are involved in more intensified and vivid manifestations of the dreaming process.

Does a mnemic activation/reorganization dimension necessarily run through all dreaming, as its point of departure? Are features of memory consolidation also present in all dreams involving imagination—in visual metaphor, verbal metonymy, ludicity, and archetypal dreaming? Findings of a memory consolidation function in mammalian REM sleep might so indicate. On the other hand, if we possessed fully developed rating systems for lucid, somatic, or archetypal dimensions of dreaming, I suggest that they too could be traced (in less developed forms) through normative memory-based dreams. Dreaming might have a linguistic and mnemic core (as does waking inner speech, the basis of everyday intelligence), yet all dimensions of dream formation may be more or less nascent in all dreams. Intensification of the dreaming process would selectively exaggerate one or more of these dimensions, leading to one of the less frequent, imaginatively based dream types. Just so, human intelligence rests on a linguistically organized semantic memory, but some individuals develop into artists, engineers, mystics, and so on— exercising nonverbal frames that are also at least minimally present in all human experience.

CHAPTER 7

Specific Imaginative-Intuitive Faculties as Forms of Dreaming

Verbal Metonymy and the Dream's Shift toward Metaphoric Assonance

E|VIDENCE of creative imagistic activity in dream formation does not encourage us to assimilate all dreaming to representational language. Still, the difficulty in evaluating when dream imagery goes beyond prior verbal understanding suggests that imagery and language must continuously interact anyway. The linguistic processes that enter dreams most readily are more presentational than representational—in that "the whole domain of verbal wit is put at the disposal of the dreamwork" (Freud, 1900, p. 376). Certainly, in many of Freud's own dreams ordinary language has been spontaneously rearranged in the form of rebuslike wordplay, visual hieroglyphics based on special turns of phrase, and above all punning, rhyming, and clang associations based on verbal phonetics. The visual products of this underlying activity intrude on, and in the extreme eliminate, the sequential story structure of ordinary dreaming. To explicate the complex wordplay in the formation processes of some dreams, we will follow Paul Kugler's important treatment of the interaction of language and image in his *The Alchemy of Discourse* (1982).

Like the linguists Jakobson and Saussure, Kugler, a Jungian psychologist, distinguishes between symbolic connections that rest on sequential *chaining* or metonymy (including syntax itself and personal associations) and connections based on *equivalance* or metaphor (including semantics and the phonetic assonance involved in wit and poetry). Although actual wordplay and neologism appear only rarely in the manifest dream (Heynick, 1981),[1] Kugler reinforces the observations made by many others (including Freud) by suggesting that certain visual intrusions are only explicable in terms of verbal assonance and other wordplay. Jakobson and Halle (1956) distinguished between two kinds of aphasic disorder: (1) disorders of similarity, equivalence, or metaphor, where naming is profoundly disturbed but syntax remains; and (2) contiguity disorders, where it is the metonymic connections that are disrupted, allowing only condensed telegraphic communications that lack most syntactic connectives and modifiers and that often fuse words based on the same etymological root and/or sound. Before examining the extent to which dreaming may lean toward such a "disorder" of contiguity, favoring immediate "presentational" fusions based on sound and image, we must look at examples of the opposite extreme—dreams based on creative metonymy.

First there are those relatively infrequent but striking dreams of narrative complexity and originality that have figured in the creative writing of several authors. Robert Louis Stevenson (1912), H. P. Lovecraft (1962), and Franz Kafka (see Hall and Lind, 1970) all "dreamed" the first versions of several famous stories. This clearly shows that the narrative story dimension of dreaming, which Foulkes makes the core of all dreaming, can be enhanced in its own right. Related but again infrequent effects include the presence of an anonymous verbal narrator in some dreams (often anticipating dream events that only unfold later) and the dream experience of elaborately detailed narrative memories, amounting to alternative lives, that turn out completely false on awakening. Certainly such dreams indicate the primacy of an imaginative narrative intelligence.

Lest such dreams seem altogether too esoteric and "literary," I offer a recent example of complex narrative dreaming, clearly creative but not dreamed by a writer, from a report by Lavie and Wollman (1985) on a seventy-year-old man who came forward because he thought (rightly) that his dreams were unusual enough to warrant study.

> One Eskimo was sensitive to cold. Many times he got caught stealing calorie-rich fish oil, and he always asked to set the thermostat of the central heating to the highest temperature. The Eskimos could put up with the theft of blubber, but not with the extremely high consumption of the expensive fuel oil. It was then decided unanimously to send our Eskimo away from his tribe and his igloo and to leave him to his fate. As he was still of a rather strong constitution, he did not sit

down on the ice and wait for what was supposed to be an agreeable death by freezing. After having walked for some distance, he met an expedition that wished to reconstruct old means of exploration. He set off by sledges drawn by dogs and with kayak in order to reach the Pole. The explorers were much impressed by the Eskimo's stories, especially by his sensitivity to the cold, and they gave him a special suit, heated by electricity. The happy Eskimo put on his new warm suit and started on his way back to his igloo-home. When he got tired he went to sleep on an ice-floe. The heat of the suit melted the ice below him, and he fell through the melted ice into the sea, where he drowned, leaving behind him a hole the shape of his body. When the members of his tribe came by this place the next day, they could not understand the hole, nor the fact that the water at the bottom of the hole was hot. The leader of the tribe came up with the explanation that their friend went straight down to Hell. This did not prevent them from coming back to the hole every day to get water for their tea.   (Lavie and Wollman, 1985, p. 114)

The subject had such dreams, reminiscent of active imagination fantasies in Jungian therapy, approximately forty times a year. He was never himself a character in these dreams. When he realized such a dream was occurring, he waited for it to finish and then awakened himself in order to write it down. This suggests not only some lucidity but a general heightening of reflective awareness. Lavie and Wollman concluded that these dreams occurred in REM sleep.

Freud was especially interested in dreams whose novel structure seemed determined by sayings or catchphrases—as in Alexander's dream of the satyr (Tyre Sa). Here again, statistics are nonexistent, but it is possible that this "rebus" format constitutes a style of dreaming for some subjects. Kenneth Arenson (1986) offers the dream of a women whose father had punished her by prolonged staring when she was a child. It tended to recur whenever anyone silently rebuked her:

I'm on the stairs looking down at two people. They have no faces.

Arenson's "metaliteral" translation: "I can't face the stares."

Such interpretations are exceedingly difficult to prove, but sometimes they provide the only clarification of ostensibly nonsensical dreams once the right saying, primed by the dream, comes to mind. At times such deciphering can have a convincing specificity, as in the following dream of mine. At a time when I was reading Primo Levi's *The Periodic Table*, I wrote down the following vague but repetitious and prolonged dream:

Periodically in the dream I was setting up tables. They were round metal ones. Then every so often I went back to setting up these tables.

I did not see any connection to the book until a friend pointed it out! Yet it is hard to see how this dream could have been formed except as a visual paraphrase of the book title itself.

The line between verbal polysemy embedded in such catchphrases (necessarily a bit quaint or we would not identify them so easily) and more general and potentially nonverbal metaphors (visual-kinesthetic patterns) is ultimately impossible to locate—and this quite apart from theoretical debates about the identity or separateness of thought and language. Consider for instance Breger, Hunter, and Lane's example of a young man, verbally attacked in a group psychotherapy session, who then stated "I feel like everything's dropped out underneath me." That night he dreamed the following:

> I was in a swimming pool . . . all the water dripped out . . . I was swimming along . . . then there was nothing left . . . Everything just dropped out right underneath me. . . . (Breger, Hunter, and Lane, 1971, p. 47)

It may be less likely that the dream "translated" his verbal statement than that both dream and statement gave different expressions to the same ultimately visual-kinesthetic metaphor.

Despite Freud's emphasis on the verbal basis of latent dream thoughts, limited in their potential translation by the conditions of representability inherent in a visual surface medium, he in fact pictured dream formation as a complex two-way interaction between visual structures and verbal expressions. Thus he states that considerations of visual representability may actually determine the formulation of the latent verbal dream thoughts themselves, selecting certain concretely expressive terms as "richer in associations than conceptual ones." Freud writes, "the dream work does not shrink from the effort of recasting unadaptable thoughts into a new verbal form—even into a less usual one—provided that that process facilitates representation" (1900, p. 379).

An illustration of what Freud calls *switch words* or *verbal bridges* and their ability to fuse polysemic meanings within dream thoughts, as well as of the way linguistics and imagistics run together in verbal metaphor, is found in a dream reported to Freud by a female acquaintance. The dream centers on a conductor friend whose career had been cut short by insanity:

> She was at the opera. . . . In the middle of the stalls, there was a high tower which had a platform on top of it surrounded by an iron railing. High up at the top was the conductor, who had the features of Hans Richter. He kept running round the railing, and was perspiring violently; and from that position he was conducting the orchestra, which was grouped about the base of the tower. . . . (Freud, 1900, p. 377)

Freud suggests that the tower is a visual metaphor for the woman's wish that the conductor should tower above other musicians. Eminence can be associated with height on the basis of verbal sayings or the kinesthesis of a prideful physical stance. In this instance, however, Freud sees the rushing about on top of the tower as a visual allusion to the phrase *fool's tower* (insane asylum). Here indeed the dream only makes sense in light of that phrase, even though it is unclear whether the dream originates in language or expressive kinesthetic imagery.

The most striking (and/or easily researched) form of linguistic expression in dreams is the determination of dream content by phonetic assonance. Sometimes assonance constitutes the only possible interpretive key to an otherwise semantically unrelated aggregate of dream objects and actions. In a few of my own dreams, for example, all objects and actions may begin with the same letter or sound, the sound perhaps being central to someone's name. In a study by Berger (cited in Arkin and Antrobus, 1978) on the influence of spoken names on ongoing REM-period content, assonance was by far the most significant determinant of incorporation into the dream, accounting for 65 percent of all rated incorporations; it eclipsed incorporations based on associations (metonymy) and direct representation. Thus the spoken word *robber* entered a dream as "a rabbit"; *Naomi* entered as a friend who said "oh show me." This expression of linguistic metaphor, its most concrete and immediate form according to Kugler and Jakobson, is also found in one of Maury's dreams (as recounted by Freud):

> He was walking along a highway and reading the number of *kilo*metres on the milestones; then he was in a grocer's shop where there was a big pair of scales and a man was putting *kilo*gram weights into the scale in order to weigh Maury; the grocer then said to him: "You're not in Paris but on the island of *Gilolo*." Several other scenes followed, in which he saw a *Lo*belia flower and then General *Lo*pez of whose death he had read shortly before. Finally, while he was playing a game of *lo*tto, he woke up.   (Freud, 1900, p. 92)

Freud of course attempts one of his characteristic metonymic (associative) explanations for Maury's dream by suggesting that such dreams are based on children's experiences of looking up risque words in dictionaries—but clearly this proclivity to phonetic assonance requires a more systematic cognitive account.

Here Kugler's contribution is invaluable. Citing Jung's early work with the word association test, he notes two categories of response—predicative (metonymic) and based ultimately on verbal contiguity, (i.e., *hut* leading to *poor* or *thatched*), and metaphoric, based on substitution via similarity. Similarity can be semantic (*cabin* to *palace*—contrastive) or phonetic (*cut* to *slut*). Kugler notes that the latter, called *clang associations* (based on puns and rhymes), constitute a major category of response only when the subject is exhausted, drunk, distracted, or forced to give an immediate rapid response. Their prominence in dreams would then suggest that the negative side of dreaming entails a contiguity disorder and that its shift toward the immediate and presentational (its "positive" competence) favours simultaneous over sequential patterning. Indeed, the emphasis on the visual in bizarre transformations may rest on the relative simultaneity of that modality in contrast to kinesthesis and especially audition.

Kugler suggests that the phonetic assonance which is sometimes the only key to the intelligibility of the dream may rest on an underlying (archetypal) image. Thus different languages show the same tendencies to link aspects of semantically different realms with the same sound pattern—perhaps suggesting a common visual-kinesthetic physiognomy. In several languages flowers are named by sounds that are also linked to concepts of violence, sexuality, and death or birth—in English, for instance, *carnation, carnal, carnage, incarnate, reincarnate*; or *violet, violate, violence*. In German we find *Blüten, bluten, Blut*. Phonetic assonance for Kugler is the core of linguistic metaphor; and it has been used cross-culturally to express these nonverbal imagistic "complexes." Such a phonetically based image complex would provide the key to dreams such as the following from a female student.

> She went with her boyfriend to the junior prom. The boyfriend brought her a *carnation*. She was very pleased and in high spirits. She wore a beautiful white evening dress. They entered the ballroom exuberantly. They went in together. They attracted everyone's attention but to her great embarrassment she first perceived some *blood* dripping from her *carnation*. The *flowers* were *bleeding*. She left the ballroom in great embarrassment. She awoke with palpitations. (Kugler, 1982, p. 20)

As Kugler points out, Freud presented a similar analysis of a dream of carnations as ultimately referring to the carnal and to violence.

Note that the more clearly linguistic patterns creatively transform the dream, the more this involves metaphor and the presentational (echoic, poetic) aspects of language rather than grammar and syntax. It also involves polysemy, since words with the same root sounds may metaphorically link semantically distinct realms of meaning. They bypass the *singularity* and *unambiguity* of reference entailed by the sequential contiguity of syntax. In other words, to enter fully into and transform the dream, language becomes imagistic and physiognomic.

It seems likely that metonymic wordplay is the actual cognitive basis of

Freud's mechanism of displacement—which creates a lacuna in connective syntax to be replaced by later interpretation. Here the loss in narrative syntactic continuity would be less than when dream content is determined by phonetic assonance or verbal polysemy. Thus we need not worry as do Palombo (1978) or Greenberg and Pearlman (1978) that Freud's linkage of semantically distant material by displacement necessarily constitutes an overemphasis on a defensive or disguise model of a dream formation—although this was in fact Freud's inclination. True "displacement" now appears to reflect an aspect of imagination involved in poetic allusion and wit (although its endpoint is typically visual and not verbal). Quite probably it could be a style of dreaming for certain individuals, as in Freud's own Byzantine dreams (see chapter 2).

Visual-Spatial Metaphor

The predominance of visual imaginative transformations in dreams, despite the periodic presence of metonymy and phonetic wordplay, suggests a bias of the dream process towards visual-spatial expression—reflected also in its metachoric perceptual core. Whatever the dream is, it is not, at least in its outward form, a poem. Although it may not fit easily with current cognitive science orthodoxy on the relations between imagery and language, dreaming can show processes of visual-spatial imagination that are not easily assimilated to background verbal processes. Of course, dream interpretation seeks to render the dream intelligible in verbal terms, but only where the roots of the dream are predominantly metonymic and phonetic does that mean that we are trying, in Kugler's terms, to *restore* "the grammar of the dream." It is more parsimonious, where evidence of creative wordplay is lacking, to conclude that the verbal interpretation of imaginative dreaming works simply by restating the visual-spatial features of the dream—thus bringing home its hitherto implicit significance. This implies that the visual structure of the dream can reflect a knowledge which goes beyond any previous understanding. We see this most characteristically in the way such restatements can provide genuinely novel insight into one's personal concerns. It is of course even more striking in the more infrequent cases in which creative insights in science come as the direct result of visual-spatial dream patterns—as in Kekule's famous spinning snakes showing the structure of benzine rings or Howe's discovery of the correct position for thread placement in the first sewing machine through his dream of threatening natives carrying spears with holes in their ends.

This is the dream realm of Herbert Silberer and C. G. Jung rather than that of Freud and Foulkes. A self-referential capacity is directly expressed within the visual-kinesthetic patterns of dreams—hard to imagine if all dream formation is a direct translation from a psycholinguistic deep structure to an epiphenomenal visual surface array. If we can only image what we know (Pylyshyn, Foulkes), how comes it that so much personal and scientific discovery originates in the visual imagery of dreams—especially when Freud and others see imagery as, at best, a concrete and primitive form of thinking? Such dreaming, however, does fit well with the more holistic-gestalt tradition of cognitive psychology and its tendency to locate the human abstract recombinatory capacity in nonverbal imagery, or at the very least to see visual-spatial imagery as its own relatively independent "frame of mind" that feeds (and is fed by) linguistic expression. Thus Rudolf Arnheim (1969, 1974), pointing to abstract art and the importance of complex visual models in the physical sciences, shows that visual imagery can itself be highly abstract. For Arnheim, abstract verbal concepts are ultimately based on metaphors drawn from the visible dimensions of physical nature. We can only speak of the "depths" of a matter of concern through the imaginal reuse (schematic rearrangement) of perceptual dimensions.

Of special significance if dreaming is assimilative and centered on long-term personal concerns, Solomon Asch has pointed to the centrality of physical metaphor for the language of human affairs. We must use "double function" terms (referring to both human and physical reality) in order to speak of "white-hot anger," "hopes being rekindled," "the height of passion," and so on. In all languages, words devoted to mental states originally (etymologically) referred to physical properties that were thereby given a metaphorical reference. For instance, the *ang* root of *anger, anguish,* and *anxiety* originally referred to a narrow physical passage (cf. *dire straits*). The physiognomic animation of nature so characteristic of the mythological thought of tribal peoples thus may reflect not so much its proto-scientific status as its sophisticated self-representation of psychological reality. Both Jung (1944) and Lévi-Strauss (1966) have reinterpreted the ostensible concentration of primitive mythology on physical reality as providing systematized mirrors for human self-reflection. If visual-spatial metaphor is the natural vehicle of psychological self-awareness, it should be especially prominent in dreams.

There are many examples of dreams seemingly based on an autonomous visual-kinesthetic imaginative faculty, whose features, once verbalized, generate novel metaphors for problematic life situations. One of my own dreams, which occurred early in my academic career, is relevant here. After a demoralizing but successfully completed period in graduate school and in my first academic appointment, I found myself deeply uncertain, both personally and professionally, and unable to undertake major research or writing—in short,

paralyzed by doubt and indecision. One night, without any obvious day residue, I had an astonishingly powerful dream.

> I was being taken on a tour through a very large insane asylum. In the very center
> of the vast building in a room normally kept in total darkness, I saw what on
> awakening I could only term the "the Ur-gorilla"—a huge, dark apelike/manlike
> beast chained to the wall. It was lying full-length and motionless but full of a
> pent-up and starkly masculine vital force unable to express itself.

This subjectively disturbing dream was a metaphoric depiction of my own
hopes, fears, and despair at that time, with implications quite different from
my own formulation of my situation. It would seem most plausible to conclude that in a purely imagistic medium I was being "told" something that at
the time exceeded my understanding.

Original visual-spatial metaphors seem to inform the dreams of Jung (see
chapter 10) and his patients. Consider Jung's "constructive" interpretation of
the dream of a woman caught in subjective paralysis and passivity, in marked
contrast to her energetic and strong-willed father.

> Someone gave her a wonderful, richly ornamented, antique sword dug up out of a
> tumulus.   (Jung, 1916, p. 75)

Jung eschewed the phallic symbolism of Freud and argued that the dream
presented the woman's deep need for the passionate unbending will possessed
by her father and symbolized in her Celtic ancestry—with which she had
hitherto been unable to identify.[2]

Finally, just as the entire structure of the dream can be taken over by
complex and original narration, dreaming can also be completely transformed
by a visual aesthetic sense, capable of producing astonishingly beautiful effects. Such dreams can at times rival works of art in their profound depictions
of basic existential issues in human life. Thus the "dream of the urn" reported
to Medard Boss by a married woman portrays the powerful sense of home and
family that characterizes the life of the dreamer:

> I was sitting at the dinner table with my husband and children. The table was in
> our dining-room, which I had made even more cosy by moving the sideboard. I
> felt safe and peaceful in this room which was so dear to me. On the walls I could
> see the really good pictures which my husband loved to collect: In the windows I
> could see flowers, and in front of me the very attractively set table. . . . I looked at
> my husband and my children and I felt extremely fond of them and very near to
> all of them, especially to my eldest son. While he had originally been sitting in his
> usual place at the opposite corner of the table he was suddenly and strangely
> transported right next to me. In the dream it did not appear strange that he had

suddenly changed places without any movement on his or anyone else's part. It was quite reasonable. Nor did it strike me as peculiar that while I was sitting so happily amongst my family, there suddenly appeared colorful bridges, reminiscent of very bright rainbows. They extended across the table between me and my family. A large and golden urn hovered on these bridges between us, and particularly near my favourite son.   (Boss, 1958, pp. 77–78)

Such a dream is a work of art in its own right.

Similarly, as an adolescent who spent much time in local woods, I would all too occasionally have vivid, powerful dreams of woodlands I had never before seen—utterly beautiful, aglow with radiant light, and conveying a sense of mystery and the uncanny that usually prevented me from exploring them. The wonder, fascination, and at times foreboding of these dreams stayed with me for years. Such dreams manage to present fundamental life issues in immediate visual-spatial structures that clearly exceed one's conceptual-verbal grasp. Simple verbal description then becomes a struggle quite different from the facile "telling" of ordinary dreams.

Somatic-Medical Expression

Dreams that directly present somatic and medical conditions of which the individual may not be consciously aware also show an operation of visual-kinesthetic metaphor largely autonomous from linguistic structures. Dreams that are metaphoric of fever states, teeth (bruxism is a condition occurring predominantly during REM sleep), pregnancy, and menstruation reflect direct visual translations of background tactile-kinesthetic patterns—as already illustrated in my dream in which my feverishly shaking legs were experienced as an advancing snake. Here we can proceed more briefly since the visual metaphor involved in somatic-medical dreams has already been exemplified.

As mentioned above, Robert Smith (1986) has tested the view, extending from classical shamanism and Hippocrates to Scherner, that dreams are medically prognostic. He found significantly more references to separation (females) and death (males) in critically ill patients who die or do not fully recover than in similiar patients who fully recover.

The related notion that specific dream content might be diagnostic of distinct conditions and/or organ deficiencies has been approached in modern research in a series of studies by Harold Levitan (1976, 1980, 1984). For instance, a small sample of migraine patients reported stark terror and physical assault in dreams that immediately preceded waking up into the full attack:

> I was in a shipwreck . . . many people were drowning . . . I managed to save my favourite niece . . . as we swam away I looked back and saw the other people being eaten up by sea-monsters . . . the heads of the people were in the mouths of the monsters . . . it was very scary. . . . Then I awoke with a terrific throbbing headache.   (Levitan, 1984, p. 163)

Whereas both pre-migraine and pre-asthmatic dreams often involved physical assaults on the dreamer (61% and 43% respectively), asthmatic attacks were also associated with active aggression by the dreamer (27% versus 0% for pre-migraine dreams). Levitan also found that personally traumatic grand mal seizures in epilepsy were later associated with dreams of the complete destruction of the body image, which are otherwise quite rare:

> Someone dragged me to the Empire State Building. They took me to the top and threw me down. I splattered into pieces at the bottom. I was dead and I was looking at the pieces. I woke up very dizzy.   (Levitan, 1976, p. 3)

Both Boss (1958) and the Jungian psychologist James Hall (1977) also provide convincing anecdotal examples of dream precursors of major medical problems occurring before any waking physical symptoms—a phenomenon also mentioned by Aristotle. Presumably, just as dreams can be elicited by ongoing environmental stimulation and hitherto unformulated personal and intellectual concerns, they can also reflect the first subthreshold manifestations of physical illness.

All these instances involve an intelligence based on complex translations across different sensory modalities (especially tactile-kinesthetic to visual). This is consistent with theories suggesting that human abstract recombinatory intelligence is made possible by just such cross-modal cortical translations, relatively independent of limbic and/or concrete motivational involvement (Geschwind, 1965; Hunt, 1984, 1985a,b). In this approach, Freud's and Foulkes's model of dream formation, based on the one-way translation from verbal to visual, represents merely one form of a series of such translations, some independent of language, which constitute the multiplicity of dreaming.

Creative Metaphors in "Objective" Problem Solving and Dreams of Direct ("Extrasensory") Intuition

The vast majority of dreams are clearly self-referential, in the narrower sense of assimilation to personal concerns. Yet some dreams are as clearly outwardly directed. As surprisingly accurate and/or creative depictions of external matters, these dreams warrant what Jung termed *objective interpretation*. In form such dreams fuse verbal and visual-metaphoric cognition to varying degrees, that is, the two sense modalities of maximum distance and objective reference. Creative breakthrough dreams in the sciences and arts, as discussed above, are based largely on visual-metaphoric patterns, whose direct implications go beyond previous verbal reflection. So-called "telepathic" or "extrasensory" dreams, at least in naturalistic terms, are best regarded as manifestations of intuition. They are extraordinarily accurate depictions of distant or future events, more or less as they actually occurred.

While many creative breakthrough dreams occur during the hypnagogic period following prolonged conscious efforts at solution, this need not be the case. Indeed, in terms of phenomenology and cognitive process, hypnagogic and REM dreams are often indistinguishable. The following night dream, occurring shortly after I began my academic career, anticipated ideas that I did not develop for several years. At the time of the dream I hoped to articulate a cognitive psychology of altered states of consciousness, but I had as yet no inkling of the importance therein of synesthetic translations across different sensory modalities, and I had not yet read Rudolph Arnheim's treatment of geometric visual imagery as basic to all abstract thought (although I owned the book). Nor did I adequately understand the importance of Werner and Kaplan's treatment of physiognomic expression as a key to all symbol formation:

I accompany a friend and colleague as he takes his cat to a local veterinarian. I wait outside while he goes in. One of my students walks by and asks if I am going to hear Heidegger's lecture. It seems Heidegger has been living here as a veterinarian and gives lectures after office hours. Upset that my friend didn't come out to get me, as he knew of my interest in Heidegger, I rush inside. It is an old house. Several rooms are crowded with people waiting with their pets. An older woman loudly weeps over an open coffin with her dead son inside. I think, rather annoyed, that she should know better than to come here with a human corpse.

My friend is nowhere in sight but I find a side door and enter a specially constructed lecture hall. Inside, my friend sits waiting for Heidegger's lecture to begin. Although I am somewhat annoyed with him, I set out to convince him that it will be interesting and important. He seems skeptical. To my amazement I see arranged at the edge of the seating area a number of brightly colored, geometrically complex three-dimensional cardboard cutouts. These have moving parts and sections that fold out and reverse, and each illustrates complex conceptual relations in Heidegger's thought. They are extraordinary and I try hard to remember what they look like. An advance copy of the lecture is also available. I look at it and it consists of a whole page of "Mmm . . . Oooh . . . Aaaah . . . " and so on. I sense that this is an interesting variant on Heidegger's approach, and I again stress to my friend that while it may look strange, there is really something to it. Heidegger appears—an older man I do not recognize. He turns on a tape machine, ostensibly to record his own talk, but it soon becomes clear that he is trying (poorly) to mouth the words of the lecture that is actually being played for us on tape. He soon turns off the recorder and goes off to one side to a small stage area, on which is a large elaborate drum set. He switches on Grateful Dead music, with drums left out, and proceeds to play with energy and abandon. I watch, utterly delighted, but also worried about what my colleague will think.

Of course, the dream contains numerous elements of day residue and long-standing interpersonal issues. In particular, I had recently moved far from the area where my mother lives and I was developing a close (but later disappointing) friendship with the colleague depicted in the dream. Most remarkable, however, is the way the dream presents the organismic-holistic cognitive psychology that I had yet to fully understand, as well as my own future development of it as an account of states of consciousness. The three-dimensional objects depicting complex intellectual relationships initiated a fascination with such possibilities that culminated in the dream diamond on which this discussion is based. The dream is still remarkable to me. Of course it may have had earlier roots in childhood foldout books and model-building. But it foreshadowed not only the fate of that friendship but the direction of my intellectual development over the next seventeen years. In a much more modest way, it is analogous to the importance of Jung's dreams (1961) of the underground phallus and ancient cellars with successively deeper layers in the development of his concept of a collective unconsciousness.

So-called precognitive and telepathic dreams represent a very different phenomenon—one impossible to evaluate here other than in the *phenomenological* sense that many persons do have such dreams (leaving aside the question of their validity or truth). Descriptively these dreams concern external matters on which little is consciously or directly known—they are "intuitive." Often, but not always, a sense of subjective reality, vividness, and portent accompanies them and marks them off as a distinct form. Most interesting in this regard is that some of these dreams are subjectively felt to be extrasensory during the dream itself or immediately on awakening. Although subsequent events may later prove them false (or sometimes not), the subjective sense of reality is such that the person remains shaken and uncertain for some time to come—often unable to return to sleep and wondering if a 3:00 A.M. phone call is in order. We have already seen that in tribal societies and classical civilizations prophetic dreaming was regarded as a major if not predominant dream type, and that sometimes all dreams, including those obviously based on personal day residues, were to be decoded as direct or indirect forms of what we now call extrasensory perception.

A recent example of this tendency to assimilate seemingly ordinary dreams immediately and intuitively to this category occurred in my presence during a hypnotic session conducted by another psychologist. It was suggested to the subject, a "trance channeler" with several "spirit guides," that he undergo a spontaneous dream. During this hypnotic dream he was to retain a lucid self-awareness that he was actually dreaming. The subject (still under hypnosis) later described a dream that included no hint of lucidity, except in his sense that he was supposed to be "doing something," probably because the dream was so visibly and emotionally upsetting. With his parents actually set to leave on a vacation the next day, he dreamed that their plane was crashing. After he emerged from hypnotic trance, his friends were reluctant to tell him the dream, and he and they were quite upset when it was finally told. Yet, on the basis of my pre-trance conversation with the subject about how upset we had both been as young children to be hospitalized for appendicitis and how devastating one's parents leaving at the end of visiting hours could be at that age, it seemed to me most likely that his dream was a classical fusion of day residue and unresolved issues from the distant past. His awareness of his parents' imminent departure, combined with older memories of upset and anger, generated a genuinely Freudian dream, the social context of which made it seem plausible as precognitive. Jung at times also tends to offer precognitive meanings for dreams that may lack the phenomenology of immediate portent that defines this type, and that can more readily be interpreted along mnemic or imaginative lines. Clearly, any existent dream form can be used as a template to assimilate all others.

However, some dreams do directly exemplify a dimension of highly accurate intuition or anticipation, often with an accompanying sense of uncanny significance and special import. Thus Boss cites Bishop Lanyi's precognitive dream of the assassination of Archduke Ferdinand and his anxious attempts to inform others before the death. Similar accounts have been put forward about John F. Kennedy's assassination. A rich and carefully rendered anecdotal literature on such dreams exists thanks to the early efforts of the British Society for Psychical Research, and Celia Green (1976; Green and McCreery, 1975) has more recently reported some instances. Boss provides a contemporary example of a young man in training analysis:

> He fell ill with pneumonia. That very night he become so feverish that he turned delirious. Throughout his delirium he believed that his mother was with him and he begged her to place her cool hand on his forehead. In the course of the following morning the mother phoned her son's boarding house. Instead of the usual greeting she anxiously asked the housekeeper, who had answered the telephone, whether her son was seriously ill, and whether she ought to come at once. She

had dreamt of her son's illness on the previous night, but had had no other information whatsoever. In this dream she had been with her son who had been lying in bed with a high fever. He had been completely delirious and had constantly asked to be cooled. Three years later when he was working in London, and while his mother was on holiday . . . he broke his right thigh on his way to the office. The following day he received another telephone call. This time the mother asked if her son's injuries were serious. She had dreamt most vividly that he was lying in a hospital bed, his right leg bandaged from top to bottom. These two telephone calls were and remain the only long distance calls that his mother had been able to afford throughout her life. If she had not been completely convinced of the reality of these dreams, she would no doubt, on grounds of economy, have made neither of them.   (Boss, 1958, pp. 177–78)

There is also Jung's own dream on the night of an unexpected death in his wife's family:

I dreamed that my wife's bed was a deep pit with stone walls. It was a grave, and somehow had a suggestion of classical antiquity about it. Then I heard a deep sigh as if someone were giving up the ghost. A figure that resembled my wife sat up in the pit and floated upward. It wore a white gown into which curious black symbols were woven. I awoke, aroused my wife and checked the time. It was 3 o'clock in the morning. The dream was so curious that I thought at once that it might signify a death. At 7 o'clock came the news that a cousin of my wife had died at 3 o'clock in the morning.   (Jung, 1961, p. 303)

Focusing on the phenomenology and cognitive processes of dream formation will spare us from essentially unanswerable questions on the causes of so-called extrasensory dreams. If we attempt to remain naturalistically oriented to the plenitude of such dreams in the literature and restrict ourselves to the descriptive, several points stand out. (1) As with lucid and archetypal-titanic dreams (see chapters 8–9), telepathic dreams typically resist free association; that is, no day residues or personal memories emerge, aside from the subjective impression of reference to significant external events. Thus the best descriptive term for such experiences is *intuitive*—allowing these dreams to be of scientific interest whether we finally try to explain them as coincidence (although death references are statistically infrequent in dreams [Tolaas and Ullman, 1979]), subliminal anticipation and processing of unnoticed cues, or extrasensory perception. (2) As with dreams in primitive societies, the immediate reaction to such experiences, in contrast to even the most visually fantastic dreams, is enactive or performative. The awakened dreamer often feels a compulsion to act on the basis of the dream, even if no action is conceivable. (3) These dreams again highlight the fact that dreams need not be private and inwardly referred but can be social in their very fabric. However it is interpreted, my "Mansur" dream (see chapter 1, note 1) shows that certain dreams constitute a *shared* form of experience. Because of the normative strategies of modern laboratory research, we lack any objective sense of how frequent dreams of this type really are—again, not speaking of "truth" but of phenomenal occurence.

We should not leave this dream type, identified in all human societies, without a brief reference to the paradoxical and challenging status of objective laboratory research on dream telepathy as reviewed by Tolaas and Ullman (1979) and Child (1985). In the 1960s, Stanley Krippner and Montegue Ullman conducted a series of carefully controlled studies at Maimonides Hospital investigating the possibilities of telepathic influence on dream experience. They achieved statistically significant results. Although attempts at replication have been marginal or unsuccessful (Belvedere and Foulkes, 1971), Irwin Child (1985) and Robert Van de Castle (1986) (one of Krippner and Ullman's original subjects and the subject in Foulkes's attempted replication) have argued passionately that fair and full replications of the earlier studies have never been attempted. Such studies are based on blind matching by judges of dream protocols and simultaneously "sent" pictures. They can be reasonably controlled while preserving some of the spontaneity of naturally occurring ESP experience, otherwise so quickly lost in supposedly more objective laboratory research. One can only bemoan the lack of adventurousness and élan implied by the failure of current dream research to properly replicate and extend these studies.

CHAPTER 8

Lucid Dreams and Nightmares: The Transition to Formal Self-Reference

Lucid Dreams, Out-of-Body Experience, and Meditational States

BECAUSE lucid dreams (and related subtypes) violate all traditional attempts to define an essence of dreaming, their study is especially useful in highlighting the dangers of such a monolithic approach. This in turn helps to explain the defensive hostility with which current research on lucidity has been greeted. Several attempts at a logicophilosophical account of dreaming (Sartre, Boss, Malcolm) have been predicated on the impossibility of what we now term fully lucid dreaming. Indeed, the analytical philosopher Norman Malcolm insists that at best we can only *dream* that we dream; we cannot *know* it as we know facts when awake. (Even if we happen to be right and can demonstrate our knowledge by prearranged signals within REM sleep?)

Similarly, both laboratory psychophysiologists and cognitivists see lucidity as violating the necessary single-mindedness of dreaming—and thereby as the exception that proves the rule (Foulkes) and/or as a sort of mental awakening within the dream (Rechtschaffen). Conveniently, this removes lucid dreaming as a problem for dream psychology proper. However, thanks to laboratory demonstrations that lucidity is accompanied by normal REM periods (Ogilvie et al., 1978, 1982; LaBerge et al., 1981) and that experienced lucid dreamers can be trained to signal their awareness of lucidity to researchers via exaggerated eye movements (LaBerge et al., 1981; LaBerge, 1985), the philosophers and experimentalists are left with an unquestionably real and distinct variant of dreaming.[1]

Clinical-dynamic psychologists are sometimes uncomfortable with lucid-control dreaming since they fear that it must tamper with the spontaneous regulative activity of the unconscious. Quite apart from the fact that most people find it difficult to cultivate lucid dreams and the unlikelihood that the dreaming process could be "forced" to go against its own grain, these psychologists ignore Freud's own observation that what is now called lucidity (and what Purcell et al. [1986] have recently placed on an empirical continuum of self-reflectiveness) is a dimension within all dream formation. However, like many who have not themselves experienced such dreams, Freud pictures lucidity as a purely defensive function of secondary revision—itself seen as the contribution of whatever is left of waking reflection. For Freud lucid dreams are a way, within the dream, to further censor threatening symbolism by the dismissive "it's *only* a dream."

The phenomenology of lucid dreaming and the closely related forms of pre-lucidity, however, indicate that this dimension of self-reflectiveness is something in its own right, open to some degree of influence by various training techniques (LaBerge, 1985).[2] Its maximum development leads not to wakefulness or simple cognitive alertness in the dream but to subjectively powerful archetypal dreams and to forms of enhanced self-awareness reminiscent of Maslow (1962) on peak experience and of meditational awareness in Eastern traditions. The following account, from one of Green's subjects, brings out the tendency of these dreams toward a special sensory clarity, expansive emotional thrill, and sense of bodily presence.

> I dreamed that I was walking by the water on the . . . shore. It was morning; the sky a light blue; the foam-flecked waves were greenish in the sunshine. I forget just how it happened, but something told me that I was dreaming. . . . I decided to prolong the dream and continued my walk, the scenery now appearing extraordinarily vivid and clear. Very soon my body began to draw me back. I experienced dual consciousness: I could feel myself lying in bed and walking by the sea at one and the same time. Moreover, I could dimly see the objects of my bedroom, as well as the dream scenery. I willed to continue dreaming. A battle ensued; now my bedroom became clearly visible and the shore-scene dim; then my bedroom would become indistinct and the shore-scene brighter. My will triumphed. I lost the sense of dual consciousness. My bedroom faded altogether from my vision, and I was out on the shore feeling indescribably free and elated. (Green, 1968, p. 160)

There is some indication that systematic attempts at dream control, once lucidity is realized, can have the effect of dampening this "lucidity sensation." It is never mentioned by those like Arnold-Forster and Saint-Denys, who used their lucid capacity only to experiment on ongoing dreams or to actively explore the nature of dream formation. Their accounts are very different from those of Van Eeden, Sparrow, and Gillespie, who pursue lucid dreaming in its own right. One of my own first (and still infrequent) lucid dreams illustrates how attempts at deliberate control can entail the progressive loss of the expansive "peak experience" quality. It shows the delicate cognitive balance involved in these states and how much they go against the single-minded grain of ordinary dreaming.

> I was walking along a favorite path in the woods, with a beautifully bound set of books under one arm, when I suddenly realized that I owned no such books and that I was in fact dreaming. The realization was accompanied by a special sense of presence and significance, which started to fade as I began to wonder what I should do next. I decided I would attempt to fly, but uncertain how to "do" that, I decided to edge out along a half-fallen tree leaning out from the hill and extending over a large lake (which had not in fact existed on that spot since the last ice age)—whence I would jump. As I edged out along the tree I became increasingly dizzy and realized that I was close to waking up. To avoid this I resolved to leap off immediately when far enough above the water. But as I was about to let go, I saw sharp rocks just beneath the surface. By now totally forgetting that these were after all only "dream rocks," I held on for dear life. As I awakened, I finally managed to let go, only to "land," completely disgusted with myself, in my bedroom.

Such dreams make clear that, while lucid dreams (like nightmares) are so vivid that they verge on full wakefulness, mere alertness and the simple knowledge that one is dreaming are quite distinct from the special sense of reality and significance afforded by these dreams.

In other words, the experience of lucid dreaming is just as distinct from 90 percent of our waking experience (which all too often is precisely marked by its lack of vividness and subjective sense of significance) as it is from 90 percent of our dreaming experience. It entails the same tenuous balance between our ordinary attitude of active participation (in which we lose ourselves in our activities equally in dream and wakefulness) and the attitude of detached receptivity that characterizes the goal of long-term meditation practice. We note in both states the same sense of clarity, exhilaration, and openness— an experiential "sense of Being"—that Maslow identified as "peak experience." In other words, the "lucidity sensation" in dreaming is a spontaneous occurrence of the state sought in meditative practice. Its occurrence, sought and unsought, in some people's dreams may reflect the fact that once asleep we are already in the physically detached and inactive state that in wakefulness can only be approximated by the social withdrawal and enforced motionlessness of the meditative posture (see Hunt et al., 1982; Hunt, 1987).

The close relation between lucid dreams and out-of-body experience helps to illuminate the cognitive processes that may be involved in both. Here of course we treat out-of-body experience both naturalistically and phenomenologically as a striking experience reported by many people—eschewing the twin "explanations" of "illusion" and "astral travel." Not only are lucid dreams and out-of-body experience statistically correlated; they also have a close logical and definitional similarity, involving the unusual development of a detached observational attitude and its tenuous balance with participatory involvement. In addition, if the out-of-body experience ends in "dream travel" to a setting that no longer includes the imagistic construction of one's own body percept, it is indistinguishable from lucid dreaming; and if the lucid dreamer attempts to become fully aware of his/her sleeping body, the situation may be indistinguishable from classic out-of-body accounts. Indeed, several empirical examples show just these continuous transitions between the two states (see Van Eeden's account in chapter 5 and Castaneda's *Tales of Power*).

In cognitive terms the out-of-body experience manifests a visual-kinesthetic version of the abstract symbolic capacity that George Herbert Mead made central for human intelligence—"taking the role of the other" or constructing one's actions and feelings as they might be regarded by someone else. In the out-of-body experience, we literally see ourselves as another would regard us. Out-of-body experience and dream lucidity, the former more characteristic of sleep onset and physical emergency, the latter of dreaming, are manifestations of the capacity for self-reflectiveness that defines a crucial aspect of human symbolic intelligence (Neisser, Bartlett, Mead, Hofstadter) and that is developed for its own sake in meditation.

Evidence that lucid dreaming is a spontaneous meditative state comes from several independent sources. First there are the meditative traditions themselves. Both Tibetan Buddhism ("dream yoga" in Chang, 1963) and Hindu yoga ("dream witnessing" in Transcendental Meditation, Alexander et al., 1987) present initiates with techniques to enhance what we now call lucid dreaming, as the form of meditation naturally available during sleep. This is borne out by findings that the physiology of lucid dreaming may be closely related to changes in EEG and autonomic measures associated with meditation (Ogilvie et al., "Lucid Dreaming," 1982; Gackenbach et al., 1987).[3]

Psychological studies by myself and Barbara McLeod (see Hunt and McLeod, 1984; Hunt, 1987) and Gackenbach, Cranson, and Alexander (1986) have shown that experienced meditators have significantly more lucid dreams than nonmeditating controls. Our study also found that the longer the meditative practice (average 5.1 years), the more lucid and control dreams were reported—to the point where some subjects could not tell whether they were having what we had defined for them as a lucid dream or whether they had awakened and were spontaneously meditating. Although "ordinary" lucidity tends to be highly realistic and true to daily life (Ogilvie et al., "Lucid Dreaming," 1982; Gackenbach, 1986), in long-term meditators length of meditative practice (and degree of lucidity) was significantly associated with archetypal or intrinsically bizarre dreams. These dreams included geometric mandala imagery, diffuse white light experiences, flying and floating, and encounters with mythological beings—all rarely seen in normative dream diaries.[4]

Stabilized lucid dreaming (a double rarity) seems to operate on dream consciousness much as long-term meditation affects ordinary wakefulness. Their common attitude of receptive detachment results in more and more striking forms of visual-spatial imagery coming forward into focal awareness, as in this dream from one of our long-term meditators:

> I am in my bedroom, it is scary and dark. I am talking to a female acquaintence about prescription drugs. Between us is a dark scary hole, which I know to be full of demons. My husband, asleep behind me, starts babbling loudly in his sleep in a voice that sounds like a teenage school girl gossiping about school work. My fear of the demons starts to grow and I float over to my husband to wake him, but it doesn't work. I almost wake myself instead and the dream starts to repeat. However, approaching me from the side of the hole was a very beautiful young girl who looks like a more appropriate owner for the voice. I sense the demons coming up through the hole but there is no escape and my fear is rising. Then I clasp the jewel at my heart within my other two hands and am repeating my mantra and rising up in the air as I do so. I rise higher and my fear starts to subside as I lift my first two arms up towards the sky.   (Hunt and McLeod, 1984, p. 23)

Geometric imagery and white light experience—more abstract imagistic effects that occur with psychedelic drug and deep meditation experience—can also occur in these lucid dreams:

> A layer of "dough" which resembles pie crust that has an outer shell in the shape of the halo of a Buddha. In the beginning I identify with the dough, a thick and heavy mass of ego and emotions accumulated over endless periods of time. Then I peel off the dough and inside is my real self in the form of a thanka, yet made out of transparent radiations from the chakras, geometric, powerful, and made of pure light. Gradually I identify with the front chakra and it softens from its geometrically concentrated power into soft golden rays that seem to come from the heart chakra. At the same time I am the source of this light. I do my mantra and pray

that I will be able to hold this state of mind for the sake of all beings.   (Hunt and McLeod, 1984, p. 23)

I was in front of my childhood home demonstrating high jumps and flying. While in the air I realized I was dreaming. I descended and it became a fall. Without expecting to land, I just stopped falling. Then I flew again. I closed my eyes and remained aware of my body floating. I became aware of a small bright light to my left. . . . I suddenly saw only light. I felt that I was floating in light. I felt prayerful and called "Father," meaning God. I remained for some time in an attitude of worship, then woke up.   (Gillespie, 1984, pp. 2–3)

We will see in part 3 how the work of Arnheim on abstract imagery and Norman Geschwind on the cross-modal basis of human intelligence allows a cognitive interpretation of such states as synesthetically based metaphors of totality in human life—the cognitive-noetic side of religious experience.

A cognitive interpretation of lucid-archetypal dreaming as the natural progression and abstraction of imagistic intelligence is also supported by the sorts of experimental measures that correlate with the tendency to lucid dreaming. In general, personality tests are the poorest predictors, measures of imagery and spatial integration the best. Gackenbach (1986) has found that lucid dreamers have unusually good physical balance and vestibular integration. Research shows a greater suppression of deep spinal reflexes (H-reflex) in lucid as opposed to nonlucid REM states (Brylowski, 1986). This is an indication of vestibular activation, since vestibular nuclei in the brain stem control normal motor inhibition during REM sleep. While all REM states entail vestibular activation, in lucid dreaming it is intensified. By itself, the association between lucid dreams and good physical balance/vestibular responsivity would lead only to the rather mundane conclusion that people with good balance are better able to compensate for the vestibular deregulation of REM sleep, and so, being less delirious and disoriented, will more likely notice that they are in fact dreaming.

However, Swartz and Seginer (1981)—(also replicated by myself and Villeneuve; see Hunt, 1987)—have reported the same statistical association between good physical orientation or balance and the tendency to report mystical experience during wakefulness. This would suggest the necessity of good balance in the special development of visual-spatial imaginative intelligence, especially if all imagery necessarily reuses modality-specific perceptual schemata. Poor balance would then be associated with disorganization and panic when imagistic processes are especially intensified, leading either to defensive suppression or intensified delirium, but not to the stabilized imagistic integrations of highly developed lucid dreaming and deep meditation.

Other studies have found correlations between lucid dreaming and the capacity for imaginative absorption (also predictive of hypnotizability), vividness of imagery, creativity, and performance on tasks of spatial intelligence and integration like the embedded figures test and imaginal rotations (Snyder and Gackenbach, 1988). Since many of these measures also correlate with the early development of dreaming in childhood (Foulkes, 1985) and high levels of dream recall in adults (Butler and Watson, 1986; Belicki, 1987), we have evidence that lucid dreaming is not a special aberration of dreaming but one potential line of its further development. In a quantitative sense it reflects more of whatever dreaming is—especially more of its visual-spatial metaphoric side.

Nightmares and Imaginal Creativity

Like other dream types, nightmares, meaning here dreams that are bizarrely fantastic and terrifying, exaggerate a potential dimension within all dream formation—involving affect modulation and the tendency, implicit in many dreams, to culminate in a physical rush of terror. Nightmares and lucidity are linked along this dimension of affect enhancement—the one is capable of producing an ecstasy of terror, the other of bliss. Common to both is a vivid intensification of the dreaming process and an enhancement of kinesthetic sensation, reminding us that it is kinesthesis, the directly felt sense of bodily presence, that is held at bay through ordinary and even imaginative dreaming. We have already seen that the orientation response constituting the physiology of REM sleep is an internally generated energization—a potential novelty/emergency reaction. Intensification of the dreaming process would thus tend toward either a maximum integration of experience (lucidity and some archetypal experience) or maximum disintegration (nightmares and what we will discuss below as "titanic" dreams). The same proclivity toward either intensified integration or dissolution is associated with psychedelic drugs and other altered states of consciousness.

Just as each dream type can be utilized as a more general attitude to assimilate all other forms of dreaming, so various relatively mundane dreams are regarded by some people as bad or frightening. We also see this in the cross-cultural tendency to regard certain dream elements as portending negative waking consequences. Kathy Belicki (1985) found that those who labeled themselves nightmare sufferers did not necessarily have more vivid, bizarre, or emotionally negative dreams than those who did not. "Having nightmares" at times reflects an attitude toward dreaming more than anything about the dreams themselves.

Among actual nightmares we can usefully distinguish several subtypes. In

addition to fantastic dreams of monsters, murders, and bizarre physical disasters, there is also the more widely researched post-traumatic nightmare (Hartmann, 1984). These individuals seem condemned to a literal, highly realistic
redreaming of actual accidents, crimes, or combat experiences, the dreams
occurring for weeks, months, or decades with little apparent modification.
Apart from Freud's suggestion of a natural destructive and disorganizing tendency to repeat trauma subsumed under "Thanatos," conventional psychiatric
wisdom has it that such repetition is a constantly renewed attempt at mnemic-
emotional assimilation, prohibited from completion by the same ever-
recurring terror. Indeed, Wilmer's (1986) study of post-traumtic combat nightmares in Vietnam veterans found that gradual amelioration followed a shift
from literal repetition to more fantastic elaboration—thus suggesting with Samuel Lowy and James Hillman that dreaming assimilates past experience only
by transforming it in terms of its own inner imagistic possibilities.

Finally there is *pavor nocturnus* or the "night terror." These experiences
originate during sleep and consist in a contentless, all-encompassing dread.
Generally the only specifiable content, aside from the belief that one is dying,
consists in various "titanic" sensations of paralysis, suffocation, engulfment, or
dissolution. It is often held that these are not really dreams, since they seem to be
attacks of sudden physiological arousal usually occurring in the midst of EEG
stage 4 sleep. Their "content" may be interpreted as a direct imagistic elaboration
of the intense arousal response itself (breath-holding, paralysis) (Broughton,
1968). However, it is also worth noting that Morrison's concept of REM state as
orientation response, with its high cortical arousal and functional paralysis,
relinks dreaming and night terrors—the latter showing the more intense "tonic"
paralysis. In laboratory research, night terror experiences have been reported
from sleep onset and EEG stage 2 (Hartmann, 1984). There are also several
accounts of REM dreams ending in the diffuse titanic sensations that are sometimes described with night terrors, as in Levitan's examples above. We will find
related accounts in the dreams of some schizophrenics.

Returning to fantastic nightmares, these show other important phenomenological and experimental parallels with lucid dreaming and its variants. In content, lucid dreams and nightmares are highly vivid, with more pronounced
mention of tactile-kinesthetic sensation than ordinary dreams. So both are
close to the threshold of awakening. They also verge on and easily develop into
the dream types we are terming archetypal-titanic. It has not generally been
appreciated how prominent are the various subtypes of lucidity in nightmare
reports. Nightmares often include dreams within dreams, self-questioning
about whether one might be dreaming, false awakenings, and "apparitional"
patterns. Green (1968) notes that the most common, if least interesting, variety

of lucid dream occurs within nightmares, when one realizes one is dreaming either in the course of terrified awakening or leading to a deliberate wakening in order to escape. The following report from a female subject with normally vivid and fantastic dreams, and occasional nightmares, illustrates the prominence of lucidity variants in some nightmares:

> I get up from bed and walk down the hallway [false awakening into completely true to life setting]. There is a strange, eerie sense and I am frightened. As I am returning to bed I pass my husband's study door and hear the voice of a small girl and I see her through the closed study door [Green's apparitional pattern]. She is repeating "Daddy? . . . Daddy?" in a strange and haunting voice. I get into bed, terrified, then in the dream I realize it was a metachoric dream [lucidity, at least in retrospect] and I say to my husband, "I just had a metachoric dream" [dream within dream] and then fall asleep.
>
> Immediately I think I hear a noise in the hallway and am terrified that someone is really in the house. Lying there, eyes open in the dark [false awakening] I see a shadow move across the hall towards the bedroom [apparition]. Terrified, I awaken my husband and pull him onto the floor. We can't hide under the bed as I want to, because we have a futon, exactly as in real life. Throughout this I give no thought to the fact that this could also be a dream. As we are hiding there, a man in a trench coat comes in and stands at the end of the bed [apparition]. I am terrified.

It is as if the vividness common to lucidity and nightmares so intensifies self-reflectiveness that the dreaming process is increasingly constrained toward the representation of one's here-and-now setting—very much as in waking perception, except for the sense of a "special reality," ultra-precise sensory detail, and uncanny portent.

Nightmare sufferers are distinguished by traits similar to lucid dreamers, although the full array of measures correlating with lucidity has not yet been tested in nightmare research. Thus, capacity for imaginal absorption, hypnotizability (increasingly interpreted as a function of imaginativeness), vividness of mental imagery, and creativity have all been associated with proclivity to nightmares (Hartmann, 1984; Belicki and Belicki, 1986). Hartmann concludes that nightmare sufferers are highly imaginative and artistically sensitive; their "thin psychological boundaries" render them more vulnerable to conflicts that are typically suppressed. Their tendency to high scores on MMPI scales measuring paranoid and schizoid tendencies is consistent with this interpretation, since highly creative people commonly show this pattern (Barron, 1969), and there is some evidence that acutely disturbed schizophrenics also perform well on some measures of creative thinking (Dykes and McGhie, 1976; Woody and Claridge, 1977).

Like lucid dreams, nightmares seem to have more of something that is within all dreaming. One can certainly predict that while nightmare sufferers do score similarly high on tests of imagination and creativity, in contrast to lucid dreamers they would be more likely to have poor spatial abilities (block designs, mental rotations) and unusually poor vestibular integration or balance—since the result of their intensified dreaming is maximal disorganization and panic. But such comparative research has yet to be reported.[5] Certainly there is some indication of a major vestibular decrement in schizophrenia (Angyal and Blackman, 1940; Ornitz and Ritvo, 1968), along with a proneness to intensely bizarre and even morbid nightmares (see chapter 9).

Since acute schizophrenia is commonly associated with especially vivid nightmares (Carrington, 1972; Hartmann, 1984) and lucid dreaming has received its major development in the meditative traditions, we see again that proneness to either exaggerated disorganization or heightened experiential integration emerges from a common dimension of intensified visual-spatial imagination. Beginning with lucidity and nightmares, and their transitions into archetypal-titanic dream forms, it is as if an excess of energy had been let into the dreaming process, as if the sleeping person had been given a psychedelic drug.

CHAPTER 9

Archetypal and Titanic Dreams: Abstract Imageries of Formal Self-Reference

Archetypal Dreams

ARCHETYPAL dreams, essentially the same as the culture pattern dreams of anthropology (see chapter 10), are more like self-sufficient cohesive visions than the patchwork mnemic reorganizations of ordinary dreaming.[1] Jung's own dreams, recounted in his autobiography *Memories, Dreams, Reflections* (1961), provide evident examples (see chapter 10 for a detailed comparison of the dreams of Freud and Jung). However, my colleagues and I (Hunt et al., 1982) have found evidence that most subjects report archetypal dreams like those of Jung when asked to provide their most "fantastic dreamlike dream" (see appendix, table 1). Thus, although statistically speaking, subjects tend to have a characteristic style of dream bizarreness, most subjects on occasion experience dreams full of uncanny numinous emotion, geometric and mandala-like patterns, flying, mythological/metaphysical thinking, encounters with mythological beings, monsters, or strange animals, and those transformations of character that Kuiken and colleagues (1983) also found to be characteristic of classical mythologies. The most fantastic dreams recalled by undergraduates typically exceeded the dream norms of Jung. The only archetypal category in which these subjects' dreams ranked lower than the typical dreams of Jung involved encounters with bizarre mythological figures—the core of Jung's theory of incipient archetypal identities.

These dreams may be rare in the dream lives of most people, yet they surely occur to many as memorable exceptions. Some, like Jung and tribal shamans, seem to dream in an archetypal style characteristically. The major defining feature of these dreams, part and parcel of their uncanny-numinous quality and aesthetically rich structure, is the powerful sense of felt meaning and portent conveyed directly within the dream. This, however, characteristically resists further articulation. It is as if this experience of felt meaning and portent were its own end. So it is not surprising that Jung chose not decoding or some other translation, but "amplification" as the natural pathway for their postdream development and utilization. Like lucid and telepathic/problem-solving dreams, archetypal (and titanic) dreams are curiously resistant to free association. Free associations to dreams usually branch out into background personal memories, but associations to these dreams tend to become more impersonal and to circle around the more striking details of the dream—conveying and heightening its "sense of reality" in a way common to all amplificatory methods. Of course it is possible to find day residue in archetypal dreams, but mnemic interpretations seem to miss the thrust of such experiences. Rather, archetypal dreams provide their own context of meaning. What stays with the dreamer is the fact of having had a powerful, nonverbal and relatively ineffable experience that "presents" major existential life themes. These dreams are not easily reduced to an earlier childhood core.

Two powerful "double" dreams, preceding a marital separation, show how these dream forms both reflect and go beyond personal mnemic sources. In the first dream, although the bald head of the "double" reminded me of my father (who also divorced) and I was also reminded of the way my young son once held my coat sleeve, it is hard to see how these "explain" the form taken by the dream. (Freud would surely have dreamed it otherwise.)

> I find myself on top of a tall building overlooking a city at night. An unknown man is sitting on a ledge near me. When I look again he is gone and I realize that he jumped, unable to stand the chaos in the streets below. I see that they are littered as if in the wake of some disaster. Dangerous and wild-looking men move about below. Suddenly I realize that the stairs are blocked, the elevator inoperative, and I have no way to get back down. A figure, up to now vague but whom I immediately realize is my "double" (although he is older and bald and does not look at all like me), begins to instruct me, somehow telepathically, how to move down the empty elevator shaft. I am overcome with dizziness, but he insists that I have done this once before, so I will be able to repeat it. I am to move down inside my own jacket sleeve. Then, if I hold on to the very tip of the sleeve with

my fingers, he and I will make a large enough circle so that we will slowly roll down the shaft, rather than plummet. I wake up just as we begin.

Of course this dream can be interpreted within the dynamic psychoanalytic tradition. Certainly it reflects my fears/hopes that I will be following in my father's footsteps (and so might at least survive the end of my marriage), but the metaphor of the double and the slow descent as dependent on gaining a needed "distance" from "myself" goes beyond any obvious mnemic residues.

The second dream, occurring within a week of the first, leaves out such personal associations to my situation entirely. It represents a more purely archetypal distillation of the double theme—except perhaps for the implication that "engaging the double" (i.e., forging a more cohesive self) would require and/or be endangered by my anger and my ability to express it:

> I am in a bare white room. Immediately I realize that I am dreaming. I sense the presence of my double. He is totally invisible except for a sense of movement and force in the air. Nonetheless I know that he does not look at all like me. I challenge him to come forward and when he does not I become angry, taunting him that he is only a dream. As I become more angry I sense his presence physically and we grapple—locked in a hand-to-hand struggle. Slowly we tip to the side, rising in the air toward the ceiling, and equally slowly we spin round and round. I awaken as we reach the ceiling. He passes right through but I do not.

Again, it is not a question of whether the dream could be interpreted in terms of personal memories. Surely it could to some extent. Rather it is a question of avoiding the false reductionism that comes from ignoring visual-spatial metaphors and their intensification and broadening of self-awareness. These metaphors go well beyond the individual's ordinary capacity for verbal formulation and lack the plenitude of associations so easily elicited with more typical dreams.

There is some experimental support for separating archetypal dreams from more ordinary mnemic dreaming. Kluger (1975) has developed a content analysis system for scoring the archetypal dimension in dreams, based on rating scales for bizarreness, rationality, everydayness, and mythological parallels. His work has been replicated and extended by Cann and Donderi (1986). Both papers found a bimodal pattern of distribution: the dreams of individuals in Jungian analysis, the most vivid dreams recalled by control subjects, and the earliest recalled dreams from childhood all showed the same archetypal profile. There was little middle ground, the dreams of the control subjects being quite low on all rating scales. The researchers agreed that approximately 20 percent of the dreams in ordinary dream diaries have some archetypal elements. Looking at dreams collected from children, Kluger found mythological parallels in 47 percent of their dreams at age 6 and in 26 percent of adults' dreams. Cann and Donderi found negative correlations between the scale of archetypal dreaming and a measure of neuroticism and a significant positive relation with intuitiveness on the Myers-Briggs Jungian-type indicator.

In further support of the view that something different is happening in archetypal dreams, I was struck in my own study on the dreams of long-term meditators by the way categories of dream bizarreness, which always correlated together in previous studies, now showed divergences (Hunt and McLeod, 1984). In previous studies the clouding categories were significantly correlated with the hallucination categories. In the lucid dreams of the meditators, by contrast, dreams with geometric content, flying and falling, mythological beings, and uncanny-numinous emotion (almost nonexistent in typical samples) also had significantly lower scores on the categories of confused thinking and recall. As with the dreams of Jung (see appendix, table 1), once archetypal dream qualities come sufficiently to the fore, clouding and confusion can drop away. The dream becomes something more like a vision—an autonomous exercise of intuitive imagination.

The cognitive processes that might generate this form of dreaming, and whether they reflect a primitive form of thought or a line of cognitive development in its own right, are taken up in chapter 12. For now I suggest that in archetypal dreams mnemic activation is deemphasized—although presumably not entirely eliminated, since the dream necessarily emerges from the life of a single individual. Its place is taken by a process of self-referential awareness centered not on verbally mediated symbolism but on increasingly abstract cross-modal visual-kinesthetic fusions. Whether these reflect the cognitive deep structure of all thought (Arnheim) or a separate imagistic frame of symbolic intelligence, they are uniquely suited to present or express life issues of encompassing import, including dilemmas of self-identity at different life stages and the various totalities of metaphysical-spiritual thought.

Here we find ourselves at the point that led Plato to resort to mythology in order to express what eludes full conceptual analysis. Jung similarly extended Silberer's notion of visual imagery at sleep onset as caused by the "apperceptive insufficiency" of sleep. For Silberer the effort to think, combined with exhaustion and falling asleep, resulted in translations of the material (and form) of would-be verbal thoughts into a more primitive imagistic medium. Jung's addition, also foreshadowed in Silberer's book on alchemy, was the suggestion that a self-referential creature would never be able to get sufficiently outside its own nature for a complete or objective self-awareness. Therefore all "ultimate" concerns will be inherently "apperceptively insufficient" and so will be generated in imagistic rather than verbal form. The imagistic capacity will be a semi-independent frame of mind in its own right, especially sensitive to novelty and to all that eludes our more discursive grasp.

The anthropomorphic animal dreams of young children are evidence of a primitive form of this imagistic self-presentation which, at least within the verbal and "left-hemisphere" emphasis of Western schooling, is later overlaid by the verbal-narrative structures so carefully traced by Foulkes. Of course, if imagistic self-reference is a frame of mind in Gardner's sense, we would also expect unusually intuitive and imaginative children to have precocious dreams—like those of Jung himself and this dream he describes of an eight-year-old girl:

> The "bad animal": A snake-like monster with many horns, that kills and devours all other animals. But God comes from the four corners being really four gods, and gives rebirth to all the animals.   (Jung, 1964, p. 229)

The archetypal dreams of long-term meditators and other highly intuitive subjects, with their geometric (mandala) designs and forms of luminosity, convey an ineffable portent that when articulated sounds metaphysical and spiritual. These are the more abstract levels of imagistic self-reference, based on structurally complex visual-kinesthetic synesthesias, with visual structures predominating. It is exceedingly difficult to see how such dreams could be based on the Freud/Foulkes model of translation from verbal-propositional thinking. They originate elsewhere.

Titanic Dreams: Self-State Sensations

The term *titanic* is borrowed, with some change in emphasis, from Herbert Silberer, for dreams (often nightmares) involving especially powerful kinesthetic sensation. They are very intense and include "primitive" forms of aggression (mutilation, dismemberment, grotesque physical attacks), sexuality (especially driven and perverse), quasi-human animals and monsters, somatic sensations of suffocation and paralysis, and kinesthetic sensations of flying, floating, falling, and spinning. Also included are diffuse (potentially explosive) expressions of energy in nature, especially wind, water, and fire.

For Silberer (1917), titanic dreams were direct expressions of Freud's sexual and aggressive instincts, in contrast to the "anagogic" dreams of autonomous self-reference, also expressed in the themes of mythology and fairy tales. But I follow Jung's original insight (see chapter 10), widely confirmed by contemporary ethology, that Freud's drives or instincts reflect specific imaginal transformation and reorganization of mammalian motivations or drives. Specifically, I suggest that the human cross-modal imagistic capability can fuse in us what are separate and distinct expressions of mating, territoriality, predation, and nurturance-affiliation in more primitive mammalian species. Thus titanic dreams can include the more or less specifically human perversities fusing sex, dominance, torture, and dependency. These are central to classical mythologies and constitute what Freud regarded as direct manifestations of id. If these "fantasies" produce torture, they also allow sexual love.

Titanic dreams are potentially overdetermined by both physiological and self-referential metaphoric processes. Thus falling, spinning, and dismemberment can function as metaphors for basic existential crises and transformations.[2] Yet they can also occur as *somatic autosymbols* (Silberer's term) for features of especially intensified and driven REM physiology. This overdetermination would seem inevitable if organismic emergency in man can come from physical, interpersonal, and cultural crises and if metaphor must reuse perceptual schemata. Accordingly, titanic imagery is the final common pathway for crises generated, if you will, from above or below.

We have already seen that the special activation of the REM state constitutes self-inflicted organismic "attack." REM-deprived cats may show astonishingly intense aggressive and sexual behaviors—the latter presumably primed by the peripheral sexual activation associated with the REM state. Similarly, deformed and monstrous dream creatures could be self-symbolizations of the diminished tactile-kinesthetic sensitivity of sleep, while sensations of suffocation and paralysis may express the motor inhibition of the REM state (as potential organismic emergency). Flying, falling, floating, and spinning would be reflections of vestibular activation during REM. Indeed Nielsen and Kuiken (Nielsen, 1986) produced such "vestibular" dreams, strikingly similar to dream reports of subjects with vestibular-cerebellar brain damage, by compressing with a blood pressure cuff the leg muscles of subjects in REM sleep.

It might seem simple to reduce these titanic dreams directly to REM physiology, were it not that they are equally or more prominent during hypnagogic sleep onset for some subjects (Oswald, 1962). And we will see below how such hallucinatory experience, dreaming and awake, seems to offer precise metaphors for the life dilemmas of acute schizophrenics. After all, the orientation response of REM (with its waking intensification in the tonic immobility of deep trance) would result whenever the organism is totally engaged by novel and/or potentially threatening stimuli. In man such activation can be externally generated in physical emergency but can be internally created in the context of species-specific emotional crises and imaginal creativity. Since such kinesthetic imagery does not occur in most REM dreams, it seems most likely that its periodic manifestation in titanic dreams reflects diffuse personal-

existential crises that select somatic features of high arousal as the most appropriate perceptual patterns to be reused as self-referential metaphor.

We have already seen the metaphoric basis of titanic sensations in the catastrophe dreams of Levitan's medically ill patients. Boss (1958) and Binswanger
(1963) have both pointed out that soaring, plummeting, spinning, and disintegrating are obvious metaphors for significant human situations and are so used in
ordinary language—for example, "soaring over difficulties," "crashing to earth,"
"spinning in confusion," and "disintegrating under pressure."

While such dreams follow from the simple physiological intensification of
REM arousal (as in Hartmann's L-Dopa research and Nielsen's blood pressure
cuff), there is considerable empirical evidence that they can occur as self-
depictive metaphors in purely personal situations of crisis and resolution.
Thus Heinz Kohut (1971) speaks of self-state dreams (based on what we are
terming titanic sensations) in narcissistic or self-pathology as markers of both
dissolution anxiety and the initial establishment of self-continuity or, in
Winnicott's (1971) terms, a cohesive "sense of Being." Kohut emphasizes that
these dreams characteristically resist free association. What seems to be thera-
peutically useful is simply their acknowledgment by therapist and patient as
indicating state of self and mode of being:

> The patient is on a swing, swinging forward and backward, higher and higher—yet
> there is never a serious danger of either the patient's falling off or of the swing
> uncontrolledly entering a full circle.   (Kohut, 1971, p. 5)

Kohut understands this dream as a metaphoric depiction of the tenuous balance between his patient's grandiosity and her transference relationship with
the therapist.

Another illustration comes from one of my own dreams, which occurred
at a point of stasis during the writing of this book, when I was attempting to
switch from literature review and my own preliminary notes to an inclusive
outline and actual writing. In the midst of this frustrating and depressing
period, I awoke early one morning from the following dream with an alertness
and clarity of mind that had hitherto eluded me and that stayed with me for
two days:

> I am in a large building when suddenly I realize that I am in danger of being im-
> prisoned in it. I wait surreptitiously until someone opens a door and I run outside.
> However, I am pursued by a man carrying a strange metal object about two feet long
> and with four sharp curved hooks emerging from its handle (a sort of grappling iron).
> He throws it at me, but it misses me, landing nearby. I debate whether to pick it up
> and throw it back; and I finally do, also missing. The man picks it up and grins. Step-
> ping quickly toward me, suddenly and with immense force, he swings the object so

that it enters my head just under my jaw. I *vividly* feel one of the points moving up inside my head and just breaking through the very top of my skull. The sensation is not painful, but strange and almost pleasurable. As the point reaches and breaks through the top of my skull, my visual field is completely filled with a brilliantly shining silver expanse, which instantly shatters into thousands of scintillating pieces. I am overwhelmed with the beauty and power of this experience and I awaken full of an unaccustomed energy and confidence.

Indeed there are possible day residues here. I had explained Maslow's concept of peak experience to my daughter the night before. A political confrontation had recently left certain colleagues somewhat annoyed with me, and once again in my life gaining the right access to legitimate anger was important. But none of this personal material could by itself have generated such a dream along the lines of normative mnemic reorganization. As for Levitan's examples, so far at least I am not epileptic. Rather, the vivid kinesthetic sensation of explosive release seems to have been an immediate metaphor (or functional autosymbol, in Silberer's terms) for the conceptual breakthrough and renewed sense of self that I so badly needed. It was a metaphoric version of "wake up and get going. What you fear is what you actually need."

A final illustration of titanic dreams as metaphors for conceptual struggle and breakthrough can be found in the famous three dreams of Descartes (Wisdom, 1947; Lewin, 1958). He connected these dreams of a single night with his final realization of the autonomy and supremacy of reason (as the highest expression of the soul) over the lower material and emotional realms. These dreams apparently marked a decisive point in the resolution of Descartes' philosophical (and personal) doubt:

> In the first dream, he "saw phantoms" and owing to an "evil spirit" he could not stand upright (feeling a weakness in his right side). A sudden wind swept him around several times and made his forward progress still more difficult, although others about him were walking about with no difficulty. In a second (hypnagogic) dream, preceded by intense philosophical reflection as he lay awake after the first dream, he heard thundrous sounds and saw sparks of light filling his room. By opening and closing his eyes he ascertained that these sensations were subjective and not real. His intense agitation was only resolved by the third dream, in which he was given several books. Because they kept appearing and disappearing before his eyes, he was able to conclude that he was actually dreaming.

Part of Descartes' famous skepticism, resolved in these dreams, was his philosophical questioning of how we can know for certain whether we are dreaming or awake. Although we might well ask whether his philosophical dualism resolves or merely enshrines the imbalance and agitation so graphically portrayed in the first two dreams, it seems clear enough that the dreams are metaphoric depictions of his intense intellectual crisis and its resolution by scientific reflection.

It is fascinating to realize that, in contrast to the specialized development of dream lucidity in Eastern traditions, leading to the conclusion that life and dreaming are equally illusory, Descartes used this lucid dream to dismiss dreaming as merely subjective and completely secondary to objective reality. The same state that led the meditative traditions to the existential bases of human reality was used by Descartes to justify the Western flight from subjectivity.

We cannot leave this attempt to establish a titanic category of dreaming, quite distinct from direct somatic-medical translations, without reference to the strikingly bizarre and often morbid dreams of that ultimate human crisis—acute schizophrenia. If titanic sensations are self-state metaphors, they should be (and are) especially prominent in early schizophrenic onset. Although not all studies of schizophrenic patients show unusual dreams (Kramer, 1969; Schwartz, Weinstein, and Arkin, 1978), those that do (Boss, 1958; Brenneis, 1971; Carrington, 1972) are so unusual compared to normal dream samples that some degree of relationship to this most extreme disorder seems clear. Especially in the early acute phase of schizophrenia, dreams are marked by intense and perverse sexuality and aggression and extremely bizarre and morbid body distortions, mutilations, and dismemberments. Boss (1958) notes that these peculiarly dislocating and upsetting dreams sometimes foreshadow or initiate a worsening of the clinical condition. Carrington lists some of the more repugnant somatic-kinesthetic dreams in a group of acute patients.

> They included a man sweeping up a girl's bones and throwing them into a sanitation truck, dead flesh decaying in layers, the dreamer lying down in a coffin from which her parents had just risen, people turning into skeletons, the dreamer raking up a huge 10-foot piece of decaying feces which was wrapped in a white sheet, and the dreamer taking a blanket off a corpse and finding it to be a sewed-up banana. (Carrington, 1972, p. 349)

Some of these dreams are reminiscent of visionary rites in classical shamanism and Tibetan Buddhism, where the initiate must undergo an hallucinatory dismemberment and reassembling—sometimes deliberately induced by visualization techniques, in other instances undergone with no warning or intent of shamanistic training. The following report is also from one of Carrington's schizophrenic patients:

> I was decapitated. My ribs were picked clean, no skin, no muscle. My body was cut in half. It was just a pile of bones. They didn't know who it was, but I still knew who I was. I wanted to pull myself together but I couldn't. (Carrington, 1971, p. 348)

Of course future shamans may show some characteristics of schizoid conflict, as do the highly creative in Western society, and we have already noted experimental evidence of high creativity in some hospitalized schizophrenics. However, the schizophrenic individual mainly presents metaphors of dismemberment, while the successful shaman literally does "pull him- or herself together" after such experience (Halifax, 1979).

Somatic hallucinations of dismemberment and internal mutilation are also common in the waking complaints of schizophrenics. While psychoanalysis and standard psychiatry have tended to interpret these anomalies as "regressions" to early stages of ego development, others, such as Harold Searles (1965), have been struck by their vivid and accurate presentation of the patient's life situation, based on metaphoric capacities well beyond the young child. Andras Angyal, in a series of original and rarely cited papers published in the 1930s, showed that typical somatic hallucinations in schizophrenia were based on the patient's hypersensitivity to background tactile, kinesthetic, and coenesthetic sensations which are present in everyone but not ordinarily open to introspection. These are the very sensitivities, we might add, that would be involved in self-state metaphoric reference with its special reuse of somatic perceptual schemata.

However diverse may be the balance of genetic, biochemical, cognitive, dynamic, and social-class determinants of schizophrenia, it most definitely represents a massive "problem-solving crisis" (Boisen, 1962; Bowers, 1974)—entailing an autonomous and totalistic self-reference as both symptom and potentially insightful solution. These bizarre experiences, dreamed and waking, of torture, dismemberment, internal damage of intestines and heart, death and annihilation, and various other examples of "cutting to the bone" are especially apt, if merciless, metaphors for the psychological catastrophe that has befallen the patient. Being "torn apart," "annihilated," "heartbroken," and so on reflect interpersonal situations so painful they cannot be faced; they must be suffered as "weird sensations" instead. Searles (1965) interprets these hallucinations as impacted and literalized metaphors which, with recovery, gradually turn back into a more accessible and imaginative, if highly painful, self-awareness.

There is some precedent for our titanic category in psychoanalytic dream theory. Just as Jung distinguished between personal and archetypal dreams (the latter clearly including much of what I term titanic), so Freud, Ferenczi, Rank, the psychoanalytic anthropologist Gesa Roheim, and most recently W. R. Bion and the French psychoanalyst Pontalis have all distinguished between dreaming based on wish fulfillment and dreams that reflect a more original function—"the psychical binding of traumatic impressions" (Freud, 1919a, p.

41). The very existence of even the most intense and emotionally overwhelming dream is proof against the still more basic tendency for dissolution into an "infinite contentless dread." Or as Pontalis put it, "Is not the wildest dream already tame?" (1977, p. 236). Roheim (1952), along with Rank (1950), called attention to the existence of a "basic dream," directly reacting to the diffuse self-awareness of being asleep, with its erratic respiration and loss of muscle tone so close to total helplessness and "death." Roheim includes as aspects of the "basic dream" sensations of sinking, falling, flying, descending to caves, tunnels, and water (being encompassed), and nature symbols of cosmic inclusiveness like sky, wind, rain, and fog. Indeed, the "guardian spirits" of dreaming in the culture pattern dreams of tribal societies are often linked to such nature symbols, and Roheim provides illustrations of "basic dream" elements from these sources—as in the following dream of a Papuan:

> Two canoes were sailing on the water with two men steering. *It was quite calm but the canoes sank down* of their own accord. The two men *climbed up* on the masts and the people on the beach were shouting. . . . Suddenly he found himself . . . with a man named Duane, *he saw a small house which was hanging by a rope from the sky.* The wind made the house whirl *round and round,* and in it they saw a man named Dabu. He asked them to come into the house and *he crawled in through a small opening while the house was spinning round.* . . . The wind came whirling and tossed the house around and the men had to crouch on all fours in order not to be thrown off. A man up in the air was holding a rope by which the house hung and they heard his voice saying, "That house I make him for wind." A heavy gust of wind carried the roof off the house. The house disappeared. Two other men sailed off in a canoe. He found a woman who lived in a house. *Underneath the house there was a hole in which she kept a pig but no one else knew of the animal's existence.*   (Roheim, 1952, p. 74; italics original)

Roheim, in true psychoanalytic fashion, interprets the basic dream as a regressive activation of the intrauterine situation and birth trauma, in a manner later followed by R. D. Laing (1982), and Grof (1980), the latter for similar experiences in LSD. However, such reductive use of biological patterns from the fetal period and birth process or, as in Grof and Jung, phylogenetically primitive behavior patterns, misses a more parsimonous cognitive account that pays full attention to the phenomenology of these powerful experiences without having to posit doubtful and ultimately untestable theories of fetal and evolutionary memory. Such basic biological behaviors are exactly the simplified and diffuse patterns sought by all forms of theoretical "structuralism"—patterns so basic that they locate all more specific and complicated forms within a more organismic general context. Piaget uses abstract concepts like assimilation and accommodation, Erikson uses incorporation, retention, elimination, and intrusion. Roheim, Laing, and Grof, by contrast, resort to concrete phases of the birth process, mistaking basic inclusive structures for causes, but to much the same effect. In other words, titanic patterns in LSD and dreams are self-referential metaphors for the basic situations of interpersonal (and all organismic) crises. Given the open-ended reflexivity of human intelligence, there is no point of final terminus for metaphoric reference. All the phases of birth, death, love, and hate are endlessly available as metaphors for each other.

A Methodological Afterword

In the dream diamond (figure 2, chapter 6), the two other panels within the apex of formal self-reference defined by archetypal and titanic dreams have been left blank. Since these levels of dreaming are essentially identical to visionary states associated with psychedelic drugs and deep meditation, it should be possible in principle to complete our typology by reference to the dimensions of such experience. Thus we can tentatively add to the archetypal and titanic level ethically performative and enactive dreams (ritual acts and commands, special names given by guardian spirit dreams)—these being formal ramifications of narrative structure—and subjectively real apparitional dreams as a further development of dreams of external reference.

On a still greater level of intensification and symbolic integration, here based on visual-spatial and not verbal intelligence, we could add various aspects of classic mystical experience (James, 1902; Otto, 1923) to categorize the same states appearing in dreams. Thus, in addition to diffuse white light (maximally abstract visual imagery, a development of the archetypal category) separate panels might represent death-rebirth crisis (maximally total kinesthetic metaphor), felt oneness and unity in all things (maximally abstract propositional thought under the aegis of visual-spatial intelligence), and sense of noetic insight (pure external reference).

In the context of this classification diamond for dreams, we may think of each dream as a "bubble" welling up from a common matrix of mnemic activation and reorganization. Most burst quickly, unable to sustain themselves long enough, in the overall context of contending personal, cognitive, and physiological forces, to reach more vivid and intense forms of imagination and self-reference. Depending on the typological features of the dream, the expanding bubble can be of any height and width—it may touch one or several panels before it bursts. In other words, any given dream could touch metonymic and/or somatic-medical and/or visual-metaphoric and/or external reference panels. As its potential vividness increases it reaches one or more of the formal self-referential dreams, or Monroe's properties of "set"—certain nightmares, lucidity, archetypal-titanic dreaming.

Where the bubble cannot form at all, it remains undeveloped, within the processes of "inner speech" beneath the lower pyramid, as repetitive, obsessive REM ruminations. This area also constitutes the matrix out of which waking intelligence unfolds, with its own frames of mind but here guided by language. The diamond shows mnemic-verbal processes as the core of normative dreaming and as the matrix from which more specialized imaginative dreams emerge. As such it may concede far too much to orthodox cognitive science and its overemphasis on language and memory. On the other hand, there is considerable evidence of mnemic day residue in even the most autonomous, imaginative dreams.

If the panels show the multiple dimensions potential within a single dream production system, then the bubbles filling the diamond will gain their "energy" from synesthetic or cross-modal fusions of verbal, visual, and tactile-kinesthetic patterns. Whatever modality most influences the others in these fusions determines which panel surface is most characteristic of the dream. The degree of intensification-vividness determines whether the cross-modal structures thus engaged will be predominantly mnemic, creative-imaginative, or formally self-referential. Normative, relatively realistic dreaming is integrated in terms of the linguistic-narrative processes of semantic memory, while dreams of abstract self-reference reflect the maximum integration open to visual-kinesthetic synesthesias. Each apex thus entails a predominance of integration over differentiation. Ordinary language binds together the everyday social order and the dreams that represent it most directly, while visual-spatial intelligence, at its maximum abstraction, generates the nonverbal intuitions of the spiritual traditions and their rare but subjectively powerful dream analogues.

Freud, Jung, and Culture Pattern Dreams: Archetypal Imagination versus Cultural Programming

The Dreams of Freud and Jung

I T is quite clear that Freud's and Jung's dreams differed markedly in style or form—yet with enough overlap to suggest that they represent variations within a single dreaming process. The old saw that Freudian patients dream Freudian dreams, and Jungians dream Jungian, also seems likely, although causation is less clear. Dreaming *is* socially malleable, but given the differences in the dreams of the founders, it may well be that people are drawn to one tradition or the other because it mirrors their lives (awake and asleep).

A continuing debate, also reflected within the anthropological literature on culture pattern dreams, revolves around whether one form of dreaming (and its corresponding method of interpretation) is somehow "deeper" or more fundamental and the other somehow secondary or defensive. For Jung (and many tribal peoples) normative dreams, based largely on mnemic assimilation and reorganization, are merely reflections of daily personal concerns, unlike the autonomous manifestations of creative imagination in archetypal or "big" dreaming. Freud and mainstream anthropology see archetypal culture pattern dreams as dominated by secondary revision—a superficial accommodation of the primary personal forces involved in dream formation to the power of society.

141

Consider first the dreams of the two men. We begin with Jung's late dream of the court of Akbar the Great, which he interpreted as anticipating his controversial *Answer to Job*. Its spiritual theme and aesthetic grandeur certainly mark it as archetypal in his own vocabulary:

> My father and I were in front of the house . . . where, apparently, wood was stacked. We heard loud thumps as if large chunks of wood were being thrown down or tossed about. I had the impression that at least two workmen must be busy there, but my father indicated to me that the place was haunted. Some sort of poltergeists were making the racket.
>
> We then entered the house, and I saw that it had very thick walls. We climbed a narrow staircase to the second floor. There a strange sight presented itself: a large hall which was the . . . council hall of Sultan Akbar. . . . It was a high, circular room with a gallery running along the wall, from which four bridges led to a basin-shaped center. The basin rested upon a huge column and formed the Sultan's round seat. From this elevated place, he spoke to his councilors and philosophers, who sat along the walls in the gallery. The whole was a gigantic mandala. . . .
>
> In the dream I suddenly saw that from the center a steep flight of stairs ascended to a spot high up on the wall—which no longer corresponded to reality. At the top of the stairs was a small door, and my father said, "Now I will lead you into the highest presence." Then he knelt down and touched his forehead to the floor. I imitated him, likewise kneeling with great emotion. For some reason I could not bring my forehead quite down to the floor—there was perhaps a millimeter to spare. But at least I made the gesture with him. Suddenly I knew—perhaps my father had told me—that the upper door led to a solitary chamber where lived Uriah, King David's general whom David had shamefully betrayed for the sake of his wife Bathsheba, by commanding his soldiers to abandon Uriah in the face of the enemy. (Jung, 1961, pp. 218–19)

Various interpersonal dynamics leap out even at the reader with a minimal knowledge of Jung's life, all of which Jung ignores in favor of his creative amplifications. Uriah, the betrayed Hebrew general, may remind one of Jung's ambivalent relations with his own father and of widespread accusations that he "betrayed" Freud. But Jung, for good or ill, was not prone to guilt in the way of Freud. He replaces "obvious" psychoanalytic associations with future-oriented amplifications. For him, the dream is prophetic of his wife's death and metaphorically anticipates his basic concerns in *Answer to Job*—the creature (humanity) who by virtue of his doubting consciousness slightly surpasses its creator (God/Nature) and thereby provides the only possible mirror (self-realization) for Creation and Creator.

As with Jung's childhood dream of the underground phallus and his late dream/vision of Zeus and Hera making love, which he takes as the sacred *Hieros Gamos* of psychic opposites rather than as "primal scene" material, there is much oedipal material in this dream—if that is what we are looking for. For Freud (and for Piaget, 1963) the child's early experience of his or her parents as omnipotent and omniscient provides the only possible source for the later personification of powerful mythological beings. However, for Jung it is just these *parental imagoes* that will later become the only suitable symbolic vehicles for the abstract and autonomous generation of the numinous concept-feeling of something that transcends and encompasses us. The oedipus complex cannot explain God for Jung, any more than the stone used in its blocks explains the design and purpose of a temple. Rather, human beings spontaneously construct, out of the raw material of these parental imagoes, an image of what encompasses us and resists discursive formulation. Likewise, for Jung, we use sexual slang (*prick, cocksucker*) not to refer to sexual practices but metaphorically to assassinate the character of those who have offended us on quite different grounds. Similarly, Jung (1953) interpreted the dream of a female patient, coddled in the arms of her gigantic therapist in the blowing wind, as an attempt to construct a healing and unifying image out of the raw material of her intractable therapeutic transference.

Jung's own dreams are experientially coherent and readily taken as cohesive unifying metaphors. Freud's dreams, on the other hand, are a loose array of personal memories and current concerns—as is his dream of Brücke, his physiology teacher, typical in its tendency toward delirium and confusion:

> Old Brücke must have set me some task; strangely enough it related to a dissection of the lower parts of my own body, my pelvis and legs, which I saw before me as through in the dissecting-room, but without noticing their absence in myself and also without a trace of any gruesome feeling. Louise N. was standing beside me and doing the work with me. The pelvis had been eviscerated. . . . Thick flesh-coloured protuberances . . . could be seen. Something which lay over it and was like crumpled silver-paper had also to be carefully fished out. I was then once more in possession of my legs and I was making my way through the town. But (being tired) I took a cab. To my astonishment the cab drove in through the door of a house, which opened and allowed it to pass along a passage which turned a corner at its end and finally led into the open air again. Finally I was making a journey through a changing landscape with an Alpine guide. . . . People were sitting on the ground like Red Indians or Gypsys—among them a girl. Before this I had been making my own way forward over the slippery ground with a constant feeling of surprise that I was able to do it so well after the dissection. At last we reached a small wooden house at the end of which was an open window. There the guide set me down and laid two wooden boards, which were standing ready,

upon the window sill, so as to bridge the chasm which had to be crossed over from the window. At that point I really became frightened about my legs, but instead of the expected crossing, I saw two grown-up men lying on wooden benches that were along the walls of the hut, and what seemed to be two children sleeping beside them. It was as though what was going to make the crossing possible was not the boards but the children. I awoke in a mental fright.   (Freud, 1900, pp. 489–90)

As ever, Freud's associations to this dream show its basis in his concerns over career and reputation. He had offered his friend Louis N. the book *She*, by Rider Haggard, but she had challenged him to provide a book of his own, one he had yet to write. Metonymic associations abound. Silver paper leads to "stanniol," a derivative of tin (stannium), and reminiscent of Stannius, the author of a dissertation on the nervous system of fish. Indeed, the scientific task that Brücke first set for Freud was on the same topic.

Yet, just as Jung's imaginatively cohesive dreams also provided rich personal-mnemic allusions, there are hints of other dream forms to be found within Freud's dream. First there is the astonishingly apt and powerful metaphor for Freud's special brand of self-analysis—dissecting one's own pelvis—a task which Brücke would certainly not have countenanced. Also there is the metaphoric depiction of his theory as formed on and over the bodies of children. Similarly, there are several indicators of pre-lucidity, as in his constant sense of surprise, which often leads to full lucidity, and the descriptions of weakness in his legs and lying down as allusions to his sleeping condition. Implicit titanic material is seen in his multiple references to heights, depths, and bodily mutilation.

The archetypal dimension, the core of Jung's dreaming, is also here, but only implicitly in Freud's associations to the works of Rider Haggard. In various books, Haggard (see Grinstein, 1980) was preoccupied with themes of ancient identity passed down over generations. Freud's associations led to thoughts of an Etruscan grave and the possibility that one's sons might have to fulfil the destiny that eluded the father. Here we see his deep concern with identity and self and perhaps his incipient identification with Moses and its opposition to Haggard's "eternal feminine." However, there is no autonomous imaginative psyche for Freud. As with his analysis of fairy tale motifs in dreams, the copious allusions to *She* throughout the dream become background fantasies introduced into the dream by a secondary revision. Just as Jung devalued the interpersonal, Freud left what we can now see as the development of self (and self-reference) as a residual and primitive narcissism. This would only be developed into a positive psychology in its own right by Jung, Winnicott, and Kohut.

The two men differ not just in interpretive attitude, amplification that further integrates versus free association that further resolves into memories, but in their dreams themselves—subjectively powerful and cohesive versus clouded and already dissolving. In my own research (Hunt et al., 1982), the dreams of Freud and Jung were categorized in terms of dream bizarreness and transformation and compared to laboratory and home samples of normative dreaming, dreams of long-term meditators, and sets of the single most vivid and mundane dreams of undergraduate subjects (see appendix, table 1). Compared to normative samples, Freud's dreams are if anything more confused and lacking in narrative cohesiveness—especially obvious in ratings of confused and inadequate thinking, clouding of attention, movement, and speech, and forgetting of parts of the dream on awakening.

What makes Freud's dreams bizarre in a positive sense is the presence of predominantly visual "hallucinatory" intrusions, as with normative dreaming. However, Freud's dreams contained only half as many intrusions rated intrinsically bizarre or impossible (content 3), when compared to reports of the normative samples; his dreams also contained only half the possible but unlikely events (content 1). What defines these intrusions in Freud's dreams is the way that actual past events and situations are presented in a fashion known to be impossible in wakefulness (content 2)—reorganized memories. Thus interpretation will restore these memories to their propositional context, connected now to the present by numerous links suggested by their dreamt rearrangement.

This restoration of propositional context can also been seen in the metonymic nature of free association, where the aim is to show how one dream element leads to another. Free association starts at the beginning of the dream and works through it in order, as if it could thereby become a coherent sequential story. The search is always for the turn of phrase or switchword that will integrate manifest dream and free associations. In the narrative disorganization of Freud's dreams, it is tempting to see just the "using up" of verbal-propositional thought he posited as part of all dream formation.

Jung's dreams, on the other hand, are more overtly bizarre, or better here, "imaginatively transformed" and significantly less clouded. Jung's cohesive dream experiences are organized around and determined by unusually high levels of geometric-mandala symbols, intrinsically impossible visual intrusions, otherworldly and/or mythological settings, uncanny-numinous emotion, and encounters with mythical beings. Compared to the single most vivid dreams recalled by undergraduate subjects, Jung's dreams were less clouded, with few somatic-kinesthetic transformations (thus sparing him the morbid somatic horrors of schizophrenic dreams), and they contained fewer identity changes and transformations (again allowing Jung a stability and clarity of dreaming). So it is not surprising that Jung takes the dream as a finished metaphoric expression to be directly amplified into a still more vivid and explicit formulation.

Freud's and Jung's methods of interpretation seem to follow from their forms of dreaming, not the other way around. It is hard to see one of these forms as somehow derivative of the other. This conclusion is supported by many years of assigning my students a project in which they are to report two dreams—amplifying one and free-associating to the other. Some students actually dream in cohesive metaphors, while others dream in more delirious aggregates; but, regardless, many will find one method of interpretation congenial and natural and the other all but impossible. Generally these students will unwittingly turn the latter into the former—really free-associating when they should be amplifying, or vice versa. No amount of instruction can change this tendency for some subjects. They are simply natural free-associaters or natural amplifiers.

Freud, Jung, and Anthropology

Most anthropologists who have written on dreams echo Jung's distinction between "little" (personal) and "big" (archetypal) dreams, for which Jung found support from his own informal studies of primitive peoples. However, beginning with J. S. Lincoln's identification of "big" dreams as culture pattern dreams in his seminal *The Dream in Primitive Cultures* (1935), most anthropologists have understood such dreams as the product of a culturally programmed secondary revision. Indeed, most observers stress the disappearance of culture pattern dreams following the inevitable secularization of sacred culture that comes with Westernization. They assimilate archetypal dreams to psychoanalytic dream theory, ignoring the latter's narrow grounding on a single dream type.

Lincoln, just as Tylor (1871) before him and Tedlock (1987) more recently, stressed the immense importance of culture pattern dreams in the maintenance of primitive cultures. Traditionally such dreams could provide and authenticate guardian spirits, totems, shamanistic powers, individual identity, membership in secret societies, and—with a cross-cultural ubiquity that seems startling in light of their near total absence in our own times—they were the original source for most native songs. However, Lincoln sharply disagrees with Tylor, who had argued that beliefs in soul and afterlife might actually be derived from spontaneous dream experiences. Such beliefs would be attempted phenomenologies of the experiential transformations associated with dreams. There are several examples of new versions of well-known myths emerging from individual native dreams, and there has long been speculation that mythologies may have originated in shamanistic dreaming. Certainly the relationship between archetypal/cultural pattern dreams and myths is very close.[1] For Lincoln, however, the basic symbols of culture pattern dreams (e.g., the thunderbird in North American Indian traditions) are in the first instance culturally determined: "the dream is not an ultimate origin but merely gives form to previously existing psychological processes" (Lincoln, 1935, p. 169). Based on secondary revision, the culture pattern dream becomes the means of confirming preexistent beliefs and maintaining group cohesion.

Of course, on a sufficiently detailed level there must be a cultural specificity to archetypal dreams—for example, dreams of birds will have a significance in Siberia very different from that in Southeast Asia (Dentan, 1987). Whatever the potential imagistic autonomy and cross-cultural commonality of some hypothetical core of religious experience, we would never expect a medieval European peasant to hallucinate or dream of the Buddha. Near-death experiences in India feature not the out-of-body pattern described by Moody and others, but black figures who carry the body away to the land of death (Pasricha and Stevenson, 1986). However, these variants can overlap across cultures—Monroe's (1985) accounts of out-of-body experience sometimes describe the "ethereal form" being lifted out of the physical body by several guides. One doubts any direct influence here because Pasricha and Stevenson's case reports are so recent.

What Lincoln missed was the spontaneous and cross-cultural features of archetypal dreaming. *Of course* the specific mythological beings will vary according to cultural definition, but some such beings—half-man, half-animal—are generally encountered, in addition to visions of geometric and white light imagery, flying, falling, and other titanic sensations, and above all the powerful sense of uncanny-numinous emotion. Rudolf Otto (1923), in his original phenomenology of religious experience, followed so closely by Jung, asserts with the sociologist of religious experience Max Weber (1960) that the subjective power of the numinous (awe, fascination, sense of wholly other, etc.) is so great that cultural schematizations are inevitable over time as a necessary taming and defense.

For Lincoln, however, these common elements are seen through the ontogenetic reductionism of classical psychoanalysis. The guardian spirit of American Indian visionquest dreams is explained as ultimately oedipal because the Indians see it as an emanation from deceased relatives on the father's side—as if that must be the cause of the experience rather than an aspect of its symbolic elaboration. The sacrificial cutting off of finger joints to ensure a powerful dream/vision is for Lincoln obviously castration anxiety—rather than, say, a graphic way of expressing a more intrinsic or existential guilt. Waud Kracke (1979), a psychoanalytically trained anthropologist, echoes this attitude when, in his analysis of the spirit dreams of an Amazonian Kagwahiv informant, he explains that the subject's tendency to dream of the ghosts of old men follows from his early loss of his father. As I have suggested already, personal-mnemic material necessarily informs all dreaming, but it cannot fully explain the distinct cognitive form of culture pattern dreams. Some dreams might, after all, be jointly determined by mnemic and creative imagistic dimensions.

Lincoln and others have missed the importance of dream phenomenology and forms of dreaming based on distinct frames of mind. Take, for example, Lincoln's own reports of two dreams from a Yuma Indian, Joe Homer. The first dream, Lincoln states, is obviously culture pattern, because it contains an encounter with the god Kumastamxo and other elements of traditional Indian belief. The second dream, following Homer's conversion to Christianity, is obviously a subjectively powerful archetypal dream from our perspective. But Lincoln does not label it a culture pattern dream because it reflects no standard themes from native culture, and such dreams are not sought as part of contemporary Christian practice.

> While at a fiesta he went to sleep. At noon he heard a voice from the air to the North. It called his name and said, "I will come back and get you." He awoke. At sundown he got sleepy again. A voice called his name again and said two or three times, "I am coming." Someone was holding his right hand. He dreamt that, "I walked out with this person who was holding my hand. It was dark and I could not see him. Now he spoke to me saying, 'Let go.' Then I walked three or four steps after I had let go. I was on the mountain Awikame." He learned four songs there. "I brought you to learn these songs to do you good," said Kumastamxo. Afterwards he showed him the place where the ceremony is held. . . . "I looked up and saw a cloud half dark and half light. Kumastamxo told me that the cloud that comes from the east will be white and that the cloud that comes from the west will be dark."

> A voice called for me in English: "God wants to see you." Several other persons were called, five young boys, and one old man, making seven in all. I walked on the road, but did not go far. . . . I saw a house with all sorts of flowers growing around it. I looked pretty. It was built after the white man's style. A negro came out with a white bulldog. He said "You had better go right up the street and go into that house and talk to God." So I started. A young man accompanied me. He was not one of the original five that started out with me. He entered the house ahead of me, but was frightened. I waited for him to come out before I went in. He had four or five books when he came out. The person inside (God) had given these to him. When he came out, he dropped all the books. He picked up some

and left others lying on the ground. I laughed at him. Then I went inside. God turned around and looked at me. He had long whiskers reaching down to his navel. He shook his head and said, "That is alright." He handed books to me which I took in my hands. . . . Then God said: "Just a minute." Then the room turned dark and he asked me: "How do you like the darkness?" I did not reply. "Look out for yourself," he said. Then came lightning and during the flash of lightning I saw a mountain . . . I went out but was very much frightened. (Lincoln, 1935, p. 198–99)

In their haste to stress the social and culturally patterned nature of all experience, many anthropologists, but not all as we shall see, have missed the possibility that the potential for altered states or numinous experience (awake and dreaming), while surely culturally shaped, might nonetheless rest on an autonomous imagistic faculty that cannot simply be reduced to "childhood" or "suggestion" because it has its own line of growth and abstraction. Certainly Jung would regard Joe Homer's two dreams as equally archetypal, correctly on empirical phenomenal criteria.

Yet there is an intriguing irony in Lincoln's rejection of Jung's interpretation of culture pattern dreams in favor of Freud's secondary revision, for it is true that in the strictest terms of Freud's own writings, Jung developed his concept of a self-referential archetypal imagination precisely from Freud's secondary revision. In later editions of *The Interpretation of Dreams*, secondary revision came to include not only rational and social influence on the dream via the capacity for self-censorship (and ultimately self-awareness), but a self-referential imagistic capacity that Freud termed *endopsychic perception*. This was his own coinage for the potential in both mythology and spontaneous hallucinatory states to depict cognitive processes that are ordinarily inaccessible (formally unconscious).

This is the same process that Herbert Silberer later termed functional autosymbolism—the tendency of sleep onset imagery to present not only what one is thinking about (material autosymbols) but formal features of one's cognitive functioning. Silberer's best-known example is as follows: While trying to sort out the theories of Kant and Schopenhauer on time, his increasing drowsiness leads him to forget first one, then the other conception. Suddenly he experiences a dreamlike image in which he is asking a morose and uncommunicative secretary for a certain file, which he does not get. This is an excellent metaphor not of his thoughts about time, but of the failure of memory itself. Silberer (1917), and Jung (using the term *transcendent function*; 1916), further developed Freud's earlier insight that much mythology is in this sense functionally autosymbolic for the *workings* of the mind; it imagistically self-presents the very processes about which the psychologist theorizes and experiments. Indeed this model was later central to Lévi-Strauss's treatment of tribal mythologies:

> Mythology has no practical function. . . . If it was possible to prove . . . that the apparent arbitrariness of the mind, its supposedly spontaneous flow of inspiration and its seemingly uncontrolled inventiveness, imply the existence of laws operating at a deeper level, we would inevitably be forced to conclude that when the mind is left to commune with itself and no longer has to come to terms with objects, it is in a sense reduced to imitating itself as object; and that since the laws governing its operation are not fundamentally different than those it exhibits in its other functions, it shows itself to be of the nature of a thing among things. (Lévi-Strauss, 1969, p. 10)

Freud agreed with Silberer that this autonomous self-referential capacity could sometimes influence dream content, as in dreams of crossing a physical threshold (a stream or path) when on the verge of waking up. However, for Jung and Silberer this self-presenting imagery became part of a developmental line in its own right (Jung called it *introversion* and later *individuation*). Freud, on the other hand, understood it first in terms of narcissism (which after all is his only manner of representing the core ability of the human mind to turn around on itself in the sense of Neisser, Mead, and Hofstadter) and later as the core of the superego—in German *über ich*, better translated "over-I."

We will trace Freud's discussion of endopsychic perception from its first presentation in a letter to Fliess, through its use in his interpretation of Schreber's hallucinations and delusions, to his final discussion of its implicit relation to deep meditation in *The New Introductory Lectures to Psychoanalysis* (1933). The close relation between endopsychic perception and Jung, Winnicott, Bion, and Kohut on a line of development based on intrinsic self-reference (introversion, sense of Being, higher forms of narcissism) has generally been missed:

> Can you imagine what "endopsychic" myths are? They are the latest product of my mental labor. The dim inner perception of one's psychical apparatus stimulates illusions, which are naturally projected outwards, and characteristically into the future and a world beyond. Inmortality, retribution, the world after death, are all reflections of our inner psyche . . . psycho-mythology. (Freud, 1954, p. 237)

> Since I neither fear the criticism of others nor shrink from criticizing myself, I have no motive for avoiding the mention of a similarity which may possibly damage our libido theory in the estimation of many of my readers. Schreber's "rays of God" . . . are in reality nothing else than a concrete representation and external projection of libidinal cathexes; and they thus lend his delusions a striking similar-

ity with our theory. His belief that the world must come to an end because his ego was attracting all the rays to itself, his anxious concern . . . lest God should sever his ray-connection with him—these and many other details of Schreber's delusional formation sound almost like endopsychic perceptions of the processes whose existence I have assumed in these pages as the basis of our explanation of paranoia. [i.e., the relation between narcissism and object libido and the withdrawal of object libido into narcissism in clinical states and sleep]. . . . It remains for the future to decide whether there is more delusion in my theory than I would like to admit, or whether there is more truth in Schreber's delusion than other people are as yet prepared to believe.   (Freud, 1911, pp. 465–66)

It can easily be imagined, too, that certain practices of mystics may succeed in upsetting the normal relations between the different regions of the mind, so that, for example, the perceptual system becomes able to grasp relations in the deeper layers of the ego and in the id which would otherwise be inaccessible to it. Whether such a procedure can put one in possession of ultimate truths, from which all goods will flow, may be safely doubted. All the same, we must admit that the therapeutic efforts of psychoanalysis have chosen much the same method of approach.   (Freud, 1933, p. 111)

Indeed, the later Freud presents self-awareness as the most basic function of the superego (better translated "over-I"), permitting its developmentally later role in self-evaluation and moral judgment. He even suggests that what we would now call first-rank symptoms of schizophrenia (patients' complaints of thoughts out-loud, made-thoughts, made-feelings) are originally accurate, if projected, self-perceptions of cognitive processes:

Psychotics . . . have turned away from external reality, but for that very reason they know more of internal psychic reality and can tell us much that would otherwise be inaccessible to us. One group of them suffer what we call delusions of observation. They complain to us that they suffer continually, and in their most intimate actions, from the observations of unknown powers or persons, and they have hallucinations in which they hear these persons announcing the results of their observations: "Now he is going to say this, now he is dressing himself to go out," and so on. Such observation is not the same thing as persecution, but it is not far removed from it. . . . How would it be if these mad people were right, and if we all of us had an observing function in our egos threatening us with punishment, which, in their case, had merely become sharply separated from the ego and had been mistakenly projected into external reality? . . . Under the strong impression of this clinical picture, I formed the idea that the separating off of an observing function from the rest of the ego might be a normal feature of the ego structure.   (Freud, 1933, p. 85)

Stripped of its pathological emphasis, Freud is discussing the self-referential capacity of symbolic intelligence, whose development makes possible the "over-I," psychoanalysis itself, and the meditative traditions.

The difference between Silberer and Jung, on the one hand, and Freud, on the other, is that the former are asserting that imagistic forms of self-reference do provide special truths for psychology. Both are in a sense more modern than Freud in their keen awareness of the intrinsic limitations of self-knowledge in an endlessly reflexive intelligence, which can never get fully outside itself for self-*representation*, but which may offer more inclusive self-*presentations* of its own nature via spontaneous visual and gestural metaphor. Here we find the echo of Plato on myth and metaphor, while Freud sides with Aristotle's devaluation of all forms of metaphoric reference as secondary to discursive reason. Jung, however, goes further than Silberer, to whom he otherwise owes a very great deal, in his suggestion that it is the self-referential (and so self-stimulating) aspect of spontaneous imagery that transforms and fuses our mammalian instinctual tendencies into the "titanic" drivenness that the later Freud terms *das Es* (the id or, more literally, the it).

> Although the existence of an instinctual pattern in human biology is probable, it seems very difficult to prove the existence of distinct types empirically. For the organ with which we might apprehend them—consciousness—is not only itself a transformation of the original instinctual image, but also its transformer. It is therefore not surprising that the human mind finds it impossible to specify precise types for man similar to those we know in the animal kingdom.   (Jung, 1960, p. 201)

Here Jung assimilates Freud in a way that foreshadows Lacan and Kohut, in suggesting that it is the superego (the capacity for imagistic self-reference) that *creates* the id—in the sense of our species-specific dilemma of fantasy-mediated "drivenness" and so-called "instinctive" perversions, not found in creatures lacking an imagination.

Accordingly, titanic and archetypal dreams are two sides (energy and form) of the same capacity for self-reference, unfolding relatively independent of personal-mnemic material—although as surely reusing childhood schemata in its initial stages. Both dream forms reflect a line of potential development, expressions of which can be relatively primitive (schizophrenia, self-pathology, human destructiveness, and sexual perversion) or developmentally advanced (aesthetics, shamanistic and spiritual traditions). Of the psychoanalysts, only Masud R. Khan (1974, 1979) has suggested a developmental link between sexual and aggressive perversion and the spiritual traditions, as did William James between alcoholism and religious experience, in that both are centered around the search for moments of experiential epiphany. Whether primitive or advanced, they constitute a very different developmental line than the more extraverted development based on social action and relationships.

In short, Lincoln and the anthropologists he has influenced are formally correct about the special relation between culture pattern dreams and secondary revision. But Lincoln followed the more popular usage in which secondary revision refers not to endopsychic perception (let alone Silberer and Jung's development of this concept) but only to the social rationalization of dreaming—dreaming transformed in terms of the "ought" in order to maintain traditional culture. Overly impressed by the tragic decline of culture pattern dreaming with secularization, Lincoln missed the continued occurrence of powerful numinous-aesthetic dreams in both modern and tribal individuals who share some of the intuitive sensitivities and imagistic creativity of the classical shaman.

With this important clarification, synthesizing the dream theories of Freud and Jung within each other's vocabularies, we can turn to more recent anthropological research on the relation between culture pattern dreaming and social structure. Here again we encounter the debate between creative imagery and ontogenetic reductionism.

Anthropological Research on Culture Pattern Dreams

Roy D'Andrade (1961) investigated the features of societies in which supernatural help is sought from dreams—the core of the culture pattern phenomenon. He found a statistical complex of dreams and dream use: supernatural beings appear in dreams and give special powers and information; religious experts (shamans) use such dreams in the performance of their role (curing, divination, soul recovery); certain dreams are required before assumption of specific roles and identities; and such dreams may be induced by techniques of fasting, social isolation, and use of hallucinogenic plants. This complex was statistically associated with hunter-gatherer societies rather than permanently settled agricultural peoples.

This finding was confirmed by Erika Bourguignon's (1972) reanalysis of D'Andrade's data in terms of her typology of trance states and their relation to social structure. She had earlier shown that most nomadic hunter-gatherer societies, more or less characterized by a single socioeconomic class, sanction trance states for all members. Typically in these societies, alterations in consciousness involve what she refers to as *vision trance*. The experience is relatively private and only later told to others; its predominant modality is visual (induced visions); and the content often involves animistic/physiognomic properties of the natural order (earth, sky, water, fire, and animal spirits).

Bourguignon found that "supernatural dreams" were statistically associated with societies she had already classified as utilizing vision trance.

Bourguignon traced a progressive decline in the social sanction of trance with socioeconomic differentiation and complexity. Thus multiclass agricultural societies, especially those with polygamy and slavery, are less likely to sanction trance for all members, and the form taken by trance experience is typically very different—she terms it *possession trance*. In possession trance, the characteristic locus of intractable problems in these societies—other people—informs the altered state experience, making it more directly symbolic of dilemmas within the social order. Possession trance is typically acted out in front of others. Its predominant modality is auditory and verbal, making it intrinsically suited to convey ethical concerns. Perhaps correspondingly, it is more frenzied and driven than the relatively quietist vision trance, and it is often associated with amnesia on the part of the persons possessed. They must be told afterward what they said and did to relay communications from more or less recognizably human spirits, powers, and gods. Whereas a majority of vision trance societies had supernatural dreams, Bourguignon found such dreams in only 50 percent of possession trance societies—apparently as a holdover in special groups and classes. They were almost completely absent as a widely sanctioned phenomenon in differentiated urban societies, although Hellenistic mystery cults might be an exception.[2]

Why in cognitive-imagistic terms should archetypal-titanic culture pattern dreams (and vision trance) characterize hunter-gatherer societies but not agricultural and urban peoples? Hunter-gatherer peoples are necessarily attuned to the properties (and expressive physiognomies) of nature. Lévi-Strauss (1966) has shown how mythologies in these people are developed in terms of a classificatory grid that organizes natural forces, colors, animals, plants, social roles, and so on into complex systems of thought. Residues of such systems are found in the I-Ching and Tarot, for example (Hunt and Popham, 1987). We have already noted the importance of physical metaphors in the language and etymology of self-reference and the possibility that the animism of tribal peoples may thereby reflect their tendency to use the properties of physical nature as expressive mirrors for human experience and cognitive operations. The fact that young children are especially oriented to animism and physiognomy need not entail that the decline of such thought in later childhood is necessary for the development of abstract cognition. Rather, animism may have its own line of potential abstraction (as imagistic self-reflection) in other cultures, less centered on quantitative modes of thought than is our own.

Perhaps we are as "primitive" with respect to self-knowledge as we find tribal peoples in science and technology. By their very impersonality and totality, physiognomically animated forms of nature would provide more inclusive and deeper self-symbols than can propositional language—as seen in the ubiquity of light and geometric symbols for the fundamental nature of mind in various spiritual traditions (Hunt, 1985b). If the reflexivity of human intelligence is based, as Mead suggests, on our ability to "take the role of the other" and see ourselves as others do or might, then imaginatively taking the role of water, fire, wind, sky, earth, and animals would create a kind of self-awareness not otherwise available in daily social interaction, where such levels of experience would necessarily be unconscious.[3] Indeed, when urban society has given birth to mysticism, with its inward psychological preoccupation, it has been via the "nature mysticism" of the romantic poets and the more abstract imageries of colors, elements, and geometric shapes involved in alchemy (Jung, 1944) and the Eastern meditative traditions (Govinda, 1960). More generally, complex society and urban living will mitigate against the natural development of a self-referential imagistic faculty as surely as they require verbal and technological intelligence. We find here a sociocultural basis for the mnemic and linguistic emphasis of orthodox dream theories and for the tendency of very young children and especially imaginative-intuitive adults to dream in a fashion more reminiscent of tribal peoples.

Of course there is a counterview based on interpersonal dynamics and its ontogenetic reductionism. Despite its obvious truth within a certain range of convenience, however, such a view must fail as a cognitive account of archetypal-titanic dreams—other than by invoking that "regression" which has always fit ill with explanations of imagination and artistic creation, even if it is "in service of the ego." D'Andrade found that supernatural dreams in a society also correlated with the distance men had to move away from the nuclear family group in marriage. Hunter-gatherer societies typically practice exogamy—the sons leaving to join other nomadic groups. D'Andrade, in the tradition of Lincoln and Kracke, suggests that the loneliness thereby imposed, combined with the necessity for individual assertiveness and autonomy among hunter-gatherers, leads the individual to seek internal help from powerful parent symbols—the guardian spirits and power allies of the culture pattern dream. The objection that shamanistic abilities and dreams occur first in early childhood (not to mention the cognitive and emotional precocity of the future shaman in many tribes) cannot be conclusive, since there is also some indication that many future shamans have troubled childhoods and may suffer the early loss of parents. Some of these individuals can appear disturbed and unbalanced from an early age (Eliade, 1964; Ducey, 1979).

Yet archetypal-titanic dreams have been regarded in all societies as directly self-curative; thus they seem to fit more clearly into the developmental line of self-psychology (re Jung, Winnicott, and Kohut) than into the developmental line of interpersonal extraversion. Jung (1961) insisted on the necessity of some degree of aloneness and social withdrawal for the path of individuation through dream and vision, and he stressed the importance of a capacity to tolerate such isolation. Certainly we saw in the 1960s the same association between leaving home and family and cultivating altered states of consciousness and Eastern meditation—along with the often cynical substitution of "family" by various cults.[4] However, while there is no reason to deny the role played by interpersonal dynamics, powerful experience in deep meditation, psychedelic drugs, and archetypal dreams also *impose* some degree of social isolation, at least initially while the person tries to consolidate and integrate the significance of these states. Of course, development along a line of imagistic self-reference must involve activation and reorganization of personal memories—predominantly, according to the literature on meditation and psychedelic drugs, in its earliest preformal stages. In these states parental imagoes come to function not only as "signifieds" but also as "signifiers" subject to an increasing degree of abstraction for potential self-reference.

The actual and theoretical ambiguity of archetypal/culture pattern dreams follow from their being necessarily both personal-mnemic and endopsychic metaphors, in varying degrees of balance. We have already seen how different dreams and dreamers can specialize in one or the other direction. Yet again, this suggests that attempts at monolithic explanations of either dream form in terms of the other are indeed false reductionisms.

PART III

The Cognitive Bases of Dream Formation in the Continuous Interaction of Image and Narrative

What, then, is a story? . . . people are presented . . . in situations that change. . . . In turn, these changes reveal hidden aspects of the situation and the people involved, and engender a new predicament which calls for thought, action, or both. The response to the new situation leads the story towards its conclusion. . . . A narrative "conclusion" is not something that can be deduced or predicted. A story that included no surprises or coincidences or encounters or recognition scenes would not hold our attention.
—Paul Ricoeur, *Time and Narrative*

What makes language so valuable for thinking . . . cannot be thinking in words. It must be the help that words lend to thinking while it operates in a more appropriate medium, such as visual imagery. . . .

Man can confidently rely on the senses to supply him with the perceptual equivalents of all theoretical notions because these notions derive from sensory experience in the first place. . . . The notion of the depth of thought is derived from physical depth; what is more, depth is not merely a convenient metaphor to describe the mental phenomenon but the only possible way of even conceiving of that notion.
—Rudolf Arnheim, *Visual Thinking*

> Let my inspiration flow
>   in token rhyme,
> Suggesting rhythm
>   that will not forsake me,
> Till my tale is told and done.
>
> While the fire light's aglow,
> Strange shadows from the flames will grow,
> Till things we've never seen
>   will seem familiar.
>   —"Terrapin Station"
>   Grateful Dead
>   words by Robert Hunter © 1977 Ice Nine Publishing
>   Company, Inc.

CHAPTER 11

Narrative Structures: Story Grammar versus Imagistics

Relations Between Image and Narrative

A NY cognitive psychology of dreaming must encounter and reconcile two statements: "the dream is a story" and "the dream is imagery." Neither statement is as obvious as it initially appears, because there is no agreement in contemporary cognitive psychology on the ultimate relation between visual-spatial imagery and language. Much evidence and theory supports both the view that a visual-spatial imagistic intelligence rests directly on and creatively reorganizes the processes of perception and the view that mental imagery is a surface paraphrase of abstract propositional knowledge, whose deep structure is accordingly far closer to verbal syntax than visual imagery. Proponents of the latter view cite copious experimental demonstrations showing that we can image only what we already know, while proponents of the former cite important scientific discoveries that seem to have been determined by novel visual imagery (often at sleep onset and sometimes in dreams). In dream theory, on the one hand, Freud and Foulkes each in his own way holds that the imagistic surface of the dream is generated by a "deeper" propositional structure. Foulkes likens dream imagery to the creative and surprisingly specific imagery we form while reading a novel, which is clearly derivative from our propositional comprehension of what is often termed the *story grammar*. On the other hand, Jung and Hillman tend to regard the narrative structure of the dream as derivative from "epiphanous" imagery formations—which surely seems to be the case in parts of archetypal and titanic dreams as well as some lucid dreams and nightmares.

If in fact we have correctly located different types of dreams and if all dreams necessarily mix and match the same dimensions of formation that, separated and exaggerated, produce these types, it follows that narrative structure and visual-spatial imagery will interact variously in dream formation— each will be capable of leading and entraining the other. The dream is an imagistic experience occurring in a creature who structures its ongoing experience in the form of "stories" to be told and understood. The imagery of the dream fills a vacuum left by a sleep-induced loss of environment, coupled with the maintenance or recovery of cortical activation (West, 1962; Antrobus, 1986). Because imagery at least shares some analogue aspect of perception (whether fundamental or secondary), it can function like perception in generating the analogue environment of the dream, but because imagery also functions within memory and imagination it can operate according to the various models of these processes as well. The interaction of imagery and narrative form constitutes the story of the dream, and there is ample evidence that dream stories can be primarily determined by either dimension. First, however, we need to look at recent evidence of the power of narrative structure over imagery, at least in normative dreaming.

Foulkes and his colleagues have made some major experimental contributions in this regard. Molinari and Foulkes (1969) and later Foulkes and Pope (1973) distinguished between two segments of REM reports—*primary visual experience*, based on perceived events generally impinging on the dreamer, and what Foulkes then termed *secondary cognitive elaboration*, covering all discursive thought, reflection, and verbalization. These categories corresponded very roughly to phasic (intense eye movement bursts) and tonic (relative quiescent) subperiods of the REM state. Foulkes and Pope found a somewhat weaker correspondence (i.e., if *specifically* asked, subjects reported cognitive elaboration during phasic periods as well). Subsequent replications (Pivak, 1978) found still more uncertain effects, leading to the current, probably overdrawn, skepticism about psychophysiological relationships.

Two points should be noted immediately. (1) Although Foulkes's colleague Molinari (1984) sees the cognitive, reflective activity of dreaming as reactive to its primary visual content, the original article stated that it was unclear whether "primary visual experience" spontaneously initiated cognitive reflection, or whether it was the endpoint or resolution of previous conceptual activity. Subsequently Foulkes decided for the latter, since "secondary cognitive elaboration" is closer to the propositional deep structure or grammar of dream formation in Foulkes's later model. (2) Primary visual experience obviously includes what I call intrusive visual bizarreness (the primary positive contribution to novelty in normative dreaming), but Foulkes's concept is much more general—too much so to address the question whether "dream grammar" is led by or leads dream bizarreness. It includes both normative, non-novel dream perceptions—which presumably often fill out an underlying story grammar or script apparent from the early phases of many dreams—and various levels of bizarreness, which at their extreme include powerful states that seem to intrude into the dream story and change its subsequent direction and nature. Foulkes now agrees with Hobson and McCarley and Antrobus that dream bizarreness, albeit loosely correlated with phasic REM activity, is a disruption and discontinuity in the core of the dreaming process. Yet this flies in the face of correlations between dream bizarreness and measures of waking creativity.[1]

Despite serious doubts about the limits of such a monolithic approach to all dream formation, there seems to be no question that imagistic aspects of normative, relatively mundane dreaming are constrained and directed by the properties of narrative syntax. Although many investigators earlier posited a right hemisphere (imagistic) predominance in dreaming, there is now evidence of a left hemisphere (linguistic) activation that may well control the ongoing development of normative dreaming. Foulkes has now reported several cases in which subjects with right hemisphere disorders of visualization report complex and often vivid dreams with little or no imagistic accompaniment. Foulkes likens these cases to the ostensibly imageless "Würzburg" dreams of the congenitally blind, in which elaborate narrative scenarios, with highly specific content, turn out on direct questioning to be abstractly "known" rather than "imagined" or "perceived" in any meaningful sense of those terms.

In an influential study with Marcella Schmidt, Foulkes demonstrated that something like a story grammar can control the unfolding of normative dreams: the longer the dream, the more apparently constrained and directed its development (Foulkes and Schmidt, 1983). They investigated changes within laboratory dreams between "temporal units" (defined as activities, characters, and settings occurring in the same time frame rather than in succession). Foulkes (1985) concluded that only rarely did both character *and* setting change in the transition from one temporal unit to another—suggesting preservation of enough continuity to allow an integrated story structure. More specifically, Foulkes and Schmidt found that the longest dream reports (in contrast to sleep onset reports, NREM mentation, typical and shortest REM reports) showed the least unit-to-unit change in dream characters. Despite earlier findings that longer dreams are more vivid and bizarre, Foulkes discovered that as the dream progresses, novel characters are less and less likely to be introduced. Foulkes interprets this as evidence of a top-down control of dream imagery by narrative structure, constraining the nature and influence of novel elements. Although this fits badly with non-normative but psychologically and culturally significant patterns of lucid and archetypal-titanic dreams, Foulkes's findings seemed to demonstrate that the storylines of dreams can constrain their novel imagery far more than clinical approaches to dreaming originally suggested.

The Propositional Structure of Dreaming

Since most dreams are narratives and since narrative structure can have a strong effect on ongoing dream imagery, we need to look more closely at recent attempts to access the structure of stories and to incorporate story gram-mar methodology into dream psychology. Story grammars (Mayer, 1983) are increasingly controversial attempts to locate the deep structure of any story—its syntax. Given the bare elements of a potential story, we automatically begin to schematize them in terms of setting, actors, plot (goals and subgoals), and resolution, treating these as quite specific "slots" that will automatically be filled to render the elements intelligible.

Donald Kuiken and Tore Nielsen (1983) at the University of Edmonton, Alberta, have approached this task most specifically. They use an elaborate classification scheme to distinguish criteria for the existence and complexity of story elements in dreams. Rules are provided for identifying a coherent action sequence and a coherent single scene as the core constituents of story narra-tives. In addition, they develop multiple dimensions for narrative perspective, setting, object character attributes, varieties of consequences, and so on—most of these with an additional rating in terms of normative expectability versus novelty and bizarreness. Using aspects of this system, Kuiken, Nielsen, and their colleagues (1983) found that REM narratives are more storylike than NREM "thinking"—the former are significantly more likely to contain the action of a character for which both initiating events and consequences are provided. They also discovered that both extraordinary dreams and myths, in contrast to ordinary dreams, include major character transformations.

At the other extreme are John Antrobus' attempts to simplify the notion of dream story by measuring only the total number of (nonredundant) words in the dream report and the number of separate "topic units" (a measure bor-rowed from Klinger's research on daydreams). Antrobus (1986) argues that higher ratios of total content recalled (TCR) to topic units (TU) reflect the single-theme, storylike quality attributed to dreams. By itself, TCR distinguished better between REM and NREM reports than did the more specific measures of total visual word count and bizarreness (assessed in terms of discontinuities), leading Antrobus to suggest that there might be no substantial difference between REM and NREM mentation other than the greater cortical activation that allows more retrieval from REM awakenings (1983, 1986). He proposes a neurocognitive model for dream formation based on TCR as an index of cortical activation and TU as a measure of raised perceptual thresholds. The more variable the environmental stimulation, the more diverse trains of thought will be initiated and the less likely will be any sustained storylike elaboration of a single theme. In his 1986 study, Antrobus and colleagues have shown experimentally that TCR/TU ratios *and* bizarreness scores are comparable between REM laboratory reports and a physically similar condition of waking rest with absence of stimulation (which actually verges on traditional sensory deprivation). These two conditions, however, were significantly different from the more thought like experiences of normal resting wakefulness and NREM stage 2 sleep. Insufficient cortical activation combined with lower perceptual thresholds would prohibit the latter two conditions from developing into sustained stories.

Apart from ignoring the likelihood that bizarreness and narrative structure reflect different cognitive processes (see below), Antrobus's findings do not rule out more qualitative differences between REM and NREM experience or between dreaming and relatively mundane varieties of daydreaming. Foulkes and Schmidt (1983) found significantly more character density in REM dreams than in NREM mentation when report length was controlled, and they found significantly more unspecified settings in NREM. This suggests that Antrobus's measures are too global to identify the more specific storylike structures of vivid dreaming. Similarly controlling for report length, Porte and Hobson (1986) found significantly more bizarreness in REM than in NREM dreams. Indeed, Antrobus ignores the likely fact that descriptions of novelty and bizarreness in dreams require more words than mundane true-to-daily-life content, making word length a consequence of bizarreness rather than the other way around. Given Foulkes's findings of significant visual bizarreness in sleep onset dreams (see chapter 12), which also involve less self-representation than do REM dreams and NREM mentation, we can infer that perhaps what constitutes the storylike structure of REM dreams is their fusion of the narrative cognitive structure of NREM mentation with the visual-spatial bizareness of hypnagogic sleep onset—a notion that begins to reflect Ricoeur's (1984–85) insistence that genuine stories are marked as much by surprise and novelty as by continuity.

Foulkes himself, in his earlier *A Grammar of Dreams* (1978), offers an intricate dream grammar midway between Antrobus's globality and Kuiken's attempt to specify story essentials. He largely assumes the basic elements of story grammars and translates all dream events into a prototypical language that ultimately seeks to operationalize Freud's method of free association. Foulkes searches for core propositions (characters and their actions) that will be the deep structure of the dream narrative. Thus all characters are reduced to self, parents, siblings, spouse, children, or peers (in terms of age, sex, and relation to the dreamer) and all verbs become interactive (moving toward, moving from, moving against, creating-nurturing) or associative (role equivalence and means/medium). The dream narrative can thereby be rendered in an abstract notational shorthand by means of elaborately detailed simplifying rules and *transform equivalents*. The manifest dream report and its free associations, treated as a unit, become progressively more singular and elemental interactions—mechanizing Freud's condensation and displacement in terms of the statistics of path analysis.

Its almost overwhelming complexity aside, the system's strength is also its weakness. In operationalizing the methods of classical psychoanalysis, the system also suffers from psychoanalytic reductionism. For instance, its inability to allow core propositions in which a self figure interacts with another self figure leaves the system unable to address the dynamics of self-awareness and development fundamental to Jung and Kohut. Thus my first double dream would be scored as a father–son (self) interaction, the second as a peer–self interaction—catching one aspect of these dreams but missing another, less studied one. Similarly, relabeling most characters as father, mother, sibling, and so on forces a classical oedipal structure on systematic dream analysis just as lifespan developmental psychologists are insisting that later developmental eras and their crises must be conceptualized in their own terms and not merely reduced to their roots in childhood. Foulkes has located and crystalized the repetitive elements of relationships, but as with the psychoanalysis he has more recently rejected, his method assumes that the dream is an aggregate of elements awaiting only its natural dissolution. Certainly we could treat a poem by Foulkes's method, but it is not clear whether that would contribute to its understanding. If we could thus miss the point of a poem, could we also miss the point of some dreams?

The Necessity of Semantics and Imagistics in Narrative Structure

Recent critiques of story grammar structuralisms have even more currency when applied to the notion that the essence of dreaming must be its narrative directedness, especially with the unexpected turns introduced into that directedness by visual-spatial intrusions and metaphors. We have already taken note of Paul Ricoeur's comment that surprise and the unexpected are essential to genuine stories. Wilensky (1983) and Garnham (1983) have argued, parallel to Ricoeur, that the experimental study of story grammars has confused *stories*, which necessarily convey semantic points, with *action sequences*, which are merely open to narration. Both psychologists point out that there is no true syntax for stories (independent of their content and meaning) in the way that there is for sentences. Would-be grammars of stories (and dreams) apply equally well to Kafka and to manuals of automotive repair. That might be fine, given arguments by Ricoeur (1984–85) and Langer (1972) that "the story" is fundamental to any definition of the human symbolic capacity, except that it ignores a crucial distinction. When someone tells us a story about recent or past events in his/her life, including episodes of automobile repair, we listen (and this seems criterial) for the point. We are as quick to detect it as to detect its absence or ambiguity.

Consider Wilensky's example of a narrative that meets all available criteria of story grammars but is better regarded as action sequence.

> John was hungry. He went to a restaurant and ordered a hamburger. When the check came, he paid it and left. (Wilensky, 1983, p. 583)

Many dreams are like this. They seem to lack any point and we may wonder not only why we are told them, but why they occurred in the first place. Perhaps rendering such accounts in terms of more fundamental propositions would provide these points. Yet by the criteria of historical and literary usage, other dreams are truly stories. They have some element of surprise or novelty that is then resolved in such a way, on Ricoeur's analysis, that it links beginning, middle, and end as a single unit. Many normative dreams are not stories in this sense, lacking the very criteria of novelty and originality that Foulkes himself makes central for dream production.

In his insistence that dreams have syntax but no semantics, Foulkes (1985) doubly misses the symbolic potential in dreaming. He suggests that dreaming cannot have symbolic intention because, unlike the sentences we speak, we cannot ask, "Did I dream that right?" in the same way we can ask ourselves, "Did I say that right?" (i.e., "was it what I intended?"). But sentences, with their specific syntax and grammar that is either correct or incorrect, are not a good model for dreaming. It is not just that a story worth telling includes the unexpected, as do the more interesting dreams; ordinary language use is also the wrong model because it misses the way dreaming resembles a phase of creative imagination. The artist is often so surprised and intrigued by his or her obviously symbolic and deeply communicative creation that the original intention is thereby changed. The artist can ask, "Is this effective, exciting, powerful?" but that may have little or nothing to do with "Does this fulfill my original intention?" Aesthetic intention is of course important, but perhaps, as with the dream, it is often intuited by the artist or writer after the creation, not before (Milner, 1957).

If semantic points cannot be eliminated in any approach to the structure of dreams, we must consider anew what makes the dream a genuine story—what gives it surprise, point, interest, and so impels us to tell it. The answer would seem to include much of what has traditionally been termed bizarreness, because it is just these image-based transformations of experience that introduce the unexpected into the dream narrative and push the dreamer toward some response (whether during the ongoing dream or upon awakening). Dream bizarreness is predominantly visual; it correlates with various measures of imaginative creativity in wakefulness; and it predominates in both the very first dreams of childhood (before the narrative element is present) and in the more personally significant dreams of adulthood. In addition, the early development of dreams in childhood (and good dream recall among adults) is correlated with visual-spatial, not verbal, abilities.

Again I turn to one of my own dreams to show that unexpected visual-spatial transformations do not so much disrupt narrative continuity as provide the dramatic sense that fulfills and completes it:

> I am traveling with my wife and children, looking for a parking place in order to visit the Tibetan National Museum. The only parking areas I can find are in highway rest areas and I realize that unless I hurry the museum will close. Accordingly, I now drive directly to the museum (a huge building with multiple wings and four or five floors). Leaving my car and family in front, I run inside. I enter a massive foyer and find to my intense disappointment that the museum has just closed.
>
> Looking about, I notice an open door to a small room off to one side. Entering, I find myself in the private apartment of an older, very thin women, who is apparently the museum caretaker. The room is primitive and archaic. The women is in one corner steadily stirring a very large pot of boiling water. As I approach more closely I see in the pot a carved wooden manikin about two feet tall. As the woman stirs, ignoring me, the room is filled with an eerie, high-pitched wailing sound. I realize with growing horror that the sound emanates from the wooden manikin, which is becoming progressively more lifelike as she stirs—its scream of pain becomes more and more shrill and frenzied and then begins to turn into an uncanny and strangely beautiful song. I realize that the price of the vivification of the manikin is the terrible agony that produces this song, and I awaken in a cold sweat.

It is hard to see how this final eerie scene, which involves a discontinuous shift in both character and setting, is implicit in or generated by the narrative structure of the first part of the dream. The first part sets up an implicit contrast between family and a more personal Tibetan interest. Certainly there is a possible contrast between *museum* (as full of "dead" things from the past) and *coming alive*, but that is only one of the many possible associations. In fact the actual image of the woman and manikin departs from the first part of the dream and certainly could not have been predicted from it or from my direct associations to it alone. Yet the scene dramatically fulfills the dream and confirms its semantic significance, casting back on and reorganizing the dream's initial events. The point of the dream becomes a contrast between death and coming alive, with the further implication that such a coming alive will be mediated by the feminine and, of course, by immense pain. The dream occurred at roughly the time of the double dreams and so constitutes a powerful metaphor for a major dilemma and an acute anticipation of its resolution.

Ostensible narrative discontinuity or bizarreness thus actually served to weld this dream together as a single dramatic whole. A visual-spatial pattern of immense emotional impact created both the element of the unexpected and its resolution with the previous narrative, which otherwise would have lacked just the point that Wilensky and Ricoeur make criteria for story. Without it the dream would have been more action sequence than story, and any point could then only have been created by transforming it into something else after awakening.

The central problem for the cognitive science perspective of Foulkes and Antrobus, and in a slightly different fashion Hobson and McCarley, can be stated in three closely related questions. Can dreaming depart from recent and past memories in ways that go beyond processes of memory elaboration and assimilation? Yes. Can visual-spatial imagery exceed what is known? Yes. And, to the extent that such departures from previous semantic knowledge rest on bizarre imagery, is that merely a randomized process of disruption, producing accidental metaphors, or it is the very fabric of dream semantics? I argue for the latter. Current cognitive science offers the view, appealing to many in an era in which intelligence is "artificial," that to the extent that creative thought requires imagistic processes these are more or less randomized patterns. The contribution of imagery would come mainly from the way it provokes taming and reorganization by propositional knowledge. Such randomization models of creativity ignore repeated demonstrations, involving both scientific discovery and dream psychology, that ostensibly bizarre imagery often directly conveys insights that go qualitatively beyond any previous formulation. This is a function of imagery basic to the accounts of Arnheim, Kaufman, Shepard, Sheehan, and most others who have studied it on its own terms.

If we can only image what we already know, and if imagery and language are separate modules with the latter generating the former as its surface array, it is deeply puzzling how the visual module could present scientific information that the linguistic system does not know and may not come to recognize for some time. Certainly in normative dreaming a narrative deep structure often seems to determine an imagistic surface. But in the more subjectively striking and impressive experiences associated with archetypal-titanic dreams, it is a powerful visual-spatial image—creatively fusing multiple dimensions of previous experience—that constrains the subsequent dream grammar and/or redefines the point of the grammar that precedes its intrusion. We arrive then at a picture of two systems, both self-referential and creatively recombinatory expressions of the human symbolic capacity, interacting in different measures to produce both normative dreaming and its imagistically predominant variations.[2]

Left Hemisphere, Right Hemisphere, and Dreaming

The model of a continuous interaction between potentially independent narrative and imagery processes must be considered against recent research on the role of cerebral hemispheres in dreaming. Whereas earlier research had suggested a right hemisphere (imagistic?) dominance in the REM state, more recent research has offered more support to Foulkes and Antrobus, "dream rationalists," in suggesting a possible left hemisphere (linguistic, propositional) control of dreaming.

The early research on hemisphericity was drawn by the now questionable assumption that since imagery processes should be a right hemisphere function, so should dreaming. A small number of reports that subjects with right hemisphere brain damage lost their ability to dream, combined with research showing a small but consistent shift to the right in hemisphere activation ratios during REM sleep, seemed to confirm this picture (Bakan, 1977). Cohen (1979) concluded that the REM state was right hemisphere predominant, with a progressive shift over the night toward left activation, so that the longest and last REM state of the night was most like the normal asymmetry of wakefulness, favoring the left or dominant hemisphere. However, these findings left a residual puzzle: why would the longest, most vivid and bizarre dream of the night occur with the highest left hemisphere activation?

More recent work has in fact introduced a considerably more complex picture. First, studies by Gaillard and Laurian (1984), Pivak and colleagues (1982), and Moffitt and colleagues (1982, Moffitt and Hoffman, 1987) found EEG hemisphere ratios to be highly variable across individuals—individual differences seemed to account for most of the experimental variance in these studies. It is true that Lavie and Tzischinsky (1985) and Bertini and Violani (1984) have shown a striking superiority in spatial tasks (right hemisphere) immediately following REM awakenings, as opposed to a superiority in verbal and mathematical tasks following NREM awakenings. Nonetheless, there seems to be no direct relationship between performance in cognitive and perceptual tasks indexed to right or left hemisphere performance and any measure of REM dream content, such as emotion, bizarreness, visual elements, thoughtlike reports (Lavie and Tzischinsky, 1985). Indeed, right hemisphere predominance (whether measured by performance or EEG amplitude) is, if anything, associated with low levels of dream recall.

Ehrlichman, Antrobus, and Wiener (1985) not only failed to find any overall difference between REM and NREM in terms of EEG asymmetry, but awakenings following momentary shifts in left versus right activation showed higher word counts for both speech and visual categories accompanying left hemisphere activation. In an earlier study on EEG changes in hemisphere asymmetry during wakefulness associated with diverse cognitive tasks, Ehrlichman and Wiener (1980) found that verbal and arithmetic tasks yielded the greatest left hemisphere asymmetries, positive affect and meditation generating the greater right hemisphere activation. Significantly, tasks requiring visual and visual-kinesthetic imagery were relatively bilateral—one of the first suggestions of a left hemisphere involvement in visual imagery. Nonetheless, it should also be noted that where imagery is self-referential (as in meditative states) and high in affect—both characteristic of some dreams—then these findings would imply a right hemisphere predominance in dreaming.

Our dream typology would certainly imply two kinds of imagery—relatively mundane imagery that fulfills propositional schemata and a more spontaneous and intrinsically novel imagery. Indeed there is some suggestion of right hemisphere predominance in bizarre dream imagery and closely related forms of altered state experience during wakefulness: Moffitt and colleagues (1982,1987) found right hemisphere activation immediately before awakening to be correlated with ratings of bizarreness. Similarly Bakan (1977) and Geschwind (1981), echoing Penfield's earlier findings, have called attention to evidence of right hemisphere involvement in dreamlike hallucinatory syndromes and in the aura and unreality states of epilepsy. Whereas left hemisphere damage fatally disrupts linguistic and mathematical abilities, it is right hemisphere damage that disrupts activity in the visual arts. Several major artists suffering left hemisphere strokes have been able to continue their painting with little or no impairment (Gardner, 1975).

Armitage, Hoffmann, and Moffitt (1988) may provide the key to this complex material. They suggest that in contrast to both NREM sleep and wakefulness, REM sleep is characterized not so much by right hemisphere predominance but by an unusual symmetry or bilateral balance in hemisphere activation. In potentially related findings Lavie and Tzischinsky (1985) found that relative right/left EEG balance during waking tasks was associated with eye movement density in REM sleep; Bertini and Violani (1984) found that subjects with smaller differences between right- and left-hand performance on a tactile recognition test performed immediately upon awakening from REM had greater recall. They later suggested that while the right hemisphere may play a greater role during dreaming, its more distinctive productions may be lost to waking memory. Indeed Moffitt and colleagues (1982) found that the smaller the shift in overall EEG patterning, including hemisphere measures, between REM state and full wakefulness, the better the dream recall.

If left and right hemisphere are characteristically balanced during the REM state, then given the preponderance of left hemisphere functioning during wakefulness (perhaps especially with Western-style education) we would expect left hemisphere processes to continue to dominate during normative dreaming. In other words, bilateral balance will continue to favor left hemisphere control, consistent with the research of Foulkes and Antrobus. At the same time we would also expect more evidence of specifically right hemisphere functions in dreams than during ordinary wakefulness, for example, intrinsically bizarre visual-spatial imageries, powerful affect, and kinesthetic self-awareness. In a relatively balanced situation the normally more powerful force may still predominate, but at the same time what is typically subordinated will make itself felt beyond its usual level.[3]

A related picture now seems to be emerging from the research literature on loss of dreaming (and imagery) with brain damage. Recent evidence that such loss is associated with neurological damage to the left hemisphere also yields more readily to a balance model. Consider Foulkes's (1978, 1985) suggestion that right hemisphere damage (or dysfunction) affects only the surface array of visual imagery, while it is left hemisphere damage to the capacity for propositional thought and inner speech that would eliminate the dreaming capacity itself. Foulkes cites anecdotal reports of loss of dreaming with aphasia and its reappearance on recovery; Epstein and Simmons (1983) have reported more such cases. There are two small studies of dreaming in subjects who underwent commissurotomy, the operation to control severe epilepsy in which the corpus callosum connecting the hemispheres is cut, leaving them as two separate systems with only the left hemisphere able to communicate verbally. Since some degree of dream reporting continued in both samples, any such dreaming must have been done by the left hemisphere alone (Greenwood, Wilson, and Gazzaniga, 1977; Hoppe, 1977). While these patients described visual content, their dreams were mundane and lacking in vividness. Again we find that certain forms and functions of imagery can be predominantly controlled by the left hemisphere and/or propositional processes.

Research by Darlene Schanfald and her colleagues (Schanfald, Pearlman, and Greenberg, 1987), however, calls into question any simple hypothesis of the dream as an exclusive left or right hemisphere process. Using stroke victims with either right or left hemisphere damage who reported a subsequent loss of all dream recall, she demonstrates that with prolonged support and encouragement (such as using drawings to bypass language problems) these patients not only could report dreams but reported dreams that seemed, as far as could be determined, normally patterned. Thus apparent loss of dreaming with aphasia is more a matter of recall than generation. Only when Schanfald attempted the same methods with patients in whom both hemispheres were damaged was no dream recall obtained (Schanfald, Pearlman, and Greenberg, 1985). The capacity to dream, as a bilateral function of the cortex, may be fully and unalterably eliminated only with corresponding bilateral damage.

This brings us to the most recent neurophysiological research on imagery and dreaming by Martha Farah and her colleagues (Farah, 1984; Greenberg and Farah, 1986; Farah, 1987). Her extensive reviews of the clinical literature showed that the loss of ability to generate visual imagery voluntarily was almost invariably associated with damage to a region in the posterior left hemisphere. This inability to generate imagery (both in everyday life and on tasks requesting subjects to image previously presented material) was often accompanied by reported loss of dreaming. Confirmation of a left hemisphere center for image generation also came in studies of split-brain patients and in experiments involving tachistoscopic presentations to left versus right visual fields in normal subjects. On the basis of these studies, Farah went so far as to state that the right hemisphere cannot generate imagery! Nonetheless this may sidestep the question whether the right hemisphere can image—since the imagery in question in Farah's research was generally externally elicited.

Following the logic of Schanfald's research, it is not clear that we are necessarily dealing here with the loss of dreaming or imagery in itself. Dream recall, even in the setting of immediate laboratory awakening, is a tenuous and variable process, involving the attempt to regenerate (reimage) a past experience. It makes sense that imagery generated voluntarily and deliberately, in response to task demands, would be located in the left (more volitional and controlled) hemisphere. The left posterior region located by Farah should perhaps be renamed the "the Pylyshyn center," since it may indeed be the place where we image what we already know. Damage to this area could affect both dream recall (to the extent that it requires voluntary effort) and that aspect of dream formation, central to Foulkes, for which imagery *is* the surface array of a propositional deep structure.

Accordingly, Farah's research may have no real bearing on the capacity for the forms of imagery associated with intrinsic dream bizarreness and waking altered states of consciousness. As much clinical evidence implies, these may still rest on right hemisphere functioning—beyond easy reach of voluntary experimental tasks. Some hint of such a possibility comes from Farah's location of a different imagery deficit, associated with failure to *recognize* previously presented materials and also involving either a total or partial loss of dreaming. This imagery deficit involves a more fundamental loss of memory—the failure to generate spontaneous or automatic imagery associated with recognition. This more severe decrement in imagery capacity was associated with predominantly bilateral or right (i.e., nondominant) hemisphere damage; it almost never involved the left (dominant) hemisphere alone. Indeed, of the seventeen cases of imagery loss cited by Farah (1984) in which dream deficit was also reported, the most frequent category was bilateral damage/recognition deficit.

Loss of dreaming associated with left hemisphere damage also entails a deficit in the ability to generate imagery voluntarily, while bilateral and/or right hemisphere damage associated with loss of dreaming entails a more total failure in the capacity for recognition. Again we find two aspects of imagery— a predominantly voluntary left hemisphere ability and a more totalistic nonvoluntary function that is either bilateral or located in the right hemisphere. Dreaming thus emerges as an interaction between the capacity to translate propositional, inner speech processes into imagery and a more spontaneous and intuitive imagery, likely to be bizarre and inherently novel, which is more variable in its appearance and may at times direct or redirect the propositional capacity of the left hemisphere. Such a model is most consistent with the actual variations of dreaming, and it still remains plausible in light of research on hemisphericity, imagery, and brain damage.

The bottom line here is that neurophysiological findings are congruent with phenomenological and cognitive-experimental evidence of two distinct cognitive processes in dreaming: a sequentially directed narrative component and a simultaneous visual-spatial component, each of which interacts with and may "entrain" the other. As with their expressions in waking intelligence, narrative sequence and visual-spatial metaphor may achieve very different effects in dreaming, although the norm, outside of brain damage and extreme specialization, must be their continuous interaction.

Propositional-linguistic thinking is the symbolic intelligence of volitional direction and control. Vowles (1970) goes so far as to suggest that the deep structure of syntax rests on the fixed sequences of limb movement in running creatures. Certainly language is articulatory and motoric. For Arnheim language is a pragmatic and communicative medium that selects sequences across the multiple possibilities of simultaneous imagistic arrays in order to direct and organize a particular social impact. Kenneth Burke (1966) somewhat similarly treats language as "symbolic action." It moves always in a "direction of definiteness," in that the effect of words on each other is a "mutual narrowing down" of potential meanings by deliberate selective order. Burke even suggests that the selection and narrowing of language is ultimately based on negation and motor inhibition. Rene Spitz (1965) calls attention to the primacy of the *no* in the earliest childhood development of consensual language use.

Part of the function of language is then the inhibition of the multiple and potential felt meanings that are naturally superimposed within imagery processes in favor of more singular and unambiguous meaning. The "swift and sudden animation of a thing by the verb that follows it is the specifically linguistic effect on the image" (Arnheim, 1969, p. 250). In other words, the pragmatic use of language (in contrast to its use in, say, poetry) takes only one direction of potential significance out of the polysemy inherent to all presentational processes. Indeed, the deeper distinction may be not so much between language and imagery as between representational and presentational symbolism. The former is based on the arbitrary relation between signifier and referent, allowing the "handling" of meaning in terms of personal and social intention—ultimately a *movement* that intends a singular unambiguous meaning. Its twin, whether evil or saving grace depending on the context, is polysemy and expressive physiognomy, where meaning remains within the multiple properties of the sensory medium.

If representation is ultimately based on motor inhibition and negation, presentational imagery is based on the *yes*—perhaps the cognitive significance of Freud's statement that the unconscious knows no negation. Presentational symbolism has its full effect in the superimposition of expressive sensory patterns. Yet this multiplicity is not arbitrary or infinite. If, with Foulkes, this makes dream interpretation completely relative and subjective, then so also for all aesthetics—which seems a more doubtful point.

Presentational processes have their root in the fascination of infants with the endless play of mirroring and mimicry—which rests ultimately on a nascent capacity to translate back and forth between the structure of things seen (the mother's face) and the pattern of things felt and done (the infant's tactile-kinesthetic sensitivity). For Arnheim, Vygotsky, and Neisser, thought (as opposed to communicative speech) is ultimately the imagistic turning around on and reuse of the patterns of the senses. Vygotsky and Geschwind share the suggestion that the cross-modal translation between the very different patterns and rhythms of vision and kinesthesis renders this recombinatory capacity possible in the first place. We will see in the next chapter that the imagery of dream bizarreness and waking altered states of consciousness reveals these same cross-modal and recombinatory operations. Certainly descriptions of artistic and scientific creation stress the importance of immediately conveyed felt meaning emerging from novel imagery. The potential right hemisphere basis of such creativity is suggested by the facts that it is involuntary, facilitated by an attitude of receptivity, and conveyed in diffuse, impalpable felt meanings.

Localization, however, is less important to us here than function and interaction. It seems that linguistic representation (and the surface array of imagery that it often controls) is a way of holding, directing, and limiting polysemic imagery to a specifically selective significance. Correspondingly, highly condensed and polysemic imagery will always be ready to emerge spontaneously from within these sequences—sometimes disrupting and sometimes reorganizing them in a new light.

The symbolic capacity requires both processes. The linguistic sequence must always lead to a sense of understanding. Simultaneous visual-spatial imagery calls for later sequential articulation and unpacking of its implications—which then either extend or transform the intentional symbolic communication. If these are two sides of symbolic functioning, they are also two sides of dreaming—the predominance of one or the other is associated with each end of our diamond of dream types.

Are Dreams Really Stories?

We must return to Paul Ricoeur's concept of story in order to ask when and how dreaming becomes a genuine story and to see the various ways that it may more typically fall short.

Just as history with its various points and lessons is more than chronicle, genuine stories (of which history is a subspecies) are more than action sequences that can be told. If Foulkes is asserting that meaning is narrative in the sense that it is based on sequential actions that can be told, then the point is trivial, for so is all of human life. That does not offer clues to the cognitive processes criterial to dreaming. In search of more useful and positive criteria of story, however, we saw that intrusive bizarreness, even given its ostensible discontinuity, may be the major element that renders dreaming something more than action sequence. Preemptory visual-spatial metaphors, with their departures from ongoing dream plot and their complex syntheses of its conflicts and ambiguities, introduce that dialectic which, for Ricoeur, defines genuine story narratives—"the competition between the sequential and the configurational dimensions of narrative, a competition that makes narrative a successive whole or whole succession." (Ricoeur, 1984–85, 2: 47).

It is crucial for Ricoeur that stories, with their necessary element of the unexpected and its successful dramatic resolution, can be followed but not predicted. Once again we stand at the hazy and shifting dividing line between human sciences that "understand" versus those that "predict and explain," with the implication that to the extent dreams approximate genuine narratives, they will transcend all logical, quantitative, or syntactic structures. Ricoeur is probably the major current representative of the *Verstehen* tradition of the social and historical sciences. He insists that narrative can never be completely reduced to a fixed system of structures, since it depends on those presentational configurations of felt meaning that James Joyce termed *epiphanies* (*Portrait of the Artist as a Young Man*). Dream psychology thus finds itself on the shores of contemporary postmodern literary criticism—with its conviction that meaning is open-ended and endlessly reversible and renewable. Better illustration could not be found than the myriad interpretations offered for Freud's famous Irma dream, continuously deconstructing before our eyes as successive generations of psychoanalysts, literary critics, and experimental dream psychologists take it up yet again.

The various structuralisms of social science and literary criticism—as techniques that simplify and organize the fundamental dimensions or deep structures of textual meanings—are not "science" in the sense sought by the psychologists of story grammars. An interesting and striking dream will no more submit without ambiguity to the various extant structuralisms than will the works of Kafka. First, the fixed structuralisms of, for instance, psychoanalysis or existential-phenomenological psychology can never be applied without interpretive uncertainty and debate. The decision how to classify a given dream (or story) element is itself ultimately literary and aesthetic, *rightly* open to different solutions. Second, very different structuralisms are put forward. All these attempts to locate basic patterns or structures so general that they will unify, without reductionism, the diversity of empirical observations in fact specify very different levels of abstraction. So there is the ambiguity of which "distance" is most suitable to one's phenomenon. As scientists of dream narratives, how do we decide whether to categorize dreams according to existential categories of being-in-time, Eriksonian life stages and social modalities (as in Richard Jones's 1970 epigenetic classification scheme), Jungian archetypes, or Piaget's cycles of assimilation and accommodation?

This necessary and at least hopeful openness in the conceptualization of human activities is even more clear in the fluid structuralisms of George Kelly in psychology and Claude Lévi-Strauss in anthropology, with the latter's focus on mythologies and their transformations. Recently Adam Kuper (1979, 1983, 1986) has extended this sort of "immanent" binary classification to dreams. Specific dreams are organized in terms of their opposing metaphoric dimensions—in my Tibetan lady dream: family versus museum, closed versus open, male versus female, old versus young. Kuper traces a series of *syntagmatic* transformations from the initial configuration of the dream in its own internal dimensions to its final structure, in terms of substitutions of character, changes in the consequences of action, reversals of sequence, and so on. In his analyses of Freud's Irma dream (of course), dreams of tribal people, and laboratory REM dreams, Kuper seeks to demonstrate "the dialectical processes by which the dreamer moves from the initial dream premise to the resolution" (1979, p. 661). Supporting the notion that dreaming naturally presses toward genuine story status, he finds that final balance and resolution among the shifting semantic dimensions of dreams are more common in spontaneous home recall than in interrupted laboratory dreams (1986). Ricoeur's point stands, however. Describing the dream in terms of its own interior dimensions and their transformations is still an interpreted act. It allows us, post hoc but more formally, to trace the dream story and its potential resolution of expected transformations, but it does not and cannot predict the structure of a given dream (or historical incident). Its successful use is another way of saying that dreams do *approximate* stories.

Yet if dreams can develop into genuine dramatic stories, they also necessarily and maybe typically fall short. Ricoeur (1984–85) posits several criteria for story narratives in addition to the resolution and reconciliation of unexpected transformations. If visual-spatial bizarreness generally creates these transformations (thereby challenging narrative patterning to their resolution), then most dreams are not stories in Ricoeur's sense. Specifically, they are not very bizarre and much of their bizarreness (especially confusional clouding) merely disorganizes and introduces discontinuity into the dream plot, which then never gets resolved—at least during the dream. Ricoeur further suggests that genuine stories (1) are structured in terms of a beginning, middle, and end; (2) expand and foreshorten in a way that reorganizes the lived time of action sequences in terms of the temporal requirements of the narrative; and (3) reflect, and potentially vary, a distinct narrative voice or point of view. With these additions it becomes more clear that even as some dreams are truly stories in every sense, with complex transformations in time and shifts in narrative and/or first person perspective, most dreams, and much of life, move at best fitfully in these directions. Thus dreams may end prematurely or falsely, may lack any genuine beginning, may go on and on with no dramatic transformations whatsoever, or may repeat the same or similar sequences to the point of serious boredom. Most dreams remain truncated, mundane, and inconclusive, lived out in immediate action sequences, and lack even a hint of narrative voice—these are not stories. Rather, they are proto-stories or *quasi-plots*, to use Ricoeur's term for quantitative treatments of history.

When dreaming really "gets going," however—as in many examples of specific imaginative-intuitive dream types—it comes closer and closer to Ricoeur's sense of story as an ur-organizational principle of the human mind. It is as though dreams (like lives?) are *trying* to become stories. If so, they tend to move in a direction opposite that taken by some experimental fiction in which criterial attributes of story are deliberately left out, producing effects that are sometimes termed dreamlike.

I received a graphic demonstration of the dream's potential to move toward Ricoeur's criteria, but here as ironic editorial commentary. This dream occurred on the night I was pondering the possible implications of Ricoeur's books for dreaming, specifically whether dreams could handle time and point of view like narrative fiction, and especially whether dreams had genuine endings. The form was rather unlike my usual dreams. As I awakened from what I even then realized were multiply nested endings, I definitely sensed that I was the object of a joke.

> I am party to the attempted solution of a mystery—in an old house that, I somehow know, was itself modernized and rebuilt over an even older house. I see graves immediately behind it as I stand looking off a second floor patio. The dream begins in mid-conversation, with much excitement and anticipation on my part as an old mystery (which is *never* further defined or explained) is being solved by my interlocutor.
> "She wanted these abstract designs [carved into the patio wall] to point toward the grave."
> "Ah! I see!"
> "Then in 1898 [free association later produced complex family references] a terribly deformed person lived and died here. Of course no one would marry someone like that."
> "Ah!" (as I sense a final clarification of a "something" whose beginning had never in fact been offered!)
> "The old inspector must have known all about this, but he never said anything."
> My sense of total resolution at this point immediately gave way to the final stages of an illustrated commentary on early buildings in the city where I live. "So [a disembodied voice now narrates] the arbors built in the flat north end stood out starkly, while those in the rolling hills of the south end only accentuated their natural surroundings." All this is seen, but immediately afterward turns into a still

photograph—taken as if from the earlier house and looking toward my university. The voice goes on to describe the photograph in terms of what can be seen from this house. Then, just as suddenly, the voice is gone and the photograph, much smaller now, is on the last page of the book I have ostensibly been reading.

As I look further down the page I see, just as I am awakening, a list of acknowledgments for assistance in preparing the book!

The "point" here is that, having fallen asleep over Ricoeur, I am told, "So, you want endings?"

Note that this dream has a narrative point, with its quality of unexpected intrusion and resolution, only because I tell you the background circumstances in which it was dreamed. Without them, and unlike some "genuine" story dreams, it is not a story in Ricoeur's sense. In particular the multiple endings only become such, and resolve an earlier ambiguity, when we know that the beginning rested outside the dream in my attempts to apply Ricoeur's analysis.

Dreaming shows a natural tendency to approximate the criteria of a dramatic story but also characteristically falls short. It is the way we spontaneously handle dreams on awakening that finishes the operation by turning the dream into a story in Ricoeur's meaning—and this in a double sense. Ricoeur specifies two fundamental types of story—history and fiction/mythology—each using the same fundamental narrative criteria to very different effect. To bring out the story in historical narrative we must go in search of the background context against which specific actions can be evaluated. In fiction, on the other hand, we remain within the story itself and aim primarily for effect and dramatic power. The story itself must have an aesthetic impact.

It is striking that where dreams lack an obvious point and so push us towards interpretation, the two general methods employed—free association and amplification—precisely parallel Ricoeur's dichotomy between history and fiction. To free-associate is to dissolve the dream back into one's personal past. Meaning arises outside the dream from its background context. Freud's intent is always historical and the most senseless manifest dream will gain its point when it affords a more full and rich tracing of one's past. And we have seen that free association seems best suited to those dreams that are predominantly mnemic in their organization. Amplification, on the other hand, takes the imaginative/metaphoric elements in the dream and seeks to make them more powerful and direct. Thus Jung often connected the dreams of his patients to major aesthetically powerful and emotionally moving mythologies. Jung and others often further elaborated the dream by means of imaginal dialogues with dream figures, actively finishing the dream by turning it into a piece of fictive dramatic dialogue. Hillman's (1977, 1978) later illustrations of dream interpretation involve rewriting the dream as a kind of poetry.

Thus, the two ways of turning a dream into a genuine story show the fundamental operations of the two general classes of narrative—history and fiction. Given the reflexive basis of human intelligence, it is not surprising that these methods of dialogue with dreams may gradually come to change the dreaming process itself in their own image—producing complex allusions to the personal past in long-term psychoanalysis and the powerful epiphanies of Jungian patients. This interpretive "framing" of dreams is in principle identical to the way we may eventually come, with time and distance, to turn around on our life situations and see them as metaphors or emblems for more general and fundamental issues. Important experiences may then offer factual clues to our personal and familial fates or may become our own personally expressive myths. A major difference between dream and life experience is that the dream, already separated from the ongoing course of experience, inherently lends itself to such framing. In addition, dreams can be transformed in their very fabric by the cognitive operations of personal memory and imaginative metaphor.

CHAPTER 12

The Visual-Spatial Side of Dream Formation

Hypnagogic Imagery, Dream Bizarreness, and Altered States of Consciousness

T HE correlation of visual-spatial forms of dream bizarreness with waking measures of imagination and creativity is not sufficient to establish the metaphoric roots of such experience. Despite recent demonstrations of cortical antecedents in phasic REM discharge, it could still be that imagistic bizarreness works on the randomization model of creativity, so favored in current artificial intelligence accounts. On that model, creative imagery would operate by destroying the continuity of on-going propositional intelligence, so that its later reestablishment would have to include novel and so potentially useful elements. The question becomes whether visual-spatial transformations in dreams and closely related features of altered states of consciousness show abstract symbolic operations in their very fabric. This goes to the heart of current debates about imagery: is it a semi-autonomous symbolic frame of mind or a secondary expression of language?

The heightening of visual-spatial transformations in hypnagogic accounts makes the relations between sleep onset experience and night dreams central to our discussion. It also appears that the most famous anecdotal accounts of major creative breakthroughs occurring in dreams (e.g., Kekule's benzine rings) involve sleep onset rather than REM dreaming. It might seem that the discovery of REM sleep as physiologically distinct from normal sleep onset would render invalid nineteenth-century suggestions that full dreaming actually forms itself out of the visual, kinesthetic, and verbal alterations of classical hypnagogic imagery. However, more recent demonstrations that dreaming is a general process that occurs whenever certain minimal conditions are met reopens the possibility that the more episodic and fragmentary reports of sleep onset might show us normally invisible (microgenetic) phases of dream formation. In some sleep onset reports we seem to find the same visual-spatial imagistic forms that make vivid dreaming so interesting, yet without the narrative-propositional structuring so characteristic of NREM and REM dreaming.

In contrast to laboratory studies of ordinary sleep onset (reviewed below), classical hypnagogic experiences are self-arousing. They are well represented in a phenomenologically rich anecdotal literature (Mitchell, 1890; Ellis, 1897, Silberer, 1909; Hollingworth, 1911; Slight, 1924; Leaning, 1925; Kluver, 1966; Van Dusen, 1972), but there have been few systematic questionnaire studies with larger groups of subjects (McKellar and Simpson, 1954; McKellar, 1957; Schacter, 1976). Only a minority of subjects seem to have hypnagogic experiences typically, a point further emphasized by their occurrence in a physiological "twilight" setting that mixes normally separate features of sleep and wakefulness. The few laboratory studies of subjects reporting this phenomenon spontaneously find either sudden increases in physiological arousal in the midst of sleep onset (Oswald, 1962) or an unusually long time spent in EEG theta, rapidly passed through in ordinary sleep onset (Schacter, 1976). In physiological terms both meditation and sensory deprivation involve a highly similar mix of sleep and wakefulness—all these being transitional states of consciousness (Zubek, 1969; Woolfolk, 1975).

Classical hypnagogic reports are surprisingly similar to those from sensory deprivation, meditation, and especially psychedelic drug states. McKellar and Simpson (1954) found a feeling of strangeness, uncanniness, or unreality to be the most common effect (after physical "sleep starts" or "jerks"). It is also worth noting that so-called paranormal, apparitional, and out-of-body experiences occur most commonly at sleep onset (Sidgwick, 1894; Green and McCreery, 1975). Bizarre verbal imagery was slightly more common than visual and kinesthetic reports in McKellar and Simpson's questionnaire study and in the careful self-reports of Van Dusen (1972).[1] Arkin (1978) and Heynick (1981) both agree that hypnagogic verbal-auditory expressions lack the linguistic competence of verbal recall from REM dreaming. Instead, various "nonsense" statements, nearly inaudible whispering, accusatory voices,

voices saying one's name, and complex and often poetic neologisms are reported.

The similarity of hypnagogic visual imagery to that experienced under the influence of LSD and mescaline has probably been the most widely remarked feature of this literature. Subjects describe diffuse lights and colors, which may develop into geometric patterns of a simple repetitive quality or into the dazzlingly complex and aesthetically beautiful designs described by Jung as mandala patterns. These may remain as such or may develop into isolated images of specific objects, often undergoing strikingly psychedelic changes in size, shape, or color. Entire landscapes may possess qualities of unusual grandeur and beauty, as in some archetypal dreams. Especially common among the images of isolated objects are bloated or distorted faces, often quite horrifying. At times all these effects can change so quickly that there is a flashing or scintillating effect.

Somatic transformations of the body image are strikingly reminiscent of psychedelic drug, schizophrenic, and/or yogic chakra experiences. Weir Mitchell describes the following subject:

> While waiting for sleep he became aware of an indescribable something, which rose from the feet and hands, and taking eight or ten seconds to reach the head, there ending in a sound like the crash of glass houses breaking in a hail-storm, with a vivid flash of yellow light, leaving him for a moment dazed, but able at once to rise, or to think. Such is the usual account given of this aura. It never varies, save that it may rise only from the belly. . . . The aura is said at times to be like a tingling, or else is described as an upwards surge of indescribable nature. (Mitchell, 1890, p. 121)

Sensations of floating, falling, flying, or spinning are also common to hypnagogic sleep onset. We also find synesthetic fusions of patterns from different sensory modalities. This may be the cognitive basis for out-of-body experience. As Irwin (1985) and I have suggested (Hunt, 1985b), incipient bodily sensations of floating, in the context of continuous awareness of one's actual physical setting, may be cross-modally translated into an imaged view of oneself as if from above. Indeed, it seems possible that the curiously distorted faces mentioned above are visual-synesthetic translations of the residual expressive sensations from one's own face during the reduced tactile sensitivity of sleep onset.

Some subjects also report brief dream scenes, usually without the representation of self typical of dream experience. Such disconnected scenes were the source of Silberer's original observations on autosymbolism—since confirmed and extended by Slight, Van Dusen, and Ulric Neisser (1967). The self-referential focus of these brief dream scenes may vary from visual metaphors of the topic of thought immediately prior to sleep (Silberer's material autosymbols), to metaphors of the form or functioning of thought and feeling (functional autosymbols), to visual-synesthetic translations of body sensation (somatic autosymbols).

Lest these classic hypnagogic reports, with their psychedelic transformations, seem completely antithetical to a narrative organization of REM dreaming and so to REM dreaming generally, it is worth noting their predominance in the sleep onset REM dreams of narcolepsy. Narcolepsy is a sleep disorder characterized by especially intense and extended REM sleep, sometimes occurring periodically throughout the day and characteristically at sleep onset, when there is a mixture of REM physiology (e.g., paralysis, vestibular sensations) with wakefulness—the same transitional or twilight state conducive to major alterations in consciousness. Narcoleptics report especially vivid and bizarre dreams that feature an unusual amount of flying, falling, and floating. Many of these subjects report an awareness that they are dreaming (lucidity), some degree of control, and an ability to think clearly and rationally in the midst of the dream (Oswald, 1962; Vogel, 1976; Van den Hoed, Lucas, and Dement, 1979; Krishnan, 1984). Again, intensified REM sleep shows a preponderance of imagistic processes over narrative-propositional ones. Whereas sleep onset dreams in narcolepsy show rapid eye movements and motor paralysis, classic hypnagogic reports do not (Oswald, 1962).[2]

At first glance experimental laboratory research on sleep onset with subjects who do not report these vivid but relatively infrequent classic transformations seems to suggest that they are absent during the normative transition to sleep. Thus the LSD-like phenomena of the hypnagogic period would be special presentational constructions permitted by transitional or twilight states— and indeed the physiology of sleep onset in subjects prone to these experiences is unusual. In a series of laboratory studies of normative sleep onset, Foulkes and Vogel and their colleagues found almost no strange voices, faces, geometric designs, synesthesias, and body image transformations. Instead, when deliberately aroused by the experimenters during the descending EEG of sleep onset, laboratory subjects reported brief "dreamlets." Without laboratory awakening these would have been completely forgotten—unlike the self-arousing effect of hypnagogic experience. A closer look at these dreamlets, however, shows that they involve the same separation and alternation between imagery entrained by narrative thought and spontaneous visual-spatial transformations that we are attempting to trace within dream formation generally.

Vogel, Foulkes, and Trosman (1966) locate three types of sleep onset dream, roughly associated with the physiological transitions from waking EEG with alpha rhythm to descending EEG stages 1 and 2. Initial phase 1 reports were characterized by a loss of control over ongoing mental content along with a shift to a passive, observing attitude. While the subject generally lost awareness of the laboratory context, the resulting experience was not necessarily hallucinatory; that is, it was not generally taken as real. Indeed, the best way to characterize these events, which Vogel and colleagues categorize as *intact ego*, is to say that they reflect an immediate imagistic translation of ongoing verbal thought (what Silberer classified as material autosymbols). In one example a concert pianist states, "I was thinking of sending clippings to a Russian pianist and I saw an envelope with fifteen cents postage" (Vogel, Foulkes, and Trosman, 1966, p. 242).

The second phase, classified as *destructuralized ego*, shows the predominance of what the authors call "regressive" content and what I regard as potential visual-spatial metaphor. These reports, in a context of greater organismic activation, would be reminiscent of classic hypnagogic accounts. The authors include in this category single isolated images, incomplete scenes or fragmented objects, bizarre superimpositions and condensations, dissociations of thought and image, and magical omnipotent thinking—in short, many of the elements of REM dream bizarreness. Here, in addition to the passivity and loss of control characteristic of phase 1, most of these reports were understood as actually occurring (hallucinatory). Thus the same pianist reports:

> [I was] observing the inside of a pleural cavity. There were small people in it, like a room. The people were hairy, like monkeys. The walls of the pleural cavity are made of ice and slippery. In the midpart there is an ivory bench with people sitting on it. Some people are throwing balls of cheese against the inner side of the chest wall.   (Vogel, Foulkes, and Trosman, 1966, p. 242)

Another subject:

> I was looking at sort of a low lazy-Suzan type of thing which was on the floor under a typewriter stand. I was in a very peculiar vantage point. I was looking down between the legs there, and never got above this. It was made out of crystal, and it was a platter type of arrangement. In the middle there was a stem and a little ball on the top, and I first saw there was blood in the little glass thing. In the middle it was full of blood; and then as it developed, the blood turned into what looked like the sort of cocktail sauce that's served with shrimp; and then as it developed more, little shrimps started appearing around the little glass where the sauce was; and then as it developed more, more shrimp appeared on the platter below; and just as you called, a dog was walking over there and was just about ready to help himself to a few of the shrimp. This was mostly in vague symbols because there was nothing realistic about this at all. The dog was strange too

because his head, you know where his snout comes down to his nose, this part was all, like it was sawed off. In other words his face was completely squared off and he didn't have any nose. I remember when I saw the dog coming out, I looked at him, made me feel uneasy. (Foulkes and Vogel, 1965, p. 239)

In the third and final stage, *restructuralized ego*, reports were typically less bizarre. Experience was still involuntary and hallucinatory, but for the first time an active self-figure was represented within the relatively mundane dream narrative—more reminiscent of the organization of experience in NREM and tonic REM dreams. Here is the pianist again: "I was driving a car, telling other people you shouldn't go over a certain speed limit"; another subject reported, "I was writing an exam, probably in histology and felt frustrated because I couldn't express myself clearly" (Vogel, Foulkes, and Trosman, 1966, pp. 342–43). To characterize this third stage more generally, subjects are describing normative dreams, where an active "I" moves through a dramatic episode in which imagistic properties have been more or less entrained by narrative sequence.

At its point of maximum activation (in our special imaginative types, narcolepsy, L-Dopa, etc.), REM dreaming reflects more of the second sleep onset phase and classical hypnagogic phenomena, where creative imagistic processes develop in their own right and may predominate over and determine narrative. In certain vivid archetypal dreams the narrative and visual-spatial phases of dream formation interact at a maximum degree of complexity. Such interaction produces the dreams of a Jung, correspondingly more rich and creative than narratively predominant dreams but less fragmented and dissociated than classical hypnagogic experience. It is only in such dreams that narration and imagery have a mutual and reciprocal influence.

There is considerable evidence that dream narrative and novel visual-spatial imagery reflect alternative and potentially independent cognitive processes. Thus Foulkes and Fleischer (1975), in a highly original attempt to develop an experimental control condition for sleep laboratory methods, periodically interrupted the ongoing mentation of subjects who were fully awake and lying in laboratory beds during the day in order to ask them about their experience. Of these reports, 19 percent were described by the subjects as hallucinatory—daydreams in which they were sufficiently engrossed to forget their surroundings and take the experiences as actually occurring. Twenty-five percent were rated as bizarre on the Vogel criteria. Not only did these reports themselves rarely overlap, but out of twenty subjects there was no overlap between the four who produced the most hallucinatory dreamlike narratives and the five with the highest bizarreness ratings. Here is an example of these visual-spatial transformations, which at that time at least Foulkes referred to as a "perceptual synthetic mode of thought":

> I was picturing this thing, this animal kind of thing . . . it was gray, grayish white in color; it was really scaly. I pictured it in mid air; it wasn't moving or flying or anything. It had little bowed legs, and regular hands and feet and all, and the face—no, there wasn't a face, there was sort of like a helmet, you know, going down over this head, and it had these huge wings that were spread out, but it was like a statue falling from somewhere, but it was more lifelike than a statue.   (Foulkes and Fleischer, 1975, pp. 72–73)

Similarly, in research on sensory deprivation Zuckerman (1970) pointed out that subjects initially oscillate among three possible responses: thinking about the experimental situation, daydreaming about personal concerns, or attending to the minimal background sensations (phosphenes, tactile sensations) that research in sensory deprivation, LSD, and meditation shows to be the preliminary phase of more elaborate altered states of consciousness. In my own research on experimental meditation and a related control condition of simple isolation (a subject seated in a bare experimental room with varying degrees of instructional set to observe immediate ongoing consciousness— Hunt and Chefurka, 1976), I found the same variations in response. Some subjects defensively worked to "figure out" the experiment, while still others similarly ignored the instructions by sinking into personal reverie (and indeed became so absorbed they often forgot where they were). Neither of these groups reported the striking alterations of consciousness that were described in periods as short as five or ten minutes by subjects who were able to follow the instructions for either visual meditation or introspection on immediate moment-by-moment awareness. These subjects described complex and often startling changes in the organization of visual and somatic perception akin to the formal transformations of hypnagogic experience and psychedelic drug experiences. They also reported sensations of trancelike absorption, feelings of uncanniness, fascination, and awe, and tendencies to animate their physical surroundings—some subjects, for example, actually felt observed or ineffably addressed by the room itself:

> I was looking at this particular brick. I could see a white tunnel with dark sides. Way at the back of the tunnel there seemed to be—well, it's hard to describe—I guess you could call it a gyroscope—that's just something I can compare it to. It was spinning and it kept coming closer and closer. It was diamond-shaped and it didn't seem to have any substance inside—just sides intersecting. It seemed to encompass the whole wall. It started with one brick and then it spread. . . . Before the brick started to move, I was staring at a little hole in the brick. After a while it

looked like an eye—not really like an eye, but I visualized the hole as staring at me—I thought the room was alive itself. Like it had blood flowing through veins and it was trying to entertain me—showing me all this stuff. It seemed to have a life of its own almost. Like I was encompassed by it.   (Hunt and Cheferka, 1976, p. 873)

In these waking altered states daydream narratives and imagistic bizarreness can occur independently, as alternatives, and run a separate course. As with dream bizarreness, the visual-spatial reorganizations of altered states correlate significantly in my own studies with measures of imaginative absorption, visual imagination, and creative use of metaphor (Hunt and Popham, 1987).

Similarly, in laboratory sleep onset research we saw a shift from imagery constructed by and illustrating ongoing verbal preoccupations (the form of imagery studied by Foulkes, Farah, and Pylyshyn) to a predominance of imagistic processes over narrative structure. In the final sleep onset phase narrative-propositional cognition is once again imposed upon imagery in the form of normative dreaming.

The following picture emerges: Novel visual-spatial transformations in dreams and altered states reflect the disinhibition of a normally contained and subordinated system of presentational symbolism, probably based in the right hemisphere. In these states it is temporarily released from its normal dominance by the verbal-representational system, presumably left hemisphere–based and engaged in the ongoing construction of the everyday social world. This shift to a presentational and immediately expressive intelligence occurs in all conditions where cortical activation is lowered just enough to blunt verbal-representational control, but not enough to prohibit imagistic-intuitive processes from coming forward. Further decrease in level of activation would also begin to affect these autonomous imagery processes in such a way that the normally predominant representational intelligence can reassert its control and direction—as in NREM and tonic REM dreaming. At still lower levels of activation, mentation is for all practical purposes unrecoverable. Much the same sequence can also occur when activation is increased to the point that adaptive left hemisphere processes become overloaded and self-inhibited, as in accounts of out-of-body experience in physical emergency, some psychedelic drug episodes, and spontaneous ecstasy.

It is relevant that especially bizarre REM dreaming is associated with the highest physiological activation of REM sleep (phasic bursts, chemically "driven" REM periods, and REM rebound). Yet EEG recordings during activated REM sleep still show a slightly lower arousal than alert wakefulness. Accordingly, the subjective intensity of many altered state experiences can be reconciled with their predominance in states transitional to actual sleep. What seems common to a wide range of transformations of consciousness—occurring in the midst of sleep, dream, or wakefulness—is the relative paralysis of dominant verbal-representational processes and an intense orientation response (verging on tonic immobility) associated with response to novelty. If visual-spatial imagery comes into its own as a system in response to novel materials that require creative reorganization of past experience, then it makes sense that relative twilight states, in which propositional organization is lessened, would be the setting for the spontaneous emergence of imagistic intelligence—whether entrained by previous attempts at reflective problem solving (as in scientific discovery) or released in its own right (as so-called altered states).

Visual-Spatial Transformations: Regression or Self-Referential Intelligence?

The predominant approach to transformations of consciousness in psychoanalysis (Freud), psychiatry (Sullivan), and cognition (Piaget, Foulkes) has been to assume their basis in regression or primitivity, a view at least initially supported by the overlap of these states with neurological and schizophrenic syndromes. Yet there is indication of an abstract intuitive self-reference in the very fabric of these states that goes beyond ordinary levels of conscious self-awareness. Such a position, of course, is widely assumed within transpersonal and Jungian circles, but this assumption is largely intuitive and practical and lacks a supporting cognitive psychology.

Several major cognitive theorists, coming from very different perspectives, have suggested that an essential aspect of all human symbolism is its capacity for reflexivity or self-reference (Hofstadter, Mead, Vygotsky) and/or turning around on and recombining its own perceptual and affective schemata (Bartlett, Neisser). In his seminal analysis of hypnagogic imagery, dreams, and meditation, Wilson Van Dusen (1972) sees even the most fragmented and isolated forms of such states as manifesting "the most profound tendency of the psyche . . . to represent itself" (p. 4)—this is also the fundamental point of Silberer's autosymbolism, Jung's transcendent function, and Freud's endopsychic perception. However, if geometric and synesthetic hypnagogic imagery and archetypal-titanic dream forms are to be taken as abstract metaphoric presentations, we are still left with a choice between a strong and a weak version of such reflexivity. The weak version would simply hold that these phenomena do not start off as symbolic operations (i.e., there is no intentionality) but are later taken as presentational symbols when we "take the role of the other" toward them and treat them *as if* they had semantic content—much as we, post hoc, see faces in clouds. Since such spontaneous imagery is diffuse and constantly changing it would, in contrast to the univocal nature of representational language, actually provide "deep" or "unconscious" meanings. Accordingly, the interpretation of these phenomena could be of genuine use while still reflecting nothing of any originating symbolic operations.

However, there is considerable evidence for the strong version that these subjective phenomena, so separate from verbal-representational processes, are enhanced and indeed created by an abstract and sustained attitude of self-reference—directly releasing the basic forms of presentational symbolism. For instance, in sensory deprivation research Eugene Ziskind (1964) demonstrated that increasing the amount of specific experimental suggestion for alterations in consciousness did not influence subsequent reports as much as did the more basic "direction" that the subject *observe* ongoing subjective experience, without any specific suggestion for the unusual or hallucinatory. In Ziskind's view, sensory deprivation creates an enhanced hypnagogic state, with the implication that naturally occurring hypnagogic effects are in part created by the very attitude of receptivity that observes them.

In my own research (Hunt and Chefurka, 1976) we found that directing subjects' attention toward their immediate ongoing consciousness, while they actively tried to avoid verbal labeling and discursive thinking *about* the situation, was sufficient to elicit some quite striking alterations of perception, affect, and cognition within very short time periods. This is precisely the attitude of "insight" or "mindfulness" meditation, but it is less well known that the classic introspection of Titchener involved the same suppression of reflective verbal thought ("avoiding the stimulus error") and receptive observation of immediate consciousness. Indeed, the experimental protocols of the introspectionists are filled with reports strikingly reminiscent of experiences in sensory deprivation, mild psychedelic drug states, the hypnagogic period, and meditation (for examples see Hunt 1984, 1985a, 1986a). It is especially significant that the attitude of reflexivity common to such states does not depend on language. Their development requires a difficult-to-sustain inhibition of normal "representational" inner speech. We see here an autonomous mode of self-reference within imagistic, presentational symbolism.

There is also evidence that the ostensibly perceptual reorganizations of hypnagogic imagery and dream bizarreness directly exemplify symbolic operations. Spontaneous variations in the dimensions of size, shape, distance, and color, emancipated in these states from their reciprocal relations within the phenomenal constancies of functional perception, are reminiscent of suggestions from Maier (1931), Arnheim (1969), and Crovitz (1970) that systematic variation in separate physical dimensions is a central part of our abstract problem-solving capacity. In these states such variation would not often be devoted to the solving of logical-intellectual problems, but to creating metaphoric expressions of personal and affective significance. Similarly, the tendency toward geometric imagery in these states, with a frequent subjective sense that these images convey a more or less ineffable felt meaning (Jung took them as autosymbols of one's general life course and character), can be understood as a direct illustration of the sort of abstract-dynamic geometric imagery posited by Rudolph Arnheim as the root processes of thought. Certainly these spontaneous variations in separate physical dimensions and their complex organization and reorganization in geometric patterns show all the transformational operations suggested by Chomsky as the deep structure of intelligence—deletion, substitution, expansion, condensation, addition, and permutation—but completely independent here of linguistic representation. We might even speculate that the structures of vision provide the only possible noncognitive template for symbolic operations, the ultimate source for operations that become symbolic with cross-modal translation.

The ubiquity of synesthesias in altered states of consciousness (and in somatic-medical and titanic dream forms) can be seen as the subjective side of the capacity for cortical cross-modal translation between the patterns of the different senses, which Geschwind (1965), and by implication Luria (1972, 1973), make criteria for genuine symbolism. The assimilation of synesthesias to the cognitive psychology of metaphor is supported by their prominence in poetry (Marks, 1978) and by the fact that they are felt by many subjects who experience them to be a form of thinking, an imagistic alternative to inner speech, not merely curious sensory anomalies (Wheeler and Cutsforth, 1922; McKellar, 1957). The common occurrence of synesthesias initiated by tactile, auditory, or visual stimuli and terminating in tactile or visual imagery, but the rarity of any resulting auditory imagery triggered by visual or tactile stimuli (McKellar, 1957), suggests that the missing category is language itself. From this perspective language itself is a kind of synesthesia—translating visual and tactile patterns into communicative auditory forms and vice versa. Given the phylogenetic (apes) and ontogenetic (infants) occurrence of recombinatory mental abilities prior to linguistic communication, Geschwind's assertion seems correct: it is the cross-modal translation capacity that makes language possible, rather than the other way around. The cross-modal bases of symbolization are in fact less immediately obvious in language than in the presentational symbolisms of the arts and the imagistic properties of hypnagogic and dream reports.

With respect to an attempted cognitive psychology of more developed altered states, there is some indication from the literature on LSD experiences (Leary, Metzner, and Alpert, 1964; Fischer, 1975), chakra or body center experiences in yoga (Govinda, 1960), and shamanistic trance (Reichel-Dolmatoff, 1975) that it is only when geometric-mandala designs, with their typical fourfold structure probably based on the four limbs, are experienced as fused with tactile-kinesthetic patterns that they "embody" and convey a deep sense of felt meaning. Otherwise they remain curious visual effects without any sense of inherent significance. Going further, we can interpret the white light/cessation experience of advanced meditation and highly developed lucid dreaming as an abstract presentational metaphor also based on cross-modal synesthetic translation.

William James (1902) was the first psychologist to suggest that the intuition of unity and special significance in mysticism is an exaggeration and exteriorization of the ordinary processes of felt meaning that subserve all thinking. The white light aspect would be based on a "turning around" on the perceptual schemata and their disassembling back to the most microgenetically preliminary quality of visual-spatial perception—luminosity. Indeed, descriptions of such light and its substages of development in Tibetan Buddhism are identical to early introspectionist accounts of "avoiding the stimulus error" during ultra-rapid tachistoscopic exposures (Hunt, 1984, 1985b). The appearance of these qualities of pure luminosity as imagery, however, would be based on the principles of metaphor generation.

Luminosity or glow is the perfect metaphoric vehicle to convey the sense of an all-encompassing, all-causal source emanating from outside ordinary space and time yet simultaneously generating and containing all specific forms—just as all more specific colors and shapes presuppose luminosity. Thus it makes sense that light would be experienced as the cross-culturally common metaphor for the sense of an absolute unity behind the diversity of appearance—whether conceptualized as God, mind, or void. However, on the present cognitive account, white light imagery would not be experienced as expressing such meaning without cross-modal translation into tactile-kinesthetic patterns. This in turn would explain the curious phenomenon that intense religious experience is so often associated with feelings of annihilation, "dying," and infinite void, since these would also follow from its cross-modal synesthetic translation into tactile-kinesthetic schemata. In other words, for the body image to *become* luminosity would also entail the imagistic cessation or "snuff-out" described in the literature on deep meditation (void) and schizophrenia (generalized blocking). How, other than phenomenal disappearance, could kinesthesis and luminosity fuse into one pattern, thereby generating a correspondingly abstract and total sense of meaning?

In fairness, of course, we should not finish quite so quickly with the primitivity or regression-release hypothesis for altered states and dream bizarreness. For instance, the organismic setting common to the wide range of altered-state effects is Morrison's orientation response, which, when considerably intensified, becomes tonic immobility—the form of total motor paralysis found in all animals in situations of overwhelming emergency (Gallup, 1974). Descriptions of yogic samadhi, catatonic schizophrenia, and shamanistic "flight of the soul" all sound very much like tonic immobility—including even the same "waxy flexibility" of body limbs and copious saliva. This might suggest a phylogenetically primitive source for altered states of consciousness (certainly including night terrors) and might confirm the brain stem discharge model of Hobson and McCarley.

However, there seem to be important differences between the "abstract" form of tonic immobility found in human altered states and the "concrete" tonic immobility occurring in animals, including human beings in situations of great physical emergency, suggesting that the former is a metaphoric reuse of the latter (Hunt, 1984). Deep trance states are associated with numinous-uncanny felt meaning and a sense of subjective cessation or "dying," while concrete tonic immobility in reaction to physical disasters like combat or violent crime is associated with affective numbing. In humans and other animals this concrete form easily develops into psychosomatic shock and physical, definitely nonmetaphoric collapse and death. If true novelty in human symbolism is mediated primarily through an imagistic frame that reuses perceptual-motor patterns, it makes sense that its fullest emergence would be associated with the orientation response (Pavlov's curiosity reflex)—reaching levels of tonic immobility for the most intense absorption in situations of maximum significance and/or ambiguity. Both deep mystical experience and acute catatonic schizophrenia have been represented as the most intense internally generated crises of meaning possible for human beings. Hypnosis, although less intense, is now understood by most researchers as a cognitive process of imaginative absorption—direct measures of which correlate with a tendency to especially novel dreams, nightmares, and lucid dreaming.

There are similar suggestions that synesthesias could not be the basis of all symbolism. Instead, they are seen as residues of a phylogenetically primitive subcortical tonus preliminary to specific sensory differentiation (Osgood, 1964) or as a concrete imagery capability replaced in human ontogeny by the more advanced linguistic capacity (Werner, 1961; Piaget, 1962; Marks, 1978).

Cytowic (1986) has reported studies of cerebral blood flow in subjects experiencing vivid synesthesias. He found decreased activation in both cerebral hemispheres and unusually high arousal in the limbic and hippocampal circuits. It is in these areas that Mishkin has located the association of different sensory modalities with each other and with affective tone.

Synesthesias, however, involve not an *association* between sensory modalities (necessary in all mammals as the source of learning), but a mutual *translation*, which in human beings would be at the base of symbolic "felt meaning." Indeed, subjects aware of vivid synesthesias often are not sure which modality has been stimulated—at first the experience may not be so much across different modalities as a "something" with no sensory attributes (Cattell, 1930; Werner, 1961). Accordingly, it seems unlikely that synesthesias are an ordinary aspect of mammalian learning, since the experience of fusion of modalities could only have a dislocating effect at lower evolutionary levels. In the context of perceptual-motor adaptation, creatures must know immediately and exactly where to locate novel stimulation. They cannot afford states in which localization is indeterminate, however briefly. Such states could have a genuine function only as the "felt meaning" of symbolism. With respect to Cytowic's findings, then, I suggest that the limbic system is used on very different levels—in animals to mediate associations between modalities and in humans as a locus of the felt meaning created by cortically based cross-modal fusions.

Finally, of course, it has been suggested that geometric imagery is the very opposite of anything cognitive or symbolic, being instead a direct release of the basic structures of the visual system (Kluver, 1966). It is true that Siegel (1983), using operant conditioning techniques with pigeons, seems to have demonstrated the "appearance" (reinforcement) of geometric designs when the birds are under the influence of psychedelic drugs. However, on the present cognitive model the point remains that the cross-modal translation of geometric designs between tactile-kinesthetic patterns creates the presentational meanings manifested directly in psychedelic drugs and the hypnagogic period and subsumed within all representational symbolism as felt meaning. Here again, capacities of the secondary association areas, functionally separate in lower animals (and to some extent the higher apes) would be integrated and intertranslated in both mandala imagery *and* as part of language. We must be careful not to confuse the separate elements of the human cognitive capacity with their functional synthesis as recombinatory creative thought.

In our rejection of approaches to vivid dreams and altered states of consciousness as "primitive" we are still left with the problem of how to deal with Piaget's more sophisticated cognitive account of dreaming and hypnagogic imagery in which dream symbolism is understood as a concrete, preoperational form of intelligence—something far short of a separate developmental line for presentational symbolism, as suggested here.

In *Play, Dreams, and Imitation in Childhood* (1962), Piaget, like Freud but in different terminology, pictures the dream as recreating the situation of the very young infant. The separation of the dreamer from his or her physical surroundings reproduces the lack of accommodation and primacy of assimilation of infancy. The resulting separation of various forms of thought, as expressed in action, imagery, and verbal schemata, recreates the separation of modalities of the early sensorimotor period and allows their mutual and "playful" assimilation in dreaming. As in my account here, the cross-modal assimilations create the metaphoric bizarreness and originality of dreaming, but for Piaget these constructions remain limited to the concrete pre-operations of the affective schemata (knowledge of self and others versus schematization of logical and physical material). The distinction between affective schemata and intellectual schemata parallels Susanne Langer's distinction between presentational and representational symbolism, but with the crucial difference that the affective schemata are inherently primitive, necessarily lagging behind the ultimate balance of assimilation and accommodation possible for logical-intellectual operations. The affective schemata of dreams can only become manifest by means of a primitive projection of ego qualities into sensory-imagistic patterns, rendering affective self-representation permanently concrete.

For Piaget the intrinsic linkage of signified and signifier (medium) that characterizes presentational symbolism/affective schemata, rather than offering a metaphoric reflection of otherwise inaccessible processes, is conceptualized as a concrete fixation. It contrasts with the decentering and equilibration of logical-intellectual operations that unfold in terms of information about the physical world. It is only the physical world that offers that ultimate resistance which will force maximum accommodation and so full consciousness (Piaget, 1973). Similarities between the play of children and dream metaphor, then, only serve to confirm the primitive concrete basis of dreams. The affective schemata of self-reference remain necessarily egocentric and concrete.

Nowhere does it seem to occur to Piaget that affective schemata might have their own line of abstract development and their own form of equilibration—as in Langer on aesthetics and perhaps the meditative traditions of systematic self-awareness. It is all too easy, given the variants of individual and cultural frames of mind, to see what is undeveloped and unsystematized in oneself as necessarily primitive in all its possible forms. At the one extreme it seems problematic to suggest that the music of Bach or the art of Picasso reflects less formal symbolic intelligence than the thought of Heisenberg. At the other extreme, while higher apes can be induced to "paint," these creative works, while important precursors of human intelligence, also have all the limitations of their visual-spatial problem-solving and protolinguistic signing abilities. If we do not find true language in chimpanzees, neither do we find genuine art, or shamanism.

Current transpersonal psychologists like Wilber (1984) and Alexander (Alexander et al., 1987), who suggest that the meditative path illustrates cognitive development beyond formal operations, simply invert Piaget's, Freud's, and Foulkes's interpretation of imagistic processes as primitive and/or derivative. It seems better to avoid all such ethnocentrisms of symbolic forms. Instead, I suggest that metaphoric self-reference constitutes its own line of development—leading toward an analogue to formal operations within the affective schemata. On a more concrete level, the diverse mythological tales and images of each culture depict the range and possibilities of human experience and at the same time imply a relativization and equilibration among them. On a more abstract level, the meditative traditions establish a receptive "witness" attitude which becomes the source of the accommodation Piaget finds lacking within the affective schemata.

The abstract or systematic self-reference of meditation creates a setting in which all emotional responses, memories, and hopes are gradually realized as equal manifestations of the same underlying mind. Ultimately these spontaneous manifestations of deep meditation, to be observed in a nonevaluative and detached fashion no matter what their nature or intensity, become more and more totalistic and abstract. They develop from personal emotions and memories, to archetypal-titanic patterns of great intensity, to more abstract geometric designs, to the cross-cultural ubiquity of diffuse luminosity as the most abstract and inclusive metaphor for the equipotentiality of cognitive-affective states. This equilibration of affective schemata is at least analogous to formal intellectual operations, although I have already suggested (chapter 1) that the developmental unfolding of each line presents different problems—reversibility for sequentially patterned logical operations, a full "spelling out" of simultaneously superimposed meanings for the affective schemata of self-reference.[3]

Visual-Spatial Imagery in Dreaming: Challenge and Response within a Nonverbal Dialogic Structure

I would like to try my hand at a cognitive psychology of the visual-spatial or visual-kinesthetic side of dreaming, predicated on the above notion that transformations of consciousness directly exemplify the processes of presentational symbolism. These processes will develop over time in terms of the same reflexive and dialogic patterns that underlie language. More specifically, several lines of evidence converge to suggest that a visual-spatial frame of intelligence is specifically *challenged* in dreaming and that its resulting incipient disorganization can also stimulate a corresponding hyperdevelopment.

1. What makes dreams bizarre in a positive sense (in contrast to their negative verbal-reflective lacunae) are visual-kinesthetic transformations—which often meet the criteria for an unusually developed metaphorical imagination.

2. There is considerable evidence that imagery and perception in the same modality share the same underlying structures and interact in complex ways (Finke, 1980; Shepard, 1984). Along these lines a recent study by Kerr, Condon, and McDonald (1985) showed that experimental disruption of physical balance specifically interfered with a task of visual-spatial cognition but not with a comparatively difficult verbal task.

3. Visual-spatial perception is deregulated and disorganized in dreaming in a way that is not the case for representational language—especially given recent demonstrations of the linguistic competence of dream language. Although both phenomenology and neurophysiology indicate an activation of visual perceptual schemata during REM dreams, this is accompanied by an absence of the continual input from external stimulation that supports perceptual functioning during wakefulness. Endogenous perceptual processes during dreaming necessarily lack the continuous organization afforded by the waking ecological array. More specifically, the physiology of the REM state is associated with an unusual degree of activation in the vestibular system, which in wakefulness is associated with sensorimotor balance and visual-motor integration, especially eye movements (see chapter 2).

With tactile-kinesthetic patterns there is a potential disparity between residual external perception and dream imagery. In other words, the residual impression of the actual position of the physical body almost always contrasts with the position and movements of the dreamt body image. The ubiquity of falling, flying, and dizziness in dreams and hypnagogic experience attests to a degree of vestibular deregulation, possibly enhanced by this disparity. While vestibular integration obviously affects physical balance, thanks to the study by Kerr, Condon, and McDonald we can add that it potentially affects and deregulates visual-spatial cognition as well.

4. Unmedicated catatonic schizophrenics and autistic children show little or no vestibular responsiveness (Angyal and Blackman, 1940; Ornitz and Ritvo, 1968). Perhaps not coincidentally, many acute schizophrenics show strikingly morbid body image distortions in their dreams (Carrington, 1972) and awake (Angyal, 1936), reporting unusual, emotionally upsetting changes

in the size and shape of body parts and weird internal sensations of movement, floating, or mutilation. Schilder (1942) and Angyal (1936) posited some vestibular dysfunction associated with these hallucinations, and both were able to reduplicate similar subjective sensations in normal subjects by means of kinesthetic and vestibular illusions.

5. On the other hand, we have already noted that Jayne Gackenbach (1986) found lucid dreamers to have especially good physical balance and vestibular responsiveness, along with vivid kinesthetic sensations within their dreams. Keeping in mind the striking phenomenological similarites between developed lucid dreams and meditative states, we can again cite Paul Swartz's demonstration that subjects especially prone to mystical and peak experience also show unusually good physical orientation and balance. In an unpublished study with Roc Villeneuve replicating that finding, we also found that such subjects were also highly imaginative and showed a tendency toward lucid-control dreaming. Such findings only make sense within organismic models of intelligence as rooted in the senses, imaginatively reusing and transforming perception—not the curiously "heartless" version of cognition current in artificial intelligence circles.

6. We have also mentioned the fascinating study by Tore Nielsen (1986), in which a blood pressure cuff inflated during REM sleep elicited striking dreams of falling, spinning, flying, and physical disorientation—dreams almost identical to those of subjects with actual vestibular-cerebellar dysfunction. Lachner and Levine (1979) produced an analogous phenomenon in wakefulness by stimulating the arm and leg muscles of subjects with a mechanical vibrator while they stood in the dark. Subjects reported sensations of falling, rotating, and rising—including the entire body spinning vertically around the head, if it was held in a harness. I suggest that such illusions—awake and dreaming—work by generating contradictory kinesthetic information, one set saying that the body is stationary while the other informs of muscular and tendon sensation consistent with vigorous movement.

7. Celia Green (1968) and Dierdre Barrett (1987) have called attention to the empirical association between flying dreams and lucid/prelucid dreaming. Rather than positing any simple vestibular basis, both authors hark back to suggestions by Havelock Ellis (1922) that flying dreams could result from the same double awareness of a dreamt and actual body position. We have seen that an analogous double awareness is necessary to account for lucid dreams and out-of-body experience—where the development of a receptive observational attitude is balanced against the more habitual attitude of active involvement. I suggest that flying and floating (generally experienced as intensely pleasurable) represent the integration of contrasting body positions in the form

of a "harmonious gestalt," while falling and dismemberment dreams indicate a failure to integrate this contrast between body perception and imagery. Either outcome is based on its metaphoric congruence with the relative integration/ disorganization of one's personal life and current circumstances, once the balance schemata of perception have been activated in the first place and so made available as potential metaphors.

8. While schizophrenics, with vestibular involved hallucinations, can report morbid dreams of body distortion, highly developed lucid dreamers like LaBerge (1985), Moss (1986), and Gillespie (1987) are able to maintain or intensify their lucid dreams when on the verge of wakefulness or to initiate a change of dream scene by deliberately somersaulting or spinning within the dream. Indeed, Nielsen reports that for two of his subjects who had some previous experience of lucid dreaming, the blood pressure cuff actually induced lucidity. Along these lines, dizziness induction is a cross-culturally common technique for eliciting altered states of consciousness (Siegel, 1979). Presumably the potential shaman (someone with heightened imagistic-intuitive intelligence, "with balance") can compensate for the resulting deregulation of visual-spatial structures, thereby allowing their special development and integration in the form of mythological visions, mandala patterns, and white light/cessation states—the line of abstraction potentially open to the processes of visual-spatial presentational intelligence.

Thus we come to a theory of why some dreams would show visual bizarreness, a potential for lucidity, *and* an overall clouding of verbal thought and reason. The vestibular activation and potential deregulation of the REM state would lead, through both perceptual and cognitive links, to a specific disorganization of visual-spatial structures. That would disrupt (and stimulate) visual-spatial imagination, with no specific effect at all on verbal intelligence. The average compensation for this disorganization would be the striking but typical forms of visual dream bizarreness, with their potential for metaphoric self-presentation. But especially poor balance (whether physical, emotional, or both) would be associated with an inability to compensate for vestibular deregulation and would result instead in the morbid body distortions of schizophrenic dreams or, on a more integrated and normal level, in nightmares with physical disorientation. If a subject possesses especially good balance, however, then the deregulation of visual-spatial structures in dreams will act as a challenge and lead by means of overcompensation to a special development of archetypal and/or lucid dreams. The latter, of course, show a total recovery of context (i.e., awareness that one is dreaming), a potential for pleasurable flying and physical release, and a tendency to develop into dreams of mandala patterns and white light (Hunt and McLeod, 1984; Gillespie, 1987). In short, the REM state destabilizes balance, interferes with visual-spatial cognition, and so leads either to striking disorganizations of visual-kinesthetic imagination or to its special development.[4]

Finally, this model can account for the relative clouding of the processes of verbal thought within most dreaming, if lower cortical activation and absence of environmental stimulation are not sufficient. In normal wakefulness, cognitive imagery and language are necessarily linked, and there has been some suggestion that imagery is especially sensitive to the context or overall significance of our verbal articulations (Kaufmann, 1980). For instance, if I say, "Meet me at the bank," it will be imagery processes that determine whether you think about money or fishing. So the destabilization of visual-spatial structures in dreaming will also necessarily disrupt our overall sense of gist or context. That would account for the relative clouding and confusion of verbal thought, while leaving specific verbal statements in the dream linguistically competent and relatively realistic.

It remains only to show that this special development and energization of visual-spatial imagination, like all symbolic intelligence, is necessarily dialogic in structure. In other words, this challenge and response sequence of transformation in dreams follows the developmental course of an inner conversation.

Our reflexive ability to take the role of the other operates on the model of an inner imaginative conversation. I speak here of the fundamental point made by Mead, Vygotsky, and the philosopher Wittgenstein that there is no such thing as private experience: all human experience is necessarily social—not so much socially conditioned as socially or dialogically structured even in its most interior forms. Whether we are dealing with language, imagery, or tactile-kinesthetic gesture, it comes in the form of an inner dialogue, and there is every reason to think that this self-reference gives rise to language rather than the other way around.

Any dialogue (whether external or interiorized as mind) has two phases or roles. First there is the more obvious active sending role—in which the message is sent in whatever medium. The successful organization and self-monitoring of such active messages requires a specific and functional use of "taking the role of the other" which, as Mead shows, has as its price a relative loss of our overall sense of context. Thus we can only see the full significance of what we have actually done or said later in more reflective moments (however brief). Correspondingly, there is a more receptive ("listening") role in any conversation. When we listen we often gain a broader sense of setting or context—precisely because our self-referential capacity is then not subordinated to organizing and reorganizing active communication for the sake of intelligibility. This stance of relative passivity and receptivity is especially prominent in the incubation period of creative problem solving and in altered states (including dreams). In these the "answering" material that addresses our focal or background preoccupations emerges autonomously and spontaneously into awareness as if sent by an "other"—again following the form of a conversation.

The relation between active sending and receptive receiving roles and representational and presentational symbolisms is not independent. Although arbitrary fixed codes of communication become increasingly automatized with development, their utilization is actively and consciously directed to fulfill previously developed intentions—which misled Foulkes into rejecting all semantics in dream formation because the person could not, as with language, check his or her intention against the dream. Presentational, imagistic meanings, on the other hand, are not fixed and automatized to the same degree; instead, they are polyvalent and multiple, creating intention as much as fulfilling it. Thus their meaning depends on a full and often contemplatively drawn out *experiencing* that necessarily entails Deikman's receptive mode or observing self as its predominant attitude. In aesthetics, presentational symbolism is primarily directed toward communication in publicly accessible sensory modalities, whereas in altered states of consciousness and highly developed dreaming presentational structures unfold as a more interior dialogue, yet one that is definitely open to sociocultural influence.

We can now see how it is that Deikman's receptive attitude (common to all settings that induce alterations of consciousness) takes the form of an interior imagistic dialogue: in a conversation that for whatever reason cannot be broken off, if we exaggerate the receiving or listening stance and refuse all active communication, we force the phenomenal "other" toward a steadily increasing and finally maximum degree of self-expression. In long-term meditation, for instance, as the receptive witnessing attitude progressively develops, two things happen: (1) the more inclusive and subjectively deep are the spontaneous felt meanings and the more phenomenally other their sensed source (whether conceptualized as mind, void, god, unconsciousness); and (2) the more the imagistic processes so released reflect the ordinarily masked deep structures of semantics—in the form of cross-modal synesthesias of varying degrees of abstraction.

With this background we can return to the potential long-term development of dreaming.

Sleep onset and the motor inactivity of sleep (further intensified in REM paralysis) constitute an enforced shift to a passive receptive role, with its inherent bias, revealed in the first dreams of childhood and the most vivid dreams of adulthood, toward spontaneous expression in a presentational mode. Thus, within presentational symbolism, visual-spatial bizarreness reflects the active sending role (i.e., it is the message sent), while lucidity constitutes the relatively rare reappearance within the dream itself of the receptive or listening role. The gradual stabilization of lucidity can modify dreaming consciousness much as long-term meditation modifies waking consciousness.

The reciprocal relationship between lucid dreaming and bizarreness seems to operate on the model of a long-term conversational shift back and forth between active sending and receptive roles. As pre-lucidity and lucidity first develop, we see a more direct manifestation of the visual-spatial bias of dreaming. First, pre-lucid dreaming seems to be associated with bizarre visual-spatial and confusional transformations, which, however, still remain within the categories of typical dream bizarreness (Ogilvie et al., 1982). The initial appearance of full lucidity, however, seems to temporarily suppress such active imagistic expressions, since normative lucid dreams are relatively mundane in dramatic theme. In other words, the first appearance of the receptive attitude within dreaming suppresses bizarreness—as we might expect in a role shift from sending to receiving within the same visual-kinesthetic forms of symbolic intelligence. But with maximal stabilization and development of lucid dreaming, imagistic forms come forward that are progressively more abstract and encompassing in meaning and qualitatively distinct from ordinary dream bizarreness.

If lucid dreaming, as the heightened form of presentational self-reflectiveness, leads to such inclusive forms of visual-spatial expressive metaphor, we can postulate a similarly reflexive but unconscious process underlying more ordinary levels of visual-spatial bizarreness. On the model of its highest development, then, the more typical forms of dream bizarreness, however discontinuous and fragmented they may at first appear, will also be based on "masked" levels of the same self-referential capacity—central to all symbolic intelligence. Thus dream bizarreness, if we follow out the line of its full development, should be interpreted not as extraneous disruptions of symbolic cognition but as potential metaphors whose understanding will follow the principles of aesthetics and literary interpretation. Evidence from culture pattern dreams (at least in their specifics), dreams of patients in long-term psychotherapy, problem-solving dreams, and dream groups indicates that dreams can unfold as external dialogues. We now see that the inner "private" levels of dream formation also conform to the dialogic structure of all human intelligence.

Figure 3 summarizes the relations between presentational and representa-

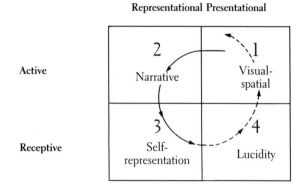

FIGURE 3: *Symbolic operations within the developmental spiral of dreaming*

tional symbolism and active and sending roles, in what could be termed the developmental spiral of dreaming. The first dreams of childhood (and the most vivid dreams of adulthood) show the presentational and active expression of "bizarre" visual-kinesthetic imagery. The verbal-representational intelligence of plot and narrative is gradually added (and so dreaming becomes increasingly dominated by the active representational intelligence of wakefulness). As Foulkes demonstrates, the self figure or self-representation (the receptive role within representational intelligence) enters last in the normal ontogenesis of dreaming—just as it does in waking cognitive development. Subsequently, for many of us, the structure of dreaming is increasingly determined (as in waking experience) by the self figure–narrative axis, with imagery filling out propositional schemata rather than the other way around. But the visual-spatial core is still revealed in archetypal-titanic forms whenever the dreaming process is sufficiently intensified.

The more infrequent appearance of the receptive role within presentational symbolism—as pre-lucid and lucid dreaming—is a direct reflection of the deep structure of all dream formation and its potential emergence into the manifest dream. This sets up a new level and balance for the dreaming process, which then allows a more direct interchange between the receptive and active roles within presentational symbolism—producing the qualitatively distinct abstract imageries of dreaming associated with long-term meditation and fully stabilized lucidity. What was hitherto the unconscious core of dream formation, and typically constrained by our normally predominant representational intelligence, now appears more and more directly in its own right, constituting the top portion of the dream diamond.

PART IV

Conclusion

"(Merrily, merrily, merrily) . . . life is but a dream."
—Traditional song, Hindu arrangement by Krishna

"Even a dream is only a dream."
—Calderon de la Barca

CHAPTER 13

Dreaming: Deconstruction and Reconstruction

What Mind Can Do in a Moment

I N beginning an overview of dreaming we could do worse than return to the nineteenth-century dream phenomenologists—who at least knew what later laboratory researchers and clinicians have forgotten, that description and classification are primary in science. DuPrel, Scherner, and Saint-Denys anticipated recent rating systems of dream bizarreness by calling attention to the positive and negative sides of dreaming. Dreaming tends always toward a delirium syndrome, but the corresponding impairment of verbal-reflective thinking allows a positive release of visual-spatial metaphor and intuition, the frames or modules of mind that are based on a relative simultaneity of expression. Carl DuPrel, like later investigators of the effects of LSD and related "mind-manifesting" drugs, stressed that dreaming is never the direct *cause* of its special "exaltations" of memory, metaphor, intuition, or discovery but instead offers an occasion or catalyst for their release. Saint-Denys suggested that what we have called the clouding of dream consciousness mitigates against forms of cognition that require sustained attention, effort, and direction—a point best expressed by Charles Rycroft in the preface of his own book: "Books, unlike dreams, do not write themselves" (p. vii).

Dreams show us what the mind can do in relative immediacy and simultaneity (thus tending toward the presentational and imagistic), and/or they show us what has already been primed for potential synthesis within a single, relatively autonomous frame of symbolic intelligence (as in scientific and artistic discoveries emerging from dreams). Saint-Denys summarizes as follows:

> If it is a matter of conceiving the overall composition of a picture, of lending an internal ear as it were to musical inspiration, of following a series of mathematical deductions in a straight line, of proceeding by intuition or simple progression, then the mind may sometimes function better in sleep than it can in the waking state. But when matters require the simultaneous exercise of a healthy critical faculty, of controlled inspiration and well considered judgment, I think the situation is entirely different.
>
> . . . In a sleeping man, concentration of the attention is sometimes difficult, the world becomes feeble and erroneous judgments are made, this is compensated by the fact that imagination, memory and sensitivity are enormously expanded. As a result, if the dreaming state does not enable us to maintain the intellectual balance that is essential for the accomplishment of any rational working of the mind, it can at least open horizons.   (Saint-Denys, 1867, pp. 90, 164)

All that is relatively simultaneous in symbolic intelligence—ultimately tending towards visual-spatial patterns, however variously directed—is available in dreams, most especially as the dreaming process intensifies. Correspondingly, all that is sequential and sustained, the judgmental, the logical-intellectual, is slowed and derailed. Dreaming is sensory and immediate. It exemplifies a presentational intelligence, in which symbolic operations appear directly within the media of expression, rather than the special intentionality of representational symbolism.

More specifically, dreaming exteriorizes the processes of cross-modal synesthetic translation and mutual reorganization that may constitute the core of all symbolic intelligence. We can see this within the multiple dream types, most of which have a predominant modality of expression with indications that this surface array is based on underlying interactions or fusions with the patterns of other modalities. Two extremes of cross-modal synesthesia are the most striking—the first characteristic of dreaming that is relatively mundane and true to daily life and the second of dreaming at its most vivid, intensified, and immediate. In the first instance we find visual-spatial imagery more or less constrained by the narrative-propositional processes that Ricoeur termed *emplotment*. What is seen and felt fulfills the narrative structure of the dream. Even the sudden visual-spatial intrusions that may initially seem unrelated to previous narrative sequence will often express creative transformations of underlying issues within the dream story. Such visual intrusions ("hallucinations of content") may be direct manifestations of visual metaphoric thinking, secondary translations of verbal metonymy and assonance, or expressions of somatic-kinesthetic states and metaphors. More generally, however, the realistic core of these dreams, at the base of our dream diamond, operates on the Pylyshyn and Foulkes model and reflects the left hemisphere predominance of ordinary wakefulness.

The tendency in normative dreaming for imagery (mnemic or imaginative) and perceptual schemata to fuse and function interchangeably introduces a characteristic vulnerability into the dream world that is absent in waking. When we are awake our ability to translate verbal and kinesthetic-technological concepts into changes in the perceived external world is limited by the necessity of planning and successive organization. In dreaming, however, the visual dream surrounding offers little or no resistance to reflective thought. Were that the case within wakefulness, we would have just the magical transformations described by lucid-control dreamers. Unsought visual transformations would seriously impair our capacity for conceptual analysis and reflective thought—since we must try to make sense of a world that can reorganize itself anew at any moment.

On the other hand, at the point of maximal intensification of dreaming, which has culturally and historically rendered the dream of religious, philosophical, and aesthetic significance, we see processes of dream formation that subordinate narrative-propositional thought to cross-modal translations between visual and tactile-kinesthetic patterns. Possibly mediated in part by an intensified vestibular activation in REM sleep, the dialogic interchange within visual-kinesthetic translations produces archetypal-titanic dreams, many nightmares, and the full development of lucidity—as well as the earliest dreams of childhood. These same processes are seen in more fragmentary form in the transformations of sleep onset. Here visual-spatial metaphoric intelligence comes forward in its own right, released from its normal subordination as the physiognomic and imagery aspects of language use. These processes of dream formation are directly manifested in major altered states of consciousness and indirectly in the aesthetics of visual-spatial forms. Geometric-mandala and white light synesthesias in these states, with their powerful sense of instantaneous and total significance, manifest the deepest processes of felt meaning ordinarily subordinated to pragmatic intelligence.

If, as Foulkes maintains, language is part of the deep structure of normative dreaming, then the relatively simultaneous visual-kinesthetic fusions mediating felt meaning are, in turn, the deep structures of all representational (left hemisphere) symbolic intelligence. Presentational and representational processes are interdependent and reciprocally related. The cross-modal fusions that are the human symbolic capacity accordingly have their maximal sequential expression in language and logical thought and their maximal simultaneous expression in these fundamental imageries. In everyday waking intelligence both function together, with a bias toward sequential propositional organization. In the more powerful dreams, on the other hand, processes of semantic deep structure become visible that make dream studies of far greater use to a true cognitive psychology than current cognitive science has so far been to dream psychology.

Dreaming and a Synesthetic Model of Consciousness

In the midst of a postmodern rejection of all conceptual absolutes, dreams become a natural focus for cognitive psychology. Their polysemy and multiplicity deny any single fixed interpretive meaning or underlying structure. On the other hand, as compelling personal narratives and emotionally powerful metaphors, dreams insist on some attempted understanding. Inherently we experience them as meanings.

Although we may rightly have lost confidence in fixed and final dream meanings (Freud) and in Foulkes's similarly monolithic version of dream formation, a still emerging psychology of the multiplicity of human cognition may, if it cannot address the why, at least outline the what and how of dreaming.

Any cognitive psychology of dreaming will search for cognitive operations manifest within the very fabric of some (if not all) dreams and for indirect reflections of symbolic intelligence within dream formation. On the one hand, Foulkes, Antrobus, and others attempt the assimilation of dream psychology to current cognitive science, with its almost exclusive concentration on the structures of language and semantic memory—all that is amenable to that artificial intelligence that pictures the human mind in its own image, as an engine for computations. These are the dream psychologies of the "head." On the other hand, the diverse phenomena of dreaming seem more congruent with organismic-holistic approaches to symbolic cognition. In this tradition, symbolic intelligence, with its reflexive capacity to take the role of the other, is understood as emerging from the cross-translation and recombination of perceptual patterns. Language is then not the source, but one (albeit critical) manifestation of the cross-modal capacity. The older but still developing organismic tradition challenges the artificialities and exclusive rationalism of current cognitive science and seeks instead to reclaim for science the lost "heart" of human cognition. On the first order of description, cognitive processes are "sentient," not computational.

Whatever else happens during dream formation, dreaming is a "becoming conscious." It is a lived experience, potentially full of an immediately sensed felt meaning. Thus the most direct clues to dreaming as a cognitive process will come from whatever we can conclude about consciousness as a self-referential, synthesizing function. Current experimental approaches to this problem turn out to undercut "head psychology" and unwittingly reestablish historical connections to earlier models of imagery, metaphor, and imagination as an "intelligence of the heart." The multiplicity and intensification of dreaming manifests cognitive processes that are ordinarily masked within the pragmatically directed functions of human consciousness.

In recent years cognitive psychologists like Natsoulas (1981), Marcel (1983), and Yates (1985) have advanced experimental evidence showing that consciousness is more than just an outward expression of nonconscious modular computations—that the "beam of light" metaphor so central to both Freud and currently dominant AI perspectives is deeply misleading. Rather, consciousness (i.e., the self-referential consciousness of human beings) *does* something. Each moment of consciousness is a synthesis, in terms of the immediate task at hand, of all simultaneously operating frames—each automatically elaborating the patterns of language, imagery, and movement. All nonconscious modules or frames are automatically and simultaneously developed on all possible levels of representation and each moment or pulse of consciousness is their creative synthesis.

Marcel's research with tachistoscopic word recognition has shown that consciousness begins from the highest level of potential processing. It is "top down." Thus, subjects can successfully guess which of two words was subliminally flashed more quickly than they can identify letters in the same words. Still more time is required to be certain that a word was actually flashed. Heinz Werner (1963) demonstrated a similar effect, within the more organismic-phenomenal tradition, when he showed that subjects could sense imagistic and metaphoric aspects of tachistoscopically flashed words before they could identify the word itself. This implies that awareness—especially when it is maximally passive and receptive as in Marcel's and Werner's experimental situations—synthesizes wholes before parts. The most complex level of processing is available to consciousness first, before its demonstrated subcomponents. Even though words are made up of letters, our awareness of the former precedes the latter.

Yates builds on Marcel's findings in demonstrating that these moments of synthesis are *amodal*—I would call them cross-modal fusions. In other words it takes longer and is harder for subjects to become aware of the sensory modality of presented information than to become aware of its semantic meaning. Seeing an event or hearing it described lead to the same knowledge, but subjects cannot accurately recall its initial medium. Along these lines Yates cites evidence showing the unconscious importance of lip reading in normal speech perception. Awareness does not "contain" separate visual, verbal, and kinesthetic components. Rather these flow together as the felt unity of each moment of consciousness.

I have suggested here and elsewhere (1982, 1984, 1985a, b, 1986a) that synesthesias and the various cross-modal translations underlying distinct forms of dreaming show this normally masked "inner" side of the synthesizing function of consciousness. Mind is a complex synesthesia. Language reflects one such patterning, in which auditory-motor fusions are predominant and imagery subordinated; visual metaphor and physiognomy represent another, based on visual-kinesthetic fusions and a relative subordination of language. Geschwind and Luria approach this same synthesizing activity of symbolic intelligence from a neurological perspective—with tertiary areas of the brain fusing and intertranslating patterns from the modular association areas of the separate senses. Of course, fixed versions of cross-modal translations—like simple language use and arithmetic—can become increasingly automatized and so can function independently of moments of conscious synthesis, without the feeling of significance or sense of meaning necesary for the open-ended and novel aspects of most human situations.

This model of human symbolic consciousness as complex synesthesia explains and reconciles the major antitheses of both cognition and cognitive theories. First, the flowing together of the distinct patterns of sensory modalities can account for the self-reference and dialogic structure of mind. The first manifestations of dialogue in infancy rest on such visual-kinesthetic translations, since the infant's mirroring of the mother's facial expressions is accomplished without any idea of the visual appearance of the infant's face, requiring only its tactile-kinesthetic feel. Second, this approach accounts for the novelty and recombinatory creativity of human cognition, for, as psychologists have long insisted, the different sensory modalities are each organized around unique and incommensurable qualities. Vision, audition, and kinesthesis do not go together in any one way, or even perhaps in any finite set of ways. Rather their intertranslations must continuously modify each other, generating novelty as they flow together and fuse on the multiple levels allowed by their differentiated qualities and stages of microgenesis. Third, the model helps to reconcile traditional rationalist versus empiricist divisions in cognitive psychology. The flowing together of the senses would create its own emergent and "a priori" categories of space/time, since each sensory modality has its characteristic ratio of simultaneity and sequentiality. Indeed, this is a naturalistic version of Pribram's holographic brain, since any situation is simultaneously "taken" from the perspective of different modalities and their different levels of articulation, creating a sort of cross-modal hologram. On the other hand, thought and world are not riven asunder by this internal structuring, since not only are the senses patterned in terms of the ecological array but the fundamental structures of the separate senses are based on the same geometric form constants that constitute the basic structures of nature, endlessly reappearing on astronomic, microscopic, and phenomenal levels (Stevens, 1974).

Equally important to the understanding of this synesthetic model of "becoming conscious," and its illustration in intensified dreaming and related states of consciousness, are its historical antecedents. This history offers the major alternative to current AI models through its insistence that the human symbolic capacity ultimately emerges out of and rests on the senses—in sentience, not computation. This cognitive psychology of consciousness was anticipated in Greek and Roman notions of a sixth or inner sense and revived and redirected in the romantic preoccupations of the eighteenth and nineteenth centuries with imagination, empathy, metaphor, aesthetics, and dreams. It also implicitly informed Freud's concept of a dissociated or repressed unconscious. In other words, something rather like the present model has been implicit or explicit in all the more phenomenological and/or organismic traditions addressing the nature of mind. Current cognitive science, it seems, lacks not only heart but also memory.

The roots of "becoming conscious" as cross-modal synthesis rest in Aristotle's notion of a *sensus communis* (*coeno-aesthesis*) or "inner sense." It was located, he thought, in the "heart," and it was responsible for the multiple integration of the senses, self-consciousness, imagery, memory, *and* dreaming! Of course for Aristotle, as for most traditional peoples, the seat of intelligence and feeling was the heart—the brain being conceived by Aristotle as an organ for cooling the blood as it flowed into and out of the heart, carrying impressions from and to the senses. Thus the ostensible gap in physiology between Aristotle and Geschwind is easily bridged, since both describe the same functioning and capacities, which Geschwind locates, presumably more accurately, in the neocortex.

On the other hand, the gap between Aristotle's understanding of the sensus communis and the present approach to cross-modal fusions as the basis of all symbolic frames is less readily bridged. For Aristotle, reason (*nous*) is an autonomous and transcendent faculty. It only touches the body at the heart and the price it pays for this necessary commerce (embodiment) is that its phenomenal expressions always require imagery. While Plato also saw reason as separate from the senses, it was the very limitations of reason that led to his use of metaphor and mythological image for matters that exceeded the formative capacity of reason. For Aristotle, on the contrary, all the psychological functions of the sensus communis are *not* criterial for human intelligence, as the later romantics and Geschwind would hold, but instead, they are common to lower animals as well. It would take a major reversal of value, associated with the romantic elevation of imagination over reason and culminating in much of nineteenth-century dream psychology, to transform Aristotle's sensus communis into a model of human symbolic consciousness.

Nonetheless, from a contemporary perspective, Aristotle's sensus communis includes the basic criteria of a symbolic intelligence more or less unique to human beings. For Aristotle the flowing together of the senses allowed self-awareness, since no single modality could otherwise be conscious of itself. Imagination and memory are similarly affections of the sensus communis, because they modify and reform outward impressions as these are conveyed inward by the blood and are fused with previous impressions within the heart. In dreaming, "internal movements" in the blood and based on impressions of the previous day sink into the heart during sleep. Periodic disturbances and activations within the heart during the night (now called phasic phenomena and localized in the brain stem and cortex) reactivate the curious amalgams of these impressions, which then rise to the periphery of the body as the novelties of dreaming. Note, however, that this view of dreaming, which so influenced nineteenth-century dream theories, implies that dreaming will spontaneously reorganize the past—producing just those creative qualities of dreaming that we suggested must be criteria for human dreaming alone.

The Roman tradition of sensus communis as a common or sixth sense, later taken up by Aquinas, added to Aristotle's synthesis of the senses something like our notion of common sense as intuition—implying that ordinary intuition and judgment were also a consequence of cross-modal integration. However, it was only the "organic associationists" who recognized that the flowing together of the senses was a creative synthesis constituting the core of mind and illustrated most directly in intuition, empathy, metaphor, and imaginative dreaming. For Addison, in the early 1700s, and Hazlitt, about a hundred years later (Engell, 1981), the multiple intertranslations of the senses meant that each was modified by the other, creating a total *impression* that was more than the sum of its parts. This was the "inner sense," or in Gendlin's modern terminology, felt meaning, which generated empathy, intuition, and multi-modal aesthetic expression. Thus Aristotle's lower mentality had become the essential defining attribute of the human mind—and we arrive again at the current contrast between the organismic cognitive psychology of Geschwind, Arnheim, and Werner and

Kaplan and the propositional/computational models of Pylyshyn, artificial intelligence, and Foulkes on dreams.

Actually, our predominant computational/neurological paradigm is itself indirectly derived (displaced?) from a fragmented and reductive reading of the sensus communis. The qualities that Aristotle terms "common sensibles" (common to the different senses) turn up again as Locke's and Galileo's primary qualities—motion, mass, quantity, and number. But with the dawn of scientific realism it was only these attributes that were amenable to scientific representation, not the "merely subjective" qualities of the different senses. The next step was inward and toward the brain, conceived as computational mechanism. Locke's primary qualities became features of nervous conduction, from which "experience" now had to be subjectively reassembled in the central nervous system. Part of the reason neurological explanations seem so fundamental and obvious to us may be that they enshrine a mechanized and digital version of an inner sense that fuses the separate perceptual modalities into a common language—once of "significance," now of "energy" and "matter."

It remains only to note that for Freud (1915) becoming conscious was a *hypercathexis* (fusion) of motor, visual, and verbal *cathexes*. Repression was based first on the withdrawal of the verbal cathexis from visual-kinesthetic patterns in the unconscious and finally on the separation of visual and motor energies—the former preserved in affectless stasis and the latter discharged directly as "symptomatic movements" and "internal affective discharge." Among psychoanalysts, only W. R. Bion has seen the direct connection between Freud's incipient cognitive psychology and the Greek-Roman sensus communis.

Eugene Gendlin's method of "focusing" to develop inchoate and implicit felt meanings literally reverses the sequence of repression posited by Freud. The individual starts by attuning to a body "sense" of contentless tension, at most accompanied by a disquieting but ineffable mood; then he or she allows an expressive presentational image to emerge as its more explicit and potential translation. That "fit" is tested by asking a series of verbal questions of this generally visual-kinesthetic felt meaning (e.g., "what does this sense want? What is so bad (or good) about it?"). This evocation of imagery and questioning is pursued until a "felt shift" occurs and, finally articulated, the original disquieting body sense disappears. Thus the client does from within and for him- or herself what the therapist's mirroring of unconscious gesture would do in making one conscious of incipient emotional expressions—a cross-modal translation from without. Likewise, the most intense and vivid forms of dreaming seem to externalize just these kinesthetic-visual fusions as powerful meta-phors for life situations.

The most appropriate mythological amplification of this model of syn-esthetic consciousness and its expression in the most vivid dream forms is not really James Hillman's (1979) descent into the Greek underworld of affectless shades. Such a metaphor applies best to the clouded delirium of less vivid, relatively mundane dreaming. The classical myth that best amplifies the more striking manifestations of dreaming is that of the Egyptian god Osiris. Osiris is dismembered by his brother Set, who had torn himself directly out of the womb before natural birth. Set exemplifies the control and power and linear sequentiality of waking cognitive functions—of all that is most readily mod-eled in artificial intelligence. Osiris is fertility and creativity. He was the bearer of culture for the Egyptians and finally the god of their underworld of eternal resurrection. His dismembered and scattered body is reassembled and revived by his sister, Isis, bringing fertility and renewal to the night world of creativity and imagination. Mind without the creative synthesis of cross-modal consciousness is like the dismembered Osiris, its separate modules and frames processing autonomously and in isolation. Vivid dreaming and related states release the sense of felt significance that is always the mark of creative insight (and living), precisely by means of the integration and flowing together of the separate limbs of the senses.

These deeply estranged brothers of linear sequentiality and intuitive imme-diacy still contend within modern cognitive psychology. However, whenever dreaming comes into its own in its maximally vivid and intensified forms, surely it is of Osiris and not of Set, since in these dream forms imagery and intuition predominate over syntax and plot. Albeit rare, these forms have been most valued by individuals and societies.

Dreaming as Ur-Phenomenon

We have seen the central role dream experience and dream interpretation, and their reflexive interactions, play in the maintenance and even creation of cultural forms in primitive societies. It has also been widely suggested that dreaming may be an autochthonous source for certain capacities basic to hu-man nature itself. Dreaming may indeed be an Ur-form for some very funda-mental cognitive capacities, in particular the narrative story as sequential configuration fusing concordance and discordance, the transformation of one situation into an expression or metaphor for another, and the metaphysical questioning of the reality of our lives—the idea, known to all peoples in all times, that in some basic sense life *is* like a dream.

The Organization of Lived Experience into Stories

The story form is fundamental to human experience, as Ricoeur, Langer, and Jones have rightly stated. All experience is and must be narratable as plot and drama, if it is to hold our interest. Even the ineffable states of mysticism or more common "secular" forms of peak or ecstatic experience are equally characterized by this special urge for articulation. They soon become tales and their significance is finally rendered as allegories of cosmic creation and destruction.

Dreams are narratives, but only the more developed forms of dreaming move toward the true criteria of story as worked out by Ricoeur and Burke, with full articulations of setting, character, agency, and act (Burke) and the preemptory introduction and dramatic resolution of discordance (Ricoeur). Were there no such things as myths, allegories, and fairytales, the simple rendition of one's dreams, from childhood on, would generate these forms.

There is an even more fundamental sense in which dreaming may be an Ur-source for the form of life we term story. Ricoeur stresses two fundamental and equally primordial forms of story—history and fiction. All fundamental attributes are the same in each, except that of empirical truth value. Historical tales (personal or collective) are asserted to have "really" happened in the same way that the ongoing life of the listener is also real, while fiction does not make such an assertion. Either the fictive quality is overt as in novels and fairytales, or, as in the various myths of world origin, the events recounted are held to have occurred in a qualitatively different space and time—a primal or sacred era.

Note however that dreams directly and immediately embody the attributes of both history and fictional narrative. The dream you recount on awakening "really happened" in your immediate past while asleep, and you tell it as such. Yet at the same time, at least for the forms of dreaming that are *interesting*, the dream events in fact did not happen at all—they did not occur within one's actual life history; they are necessarily fictive and fantastic. Dreams are equally and at once history and fiction—suggesting that both story forms could have emerged out of telling dreams.

The Framing of Experience as Metaphor

It is not just not that dreams generate powerful metaphors from and for the dilemmas of waking life. Metaphor is the framing or selection of one situation (in whole or part) as a medium for understanding a second situation. This was the process Wittgenstein termed *seeing as*—we see one situation or process *in terms of* another. For Wittgenstein (especially in *On Certainty*), a source of the curious openness of human existence is that no one episode or phenomenon is necessarily primary with respect to any other—anything can be framed as a lens through which to see anything else. So pervasive is this "seeing as" structure that we may not really ever see anything inherently or in itself—but only through comparison with something else. Contrary to popular assumption, we do not know more about the situation we use as a lens or metaphor than about its referent. Metaphor is the illustration of something unknown, *not* by something known, but by something treated "as if" it were known or known "well enough." When I say, "Language is a complex synesthesia," that does not mean I understand more fully the nature and source of synesthesias than of language. Rather I take the one as known in order to cast light on the other, which in this particular context alone seems more problematic. A linguist might say instead, "Synesthesia is a language," making the opposite assumption about what is closed and what open and unknown. Ultimately metaphor and referent are equally open and problematic, but we render one subservient to what we acknowledge as our problem or focus.

Any human situation, then, can be framed or taken as a metaphor for some other situation. But the closer we are to the direct living of a situation, the harder it is to turn around on and see it as a metaphor for something else. Usually only time allows the difficult and painful situations of the past to be "seen through" and used as exemplars of more general life issues. What we were once grateful to have simply survived eventually begins to serve as a model that illuminates and orders the teeming present—also a goal of psychotherapy. This brings us to dreams as an Ur-source of metaphor, for the dream comes to us already separated from ongoing life experience by the conditions of sleep, already potentially framed as a possible metaphor. It is of course both problematic in its own right (so we use life situations as a lens to make sense of our dreams) and an abstracted pattern that exemplifies and exaggerates issues of our waking lives. But simply waking up begins the distancing from the dream episode that is so difficult to achieve from waking experience. The dream thus moves immediately from ongoing experience to "frame," precisely the initial and difficult move in any "seeing as."

It is central for a cognitive psychology of dreams that the fantastic transformations of experience in dreams show metaphoric activity *within* dream formation. But even in the absence of any more specific and precise disassembling of past life, the dream as a whole presents itself as instant metaphor. As with story, if there were no metaphors, dreaming could invent them anew. Is it perhaps true that in human prehistory dreaming generated them in the first place?

The Questioning of Reality as Illusion

Dreams, which seem real while they continue, ephemerally disappear into illusion as we awaken. Our typical inability to recognize a dream as a dream until it is over has been taken in all places and times as a primary metaphor for life itself. In our waking lives do we not just as thoroughly lose ourselves within our ongoing involvements, often taking them far too seriously and forgetting the ephemerality of life and its inevitable end? Indeed, the meditative "waking up" to this more inclusive context of human life is analogous in every way to the lucid realization that one is dreaming. The metaphor of waking up has been used by both the Eastern meditative traditions and Western philosophy to separate reality from illusion and/or to emphasize the relativity of all experience. It appears that the universal experience of awakening from an ostensibly real dream inherently *affords*—in Gibson's ecological sense—concerns about the ephemerality of life, its brief flash in the midst of something far more inclusive, and the uneasy question of what an "awakening" into that could be.

Given the primacy of the "life as dream" metaphor, we must also note the fundamental difference in the way it has developed in Eastern and Western cultural traditions. As Wendy O'Flaherty points out in her important work *Dreams, Illusions, and Other Realities* (1984), Eastern stories and myths about dreams being mistaken for reality and vice versa stress that the full realization that life is a dream constitutes liberation—a release from clinging to the events of daily life and from the endless cycle of rebirth. The adept is freed when long-term meditative practice renders the experience of waking reality as ephemeral as a dream. In the West, however, at least since the positivism and rationalism of Descartes, seeing life as a dream has been regarded as a metaphysical horror to be refuted at all costs. The curse of pointlessness with no escape, it stands in marked contrast to our attempts, religious and secular, to look ahead or back to a time that will be or was truly real, or at least "better." In clinical psychoanalysis and psychiatry the feeling that one's waking experience is dreamlike, or felt uncertainty about whether one is dreaming or awake, is regarded as a schizoid loss of reality—a symptom of withdrawal and isolation on a natural continuum with schizophrenia, a privatized version of despair.

Whereas it is schizoid to question reality and find it dreamlike in the modern West, in the Eastern tradition it is "deluded" not to question reality. To sense one's daily life as ephemeral, like a mirage or dream, is the beginning of meditative realization. If Angyal (1965) is correct about the "universal ambiguity" of human experience, then no single or specific attitude or feeling is in itself pathological or healthy. Rather, its status as symptom or realization is determined by the overall context of optimism or despair and withdrawal. Given the inherency of "life as dream," it seems especially unlikely that in itself it could be sick or healthy. It is simply always there as a potentially and powerfully felt insight, whether that entraps or releases, whether it confirms one's innermost despair or brings relief and laughter. Certainly it seems plausible that the basic dimensions of metaphysical and spiritual thought could have been cross-culturally generated by the contemplation of dreaming and its complex relations to waking.

Dreams and Primary School Education in the Humanities and Social Sciences

Liam Hudson (1985) has questioned whether dreaming will survive in a technological, utilitarian world society based on ever increasing materialism and "success." If dreaming becomes more and more mundane and even subjectively ceases in the lives of many modern adults, then could this same fate not become general—as a postmodern but not post-money mentality works its way pervasively through people's lives. Perhaps. Yet given the correlations between vivid dreaming and aesthetic ability, creative imagination, and intuition, and the Ur-relations between dreaming and literature, metaphor, and metaphysical thought, it seems more likely that certain individuals will continue to develop the full multiplicity of dreaming relatively independent of social sanction. Although modern tribespeople complain to anthropologists that there are no more "big" dreams, we have seen that a few modern secular subjects continue to report dreams meeting these criteria.

There is an alternative possibility for the fate of dreaming in a modern mass society. While early education for the symbolic frames that "do" and "control"—reading, writing, arithmetic—is excellent, no comparable emphasis exists for the abilities and sensitivities that feed into history, literature, the arts, and spirituality. Indeed, it is commonly held that systematic early education in these more aesthetic-expressive fields is impossible and that such development will take care of itself in the especially gifted anyway—despite continuing evidence of a separation between "two cultures" and their chronic imbalance.

Given the close relation between dreaming and creative imagination and the centrality of dreamtelling in primitive cultures, it seems to me that there is an equally fundamental way to teach the roots of aesthetics, literature, and philosophy to very young children. The bases of these humanistic disciplines would be truly and soundly laid were elementary teachers to encourage children to tell their dreams, to compare them with those of other children and other possibilities of dreaming, and to listen to the dreams of teachers and parents. I have been especially struck, as have many others, by the enthusiasm and vigor with which children take up such opportunities. Perhaps that is not an accident.

Certainly it would be very surprising if we were equally "civilized" in all aspects of potential human symbolic capacity and even more surprising if "primitives" were just exactly that in all things. As we move so gradually toward a single world civilization whose incipient values often inspire more fear than hope, if our aim is not merely dominance but some form of pluralism within the possibilities of the human mind, then listening to and encouraging the dreams of young children might prove a simple and foundational step in that direction. Might be good for adults too.

APPENDIX

Variations across Multiple Groups in Forms of Dreaming

T HE following table, depicting percentages of different perceptual, cognitive, and emotive transformations occurring in dreams, is discussed periodically throughout the text. It represents several years of research with my own content analysis system for the varieties of dream bizarreness, derived from a more extensive range of categories pertaining to the full range of altered states of consciousness (see Hunt et al., 1982). Samples included here, for purposes of mutual comparison, are home diary recall, laboratory REM reports, and self-selected "most fantastic" and "most realistic" (true to daily life) dreams, all from university undergraduates, along with the dreams of Freud (as reported in his *Interpretation of Dreams*) and those of Jung (as reported in his autobiography *Memories, Dreams, Reflections*), and the lucid and nonlucid dreams of long-term meditators (average practice 5.1 years).

While normative home and laboratory dreaming is not as bizarre and/or transformed from everyday experience as one might expect from the earlier clinical literature, nonetheless the average undergraduate ranges from his or her normative style of dreaming toward quite fantastic and hallucinatory variations. Correspondingly, even the most mundane dreams show some degree of clouding or confusion of consciousness. Although Freud's dreams are more clouded and fragmented than average, it is only the dreams of Jung and the lucid dreams of the meditators that approach or occasionally exceed the "most fantastic" of the undergraduate dreams in terms of the more hallucinatory/ psychedelic/mythological categories. (High levels of clouding/confusion in meditators' dreams reflect the occurrence of hitherto infrequent subtypes of change in memory and thinking which in hindsight should have been allotted separate categories.)

While it is true that such comparisons cannot be controlled for age and intelligence, nonetheless, since educational background is somewhat compara- ble (university graduates) and dream bizarreness has not been demonstrated to increase with age, the most plausible interpretation of these variations is that they reflect differences in imaginative transformation within dream formation.

Table 1: Categories of Dream Bizarreness and Transformation: Percentage of dreams with one or more (and two or more) anomalies

Scoring categories	Normative home recall (N = 479) 47 subjects		Lab recall (N = 166) 29 subjects		Most fantastic (N = 35) 35 subjects		Most realistic (N = 35) 35 subjects		Freud's (N = 32)		Jung's (N = 34)		Dreams of meditators Lucid (N = 71) 18		Dreams of meditators Nonlucid (N = 157) subjects	
	1	2+	1	2+	1	2+	1	2+	1	2+	1	2+	1	2+	1	2+
Hallucination: Perceptual transformations:																
Visual																
Form[a]	13%	2%	11%	2%	43%	14%	6%	3%	16%	0%	24%	9%	38%	17%	21%	6%
Content 1[b]	26	7	23	5	43	3	6	0	16	3	15	3	25	4	25	6
Content 2	14	1	19	2	34	11	3	0	38	9	53	12	14	3	21	3
Content 3	27	8	16	5	54	26	0	0	13	3	32	12	38	18	56	28
1,2,3 combined	47	—	44	—	86	—	9	—	47	—	80	—	49	—	72	—
Somatic																
Form	4	0	1	0	9	0	0	—	3	0	0	—	20	7	4	1
Combined content	10	—	5	—	43	—	0	—	6	—	9	—	17	—	30	—
Auditory																
Content and form	14	—	4	—	26	—	6	—	13	—	32	—	35	—	32	—

223

Table 1: (Cont.)

Scoring categories	Normative home recall (N = 479) 47 subjects		Lab recall (N = 166) 29 subjects		Most fantastic (N = 35) 35 subjects		Most realistic (N = 35) 35 subjects		Freud's (N = 32)		Jung's (N = 34)		Dreams of meditators			
													Lucid (N = 71) 18		Nonlucid (N = 157) subjects	
	1	2+	1	2+	1	2+	1	2+	1	2+	1	2+	1	2+	1	2+
Clouding/confusion:																
Abrupt change in scene, gaps	20	6	20	5	51	14	11	0	25	3	18	3	28	7	43	18
Confusion in thought[c]	41	17	42	20	54	31	29	11	50	38	35	9	61	28	63	25
Memory within[d]	15	1	12	1	29	9	11	3	19	0	12	3	44	6	33	11
Memory about[e]	30	4	55	22	31	14	11	0	53	25	9	0	17	1	40	5
General:																
Uncanny emotion	4	0	8	1	17	0	3	0	3	0	38	0	9	0	4	0
Mythic/overinclusive thought	3	0	5	1	26	6	0	0	9	0	38	6	14	6	8	1
Bizarre personification[f]	4	0	4	0	34	9	0	0	6	3	53	9	18	0	8	0
Observational attitude	10	0	8	0	20	3	3	0	22	0	15	0	24	0	23	0

[a]Psychedelic transformations of formal properties of vision (Kliver).
[b]Content 1, 2, and 3 represent degrees of unlikeliness in objects perceived, without formal distortion.
[c]Disorganization and confusion in reasoning, irrational insights.
[d]Anomaly of memory within the dream.
[e]Difficulties in detailed recall after awakening.
[f]Uncannily fascinating or terrifying others, strange creatures, animism.

Notes

1 DREAM STUDIES AND THE FUNDAMENTAL QUESTION OF MEANING

1. Robert Haskell (1986) has rightly asked why verbal parapraxes might not involve *both* syntax and semantics.

2. An example of such interpersonal overlap in dreaming might be in order.

In the midst of a long dream, I returned to my parked car only to see a parking ticket on the windshield. Further inspection showed it to be a notice that the police had returned to me a small antique silver case with the name *Mansur* engraved on it—since I was the nearest living relative to his family. (Indeed, I had an ancestor James Mansur who was a soldier in the Civil War, but I almost never think of the Mansurs in connection with the Hunts, in contrast with the several other families who are also part of my ancestry.)

At approximately the same time and in the same bed, my fiancée, in the midst of a dream of herself and her family preparing a holiday meal, suddenly noticed one of her elementary students, Chris Manzer, who stood in the kitchen and berated her. (As in my dream, her student intruded into the overall dream and there was no specific day residue basis for his presence.) Note that there is nothing here that forces us to resort to notions of telepathy. Either she or I could have said the name while sleeping, triggering the intrusive dream element in the other. What it does show is the *potentiality* for a social intertwining in dreams that renders them anything but private.

2 FURTHER ANTINOMIES OF DREAMS, DREAMING, AND DREAM RESEARCH

1. The lack of causal specifity in REM psychology is further illustrated in the fate of research on REM deprivation. Inspired by the safety-valve hypothesis of dreaming as a nightly "madness" protecting us from hallucinations during the day (common to both Freud and Jung), early research on the enforced deprivation of REM sleep seemed to show that deprivation produced a dysfunctional psychological condition and a postdeprivation rebound in the amount of REM sleep. In animals, more radical chemical and behavioral methods of prohibiting REM sleep produce hypersexual behavior in cats and significantly lower thresholds to electrically induced seizures (Cohen, 1979; Ellman et al., 1978). But almost all recent studies of REM deprivation in human beings find only small cognitive and emotional effects—certainly not the hallucinatory syndrome reported (and expected) in the first studies. It is true, however, that humans deprived of REM sleep at levels comparable to those of animal studies—chronic abusers of alcohol, barbiturates, and heroin—do, on withdrawal, experience a massive REM rebound effect. At its extreme, it is associated with especially vivid, nightmarish dreaming and waking hallucinations typical of delirium (delirium tremens or DTs). However, these substances have effects far more general than REM suppression. They are all massive inhibitors, depressing cortical and automatic activation of which the REM period is but one homeostatically regulated form. Indeed, these arousal rebounds seem to be far more general and powerful than that associated with the REM rebound effect—leading to a massively overactivated state of arousal equally distinct from normal sleeping, dreaming, and waking. Thus any specific link between REM deprivation per se and hallucinatory syndromes must be questioned.

2. If fetal and neonatal maturation were the only function of the REM state, we would expect its complete disappearance after six months. The REM state appears thus to be a prime example of nature's multiple reuse of basic processes.

3. Winson (1985) suggests that monotremes and dolphins, both without REM sleep, have enlarged forebrain areas relative to the rest of the brain because they are needed for memory consolidation in the absence of REM.

4. I do not consider here more general concerns about whether psychoanalysis is a "science" (Grunbaum 1986), since we have already seen the complexity of that issue in light of the debates over the nature of the human sciences. Certainly skepticism about the predictive validity of psychoanalytic hypotheses (i.e., childhood sexual etiology for all later pathologies) does not prevent us from considering psychoanalysis as a sophisticated descriptive and classification system organizing experiences and behaviors that otherwise elude systematic study. In this sense, psychoanalysis is clearly an empirical science, although it is not necessarily fully amenable to the experimental method. The notion that psychoanalytic formulations cannot be empirically falsified is refuted by the very changes in Freud's dream model proposed on the basis of psychophysiological discovery and further psychoanalytic observations.

5. I owe this suggestion to Kate Ruzycki-Hunt.

6. George Gillespie (1987), a meticulous observer of his own unusually vivid lucid dreams, reports no difficulty in forming a visual memory image during the dream and experiencing it in the same manner as when awake—i.e., it does not obscure the dream scene or replace it as a new scene. On the other hand, Mary

Arnold-Forster (1921), whose lucid dreams seem less vivid and more centered on con-scious control, reports what Foulkes would suggest must happen—that objects deliber-atey imaged in the dream quickly become dream percepts. It is likely that processes fused at lower levels of dream intensity separate out more clearly as vividness increases.

7. Herman's conclusions might be supported by the demonstration of Rechtschaffen and Buchignani (1983) that laboratory subjects could match their recall of dream perception to photographs varying in dimensions of illumination, color satura-tion, figural clarity, and background clarity. Dreams were rated as less color-saturated and, most relevant here, having less clear backgrounds, but since the effect also corre-lated with subjective estimates of poor recall, it was impossible to determine whether the lack of background clarity produced hazy recall or poor recall was directly responsi-ble for the clarity estimates.

Similarly Herman's findings of reduced amplification in REM-state eye movements might be consistent with the claims of some experienced lucid dreamers, who can inspect and question their dreams while they are dreaming, that their dreams are without peripheral vision (Gillespie, 1984; Shields, pers. comm.). But eye movements are under more voluntary control in lucid dreaming (Tholey, 1983), and the enhanced cortical vigilance of most lucid dreams could also entail a tunnel-vision effect specific to dream lucidity and absent in ordinary dreams. And a lack of peripheral vision could be consistent either with imagery or with perception under reduced conditions. Al-though tempting, it is difficult to make inferences about ordinary dreaming from lucid dream observations since lucidity is a transformation of ordinary dreaming.

8. Foulkes's suggestion (1978, 1985) and Farah's recent confirmation (see chap. 11) of a loss of dreaming when there is neurological damage to functional imagery does not serve to separate dreaming from perception. Most experimental measures of imagery in these studies are of Galton's "imagine your breakfast table" variety rather than of the imaginal processes of creative problem solving, and so they amount to verbally mediated forms of that associative-reproductive imagery that Neisser places within the cycle of perceptual activity.

9. While this discussion rests on a widely shared view that recombinatory cogni-tion appears first in higher primates, Maier (1964) has presented evidence for the reor-ganization of prior experience in maze and direction-finding studies of rat behavior. Nonetheless, I take the recombinatory insight with and without tools, seemingly delib-erate deceptions, and incipient signing behavior of apes, along with their evolution of cortical intersensory translations, as the first evidence of a capacity for schematic re-arrangement that spontaneously permeates the natural life-world of a species.

However, if mammalian dreaming exists and if the special features of REM physiol-ogy entailed that such dreaming transform and reorganize the more typical patterns of waking, then such dreams are, in the interesting phrase of the psychoanalyst W. R. Bion (in a somewhat different context), "thoughts with no one to think them." Were that possible then dreams would be not only the origin of culture, as several have suggested, but also the first evolutionary sign of the capacity for recombinatory intelligence—awaiting "only" the evolution of means–ends structures that could gear this ability into the actual physical and social environment and so reorganize it. It would be not so much that dreaming is a form of thinking as that thinking as a potential cognitive function originates in mammalian dreaming. While logically possi-ble, such considerations surely take us beyond the limits of methodological determination. It has seemed more fruitful to sketch a middle way in which forms of consciousness (and dreaming) are inferred from behavioral capacities.

10. These differences cannot be explained solely by laboratory evidence that show a progression over the night toward more vivid and fantastic dreams and that find dreams of late night and early morning more likely to be spontaneously recalled. As we will see, the dreams of Freud and Jung, which helped to call attention to dreaming as a significant area of study, are more elaborate, vivid, aesthetically intricate, and emotionally powerful than early morning laboratory dreams (Hunt et al., 1982).

11. This supports Freud's notion that dream incorporation of external stimuli actually protects sleep.

3 PAX MEMORIA: MEMORY VERSUS IMAGINATION IN THE PSYCHOLOGY OF DREAMING

1. Koukkou and Lehmann (1983) have suggested a physiological basis for early memories in dreams. The less differentiated EEG patterns of REM and NREM sleep would be similar enough to the less developed waking EEG of childhood to provide a "state-specific" augmentation of early memories.

2. Presumably the hippocampal circuits necessary for memory consolidation would not be similarly "loaded" during wakefulness, because the orientation response would then be *specific* to the external initiating stimulus, while the dream, the endpoint of an internal activation, would raise all recently primed but nonconsolidated novel material more or less "at once."

3. There are differences between hippocampal neural activity in waking and in REM sleep—perhaps associated with both the internally driven mnemic loading of REM and various deficits of phenomenal memory while dreaming. Specifically, animal and human studies show that while areas projecting to the hippocampus are intensely activated in both REM and waking, single unit neural activity in the hippocampus itself is inhibited during REM (Halgren et al., 1978; Ravagnati et al., 1979). However, specific functional conclusions are hard to draw since this inhibition seems to be subcortically mediated and possibly part of the overall inhibition of the REM state.

4. Foulkes downplays the condensation effects common to episodic remembering and dreaming because he regards all forms of dream bizarreness as formal "errors of production" rather than as positive functions in their own right.

5. One of Foulkes's more questionable moves is to make the difficulty in remembering dreams a subspecies of the difficulty in recalling "recollections" in contrast to the content that is being recollected. He suggests that dreaming involves a recollective rather than an encoding mode—ignoring dreams whose startling impact is so eidetically encoded that they stay with one for a lifetime. His point might be better made about daydreams than dreams, which are difficult to recall in a way qualitatively different from both dreams and waking experience.

6. Of course we cannot know whether a non-self-referential, eidetically based episodic memory and/or dreaming in mature animals could be characterized by condensations and superimpositions. In principle they could be, but presumably only the development of symbolic self-reference would allow lucid dreams or the more extreme imaginative forms of bizarreness.

7. Hobson and McCarley make a significant contribution in linking such dreams

to variations within the sensory and motivational systems (such as flying dreams understood in terms of vestibular activation). However, in missing the sensory basis of metaphors and the way imagination necessarily reorganizes perceptual categories, they also miss the possible sources of such dreams in symbolic imagination. They fall victim to a sensorimotor reductionism almost as complete as the reductionism of memory theories.

8. Interestingly, Jung initially conceptualized the vivid, bizarre imagery of archetypal dreams as expressions of a *collective unconscious*, such that the fantastic ultimately had its lived origin in prehistorical and evolutionary experience. Here all novelty comes from the past, the more novel from the more distant past. We can also include here R. D. Laing's recent forays into fetal "memories" as the sources of imaginative mythological patterns. Jung gradually distanced himself from this undemonstrable mnemic hypothesis in his later writings, in favor of the notion, further developed by James Hillman, that such dreams show the striking and curiously impersonal autonomy of creative imagination.

5 THE MULTIPLICITY OF DREAMING IN ANTHROPOLOGY, THE ANCIENT WORLD, AND THE NINETEENTH CENTURY

1. Sadly, of the major contributors to this literature, only Saint-Denys (1867), DuPrel (1889), and Henri Bergson (1901) have been translated into English. The failure to translate Scherner, Maury, Hildebrandt, and Volkelt is especially damaging to any contemporary phenomenology of dream diversity. Major sources for this material in English, include, of course, Freud's encyclopedic review in chapter 1 of *The Interpretation of Dreams* (1900), chapter 5 of Ellenberger's seminal *Discovery of the Unconscious* (1970), and Havelock Ellis's *The World of Dreams* (1922).

2. Scherner's use of dreams for medical diagnosis has been formalized somewhat in recent studies by Levitan and Smith (see chapter 7). The latter's finding that seriously ill hospitalized patients who do not recover report significantly more dreams of separation (in women) and death (in men) raises the problem that dream typology poses for standard dream content analysis. At what point should we cease to rate such content as projective expressions of interpersonal relations and personality and regard them instead as the somatic-medical indicators they can also be? Scientific content analysis would seem to depend on initial decisions about dream type that have yet to be made in contemporary dream research.

3. Thus Schweder and LeVine (1975) show that Hausa children pass through much the same stages of conceptualizing their dreams that Piaget found in Western children. From their earliest sense that dreams are external and real they come to later insight into the unreal and internal psychological status of their dreams. Yet as O'Flaherty (1984) points out, this does not prevent Hausa adults from understanding certain sacred dreams as more real than ordinary wakefulness, as a special valuative decision. The progression in Hausa understanding of dreams from Piagetian stages in children to the adult reevaluation of certain dreams contradicts the notions, from Tylor to Werner (1961) and Hallpike (1979), that "primitive" people are fixated at preoperational cognitive stages.

4. Note that the importance of lucid dreaming in shamanistic traditions does not have to rely on two popular anthropological accounts now widely held to be

fictional—Kilton Stewart's Malaysian Senoi and Carlos Castaneda's realm of Toltec Sorcery (actually reminscent of the Raramuri, also of northern Mexico). It now appears (Domhoff, 1985), notwithstanding the popular workshops that teach "Senoi dreaming," that the Senoi do not teach their children these methods, neither lucidity nor the deliberate confrontation of dream monsters and so on—although, like most tribal peoples, the Senoi do distinguish between "big" dreams (artistic, shamanistic) and "little" dreams (based on personal memories and wishes). Stewart's endless enthusiasms may have led him to confuse what his informants told him with his own highly original use of guided dreaming under hypnosis with these same natives and later with Western patients in psychotherapy.

Castaneda's accounts present a greater evaluative problem. Several anthropologists have called attention to the way that his successive books become less and less "Indian." Yet the system Castaneda claims to have been taught involves the deliberate induction of lucid dreams and out-of-body experience. Indeed, many of the ostensibly real episodes he describes have a striking dreamlike quality—including passivity, loss of volition and reflective judgment, sudden explosive emotional states, amnesias and gaps in recall, hallucinatory transformations of otherwise plausible settings, and elaborate "false" memories and alternative pasts spontaneously remembered and as quickly lost again. Given Castaneda's own assertions (in an interview with Cravens, 1973) that he deliberately "dreamed" (i.e., rehearsed in his lucid-control dreams) episodes from his "fieldwork" before writing them, it seems possible that whether or not veridical fieldwork notes exist as the original source of these dreams (see DeMille's [1978] strident rejection of this possibility), the books offer phenomenologically informative accounts of potential developments of dreaming. The books become progressively more dreamlike, as would befit someone who was practicing the system described. Whether that system was taught to Castaneda by Don Juan, Don Genaro, Silvano Manuel, and others (and whether these represent an eclectic modern network of Indian and non-Indian sorcerers as Castaneda now claims) or whether the system is a composite created out of reports from the small number of contemporary anthropologists who did in fact apprentice themselves to Indian shamans, is known "for certain" only to Castaneda himself and, of course, DeMille.

Perhaps I am slightly soft on Stewart and Castaneda. They may indeed be disgracefully poor anthropologists but as psychologists their work is still of interest. Theirs would not be the first "fictions" that when actually practiced somehow managed to "work." One thinks of the immense impact of Don Quixote, or of a quite possibly stolen body from a Galilean tomb, and the resultant wave of hallucinatory and dream visitations that mediated the immense historical shift from pagan to Christian culture.

5. Given this maximal utilization of dreams in traditional tribal societies in contrast to our own benign neglect and privatization of dreams, it is imperative that skilled native dreamers participate in EEG studies. We need to determine whether they would show the same slight decrement in electrophysiological activity during REM sleep—especially since mammals other than man do not—and whether measures of hemisphere balance are similar to typical Western subjects.

6. O'Flaherty (1984) points out that in traditional Indian civilization there is similarly no essentially good or bad dream in an absolute sense. A dream might foretell personal disaster for an average villager yet be deemed "positive" from the perspec-

tive of one seeking Yogic spiritual liberation—since for the latter all personal and social ties must be rejected. And vice versa, a "good" dream from a secular perspective (acquiring new possessions) is "bad" for the would-be nonreturner.

7. As Freud points out, it is because of their frequent basis in verbal metonymy that the dream books of the ancients, like the *Oneirocritica* by Artemidorus, seem such nonsense to us now.

8. In this regard Hippocrates anticipates the modern psychologies of "robustness" associated with Karle et al. (1980) and Mahrer (1986). Ignoring the relationship between dream bizarreness and creativity, these psychologists hold that psychologically healthy dreaming will be true to the deliberate activity, forcefulness, and extraversion that they value in everyday waking life. So much for diversity in living, let alone in dreaming.

9. Julian Jaynes cites the ubiquity of visitational dreams in the oldest written texts of ancient civilization. Such dreams lack the vicarial (active self present in the dream) and the translocative (the dream in a setting different from one's bedroom) features of modern adult dreams. He takes the historical primacy of visitational dreams as evidence for a distinct "bicameral consciousness" in early human beings—a theory of historical development very similiar to Foulkes's stages of dream ontogenesis. However, what Jaynes misses is that such visitational/apparitional dreams still occur, as in Green's (1968; Green and McCreery, 1975) accounts of false awakening dreams, lucid dreams, and apparitional metachoric experiences at sleep onset. It seems most likely that the prominence of such dreams in the earliest literary sources does not make them the original norm of dreaming, any more than they are in current primitive societies that value them so highly—it may stem instead from the greater emphasis on the sacred in preclassical civilization, combined with the fact that such dreams, then and now, are powerful and subjectively overwhelming. These are the dreams that would be worth recording at the earliest phases of formal writing. Their vividness and numinosity have continued to warrant special emphasis in Boss's phenomenology of dream multiplicity and, of course, in the psychology of Jung.

10. The visitational dream remained as a literary form, as in the possibly apocryphal dream of the Roman Scipio (149 B.C.) His ancestor Africanus appears to him with prophesies of his later military and political achievements, culminating in an archetypal vision of the physical and spiritual cosmos. Africanus includes this very special comment on the folly of deliberately seeking fame: "What difference does it make whether you will be remembered by those who come after you, when there was no mention made of you by men before your time? They were just as numerous and were certainly better men" (Macrobius, *The Dream of Scipio*, p. 75).

6 BASIC DIMENSIONS OF THE DREAM DIAMOND

1. If Titchener and Wundt could do this for the qualities of color, touch, sound, and so on, why should it not be equally clarifiying for describing the varieties of dreaming?

2. In effect this three-dimensional structure is based on an attempt to "fold over" the two-dimensional diagram with which I represented dream types in my 1982 monograph "Forms of Dreaming."

7 SPECIFIC IMAGINATIVE-INTUITIVE FACULTIES AS FORMS OF DREAMING

1. Werner and Kaplan's *Symbol Formation* (1963, chapter 15) provides numerous examples of verbal neologisms and metonymy in dream reports.

2. Freud's interpretation of visual-kinesthetic sexual metaphors in dreams, adapted from Stekel's direct intuitive approach to sexual symbolism and introduced into later editions of *The Interpretation of Dreams,* has much more in common with Jung's demonstration of more inclusive visual metaphors than it has with Freud's complex verbal metonymies. Weapons, caves, and stairs are, after all, linked to sexuality on the basis of structural similiarities. Their occasional association with dream orgasm, without any ostensible sexual content, implies that the relationship is not just in the eyes of the dream interpreter.

8 LUCID DREAMS AND NIGHTMARES: THE TRANSITION TO FORMAL SELF-REFERENCE

1. Just to reinforce the relation of lucid dreaming to the general processes of all dreaming, lucidity is not restricted to REM sleep but can also occur at sleep onset (Tholy, 1983) and in NREM sleep (Dane, 1986).

2. Roughly following Green's typology, pre-lucid dreaming includes dreams in which one questions whether one might be dreaming but cannot decide or rejects it, dreams within dreams, dreams of false awakening—such dreamt reconstruction of one's bedroom also being typical in apparitional hallucinations (with or without ESP concomitance)—and dreams of flying and other forms of conscious dream control (without fully lucid awareness). Barrett (1987) has recently confirmed a statistical association between subjects with lucid dreams and those who dream of flying.

3. Gackenbach et al. (1987) found a further difference between lucid dreams in nonmeditators and full witnessing in an experienced practitioner of Transcendental Meditation. The latter evinced a hypoarousal and reactivity pattern during his lucid dreams remarkably like his EEG and autonomic responsiveness when meditating. This suggests that witnessing is a developed and stabilized form of ordinary lucidity.

4. Faber, Saayman, and Touyz (1978) and Buzby and DeKoninck (1980) have also reported a relation between dream bizarreness and meditative practice.

5. In an exploratory study with Aurelia Spadafora (1988), in which we compared small groups of archetypal, nightmare, and lucid dreamers, we found data confirming this model. Although there were correlations among the three dimensions, archetypal dreamers were significantly superior to nightmare sufferers on measures of imagination, while archetypal and lucid dreamers generally were significantly better than the nightmare group in several tests of spatial ability and balance. A mixed group, especially high on nightmares and archetypal estimates and probably similar to Hartmann's unusually intense nightmare sample, were on a level with the purely archetypal dreamers in imaginativeness, lowest among all groups on the measures of spatial ability, and highest on questionnaires measuring stress. Intensified dreaming, coupled with poor spatial and vestibular functioning, seems to result in more negative disorganized dreams.

9 ARCHETYPAL AND TITANIC DREAMS: ABSTRACT IMAGERIES OF
FORMAL SELF-REFERENCE

1. I use *archetypal* here in a purely descriptive sense to indicate a certain kind of empirical dream experience. My use of it has no theoretical implications re a collective unconscious in the sense of a racial or phylogenetic psyche. Jung himself shifted from this earlier more questionable usage (racial memories) to an almost exclusively phenomenological emphasis. In his final years, he used the term *objective psyche* to describe the source of experience that, while rationally subjective, feels as if it is more real than ordinary life (i.e., numinous in Otto's sense [Fordham, 1958]). *Archetypal* thus refers to a quality of imagistic cognition for which Werner and Kaplan come closest to providing a cognitive psychology (see also Hunt, 1984, 1985a, b, 1986a). It has no connotation here of any quasi-biological theory of mind.

2. In Jung's terms (1959) titanic dream sensations reflect "archetypes of transformation" rather than "archetypes of identity."

10 FREUD, JUNG, AND CULTURE PATTERN DREAMS; ARCHETYPAL
IMAGINATION VERSUS CULTURAL PROGRAMMING

1. Kracke (1987) offers a differentiation between myths and dreams in terms of predominant modality: whereas dreams start as mainly visual experiences that are translated into language as a significant means of group communication, established myths are narratives whose telling generates vivid imagery in the listeners.

2. In more complex classical civilizations, Bourguignon's typology is reproduced in what Max Weber (1963) called "radical salvation movements" that appear at points of major social change. Such movements are based on a spontaneous arousal and reschematization of numinous trance experience (charisma, for Weber), which may later become the new orthodoxy for society at large. Weber distinguished mysticism—aesthetic, vision-centered, and in its purest form restricted to small groups who tend to come from the aristocracy (Buddha)—from propheticism, more ethically and socially directed and tending to originate in the lower middle classes of artisans and merchants (Christ). We can see the same tendencies in the religious fervor (often Old Testament based) of revolutionary movements in the third world and the Western turn to the East and to psychedelic drugs in the 1960s.

It is also worth noting some parallel between Bourguignon's (and Weber's) typology and Otto Rank's (1950) division of cultural stages between animism (where immortality is immediately provided by and in "the dream"), the sexual era of inherited name and property associated with agricultural societies (and their concern with future prophecy), and the modern era of the secular individual, poised between neurosis and immortality through artistic and scientific achievement.

3. Such metaphorical self-reference would also create the special anxiety and "superstition" associated with mythological thought, as detailed by Freud in "The Uncanny" (1919b).

4. I owe this suggestion to Kate Ruzycki-Hunt.

11 NARRATIVE STRUCTURES: STORY GRAMMAR VERSUS IMAGISTICS

1. Recent findings (Reinsel, Wollman, and Antrobus, 1985) that the relation of visual imagery and bizarreness with phasic REM measures varies by time of night further stresses that psychological processes must still be researched independently of their purported physiological correlations. On the other hand, failure to replicate associations between phasic REM and bizarreness may also stem from the common use of Foulkes Dream-like Fantasy Scale, which inserts bizarreness at multiple points along a supposedly ordinal scale and seems to place more weight on whether the content is perceived and believed to be real ("hallucination") than on its degree of novelty or transformation of the waking environment. Our own work at Brock University (Ogilvie et al., 1982), using a much more specific measure of bizarreness, has found significant associations between dream bizarreness and middle ear muscle activity (MEMAS), as Watson did for phasic integrated potentials (PIPs) (Watson, Butler, and Liebmann, 1982)—both indicating phasic discharge that probably stems from an interaction of cortex and brain stem.

2. I received a personal demonstration of how striking imagery can constrain and determine story grammar. A theater preview for a recent foreign film, appropriately enough titled *Kaos*, consisted of rapid, largely stationary, scenes—repeated shots of a full moon, a woman hiding behind a shuttered window and a hand suddenly reaching in to grab her, an overview of an abandoned castle on a huge cliff, bandits seen in a courtyard from above, a crow flying with a bell around its neck, an ancient sailing ship, and a strange and eerie dance performed by dozens of men around a large earthen jar with a man crouching inside it. Knowing that preview scenes are typically not seen in the order they appear in the film, I had no problem in beginning to assign its scenes to potential slots in a single story grammar—which then seemed to me so exciting and intriguing that I convinced my companion to a change of plan, so that we went to see it. I was very surprised indeed to learn that what I had taken to be a single, powerfully mythological story was in fact five separate, basically unrelated, and much more mundane tales. In such instances it is the subjective epiphanies of imagery that generate sequential narrative structure, in marked contrast to the model of imagining what we read in a novel.

3. This balance model of hemisphericity also works for lucid dreams, suggested by LaBerge (1985) to be left hemisphere predominant because they seem to involve verbal-cognitive reflection ("I am dreaming") and because they are most likely to occur during later REM periods (more left hemisphere activated). However, on Armitage, Hoffman, and Moffitt's (1987) approach, later REM periods are both more activated and more balanced. Furthermore, lucid dreaming is much more than a verbal or intellectual realization: it generally involves an affective "high" similiar to Maslow's peak experience and is characteristically accompanied by kinesthetic sensation (Gackenbach, 1986). Luria (1973) notes that kinesthetically based self-awareness is a function of the right parietal lobe, damage to which is characteristically associated with a radical failure to appreciate the nature of any other neural deficits. The patient may then actively deny quite glaring disabilities. Accordingly, lucid dreams would require or might even intensify the same hemispheric balance that defines REM sleep generally (Gackenbach et al, 1987).

12 THE VISUAL-SPATIAL SIDE OF DREAM FORMATION

1. Why the predominance of verbal-auditory transformations in hypnagogic reports, but the visual predominance in REM? Perhaps it is a matter of ease of recall (hypnagogic experiences are self-arousing). But only Watson (1972), questioning subjects about their experience immediately prior to REM awakening, has reported verbal anomalies to the same degree as visual bizarreness, and his study involved only four subjects. Both Heynick (1981) and Arkin (1978) found that linguistic competence is preserved in dream recall; neologisms and nonsense statements are characteristic only of sleep onset. Indeed, the collection of bizarre "dream speech" in Werner and Kaplan (1963) seems to be predominantly from sleep onset.

Perhaps it is the construction of narrative sequence in dreaming that utilizes a propositional deep structure and so leaves no room for complex wordplay in the manifest dream, whereas the visual setting emerges from simpler perceptual sources that allow for a later emergence of creative visual metaphor.

2. The occurrence of lucidity, control, and conceptual reflection in narcoleptic dreams has led some to suggest that lucid dreaming might be a variant of narcolepsy. This seems especially wrongheaded. Certainly similar effects can be released by very different causal settings, but more fundamentally most major alterations of consciousness—including narcolepsy, meditation, sensory deprivation, and lucid dreaming—seem transitional between sleep and waking. Very different processes may be involved in creating this twilight state in each setting. Lucidity is no more likely to *be* narcolepsy than the other way around.

3. If there is an omission in this cognitive psychology of the multiple dimensions of dream formation it is in my subsuming feeling, affect, and emotion under visual-kinesthetic and visual-spatial structures of self-reference. An equal danger lies in restricting cognition to the structure or pattern aspect of all experience as in restricting affect to its energy dynamics. The presentational symbolism of the arts, for instance, clearly entails feeling not in the sense of any simple discharge but precisely through the complex reorganizations of sensory media—very much a cognitive operation in the sense of "higher," abstract, structured, and symbolic. What we call *affect* is anything but emotionally primitive, as Langer rightly insists.

Yet it is all too easy for even this organismic-holistic cognitive psychology of dreams to miss the primary fact that the fullest manifestation of the dreaming process involves the release of strong and powerful feeling. With more space, time, and certainty part 3 should perhaps have included a third section entitled "The Kinesthetic-Affective Dimension of Dream Formation." Developing from Lowy's affect metabolism, such a line of study is best represented by the work of Hartmann and Kramer on nightmares, Kramer on mood regulation, Cartwright on the assimilation of stress, and Kuiken on the psychophysiology of affect and felt meaning.

Certainly the appearance of vivid kinesthetic sensation in dreams—flying, strong pleasure or fright, lucidity, and so on—is an index of the total transformation of the dreaming process by visual-kinesthetic self-reference. It is here that dreaming truly comes into its own.

The transformation of dreaming by spontaneous and novel visual patterns allows their potential kinesthetic embodiment, so that they release "feeling" and gain a potential metaphoric significance. In normal wakefulness and relatively mundane dreaming, the sequential representational structure of language subordinates kinesthesis. In other words, language is articulatory and so motoric, and it entrains and subordinates felt meaning. The shift of kinesthesis from verbal patterns to the "embodiment" of the structures of visual imagery would allow the archetypal-titanic and lucid forms of dreaming. What we usually mean by *consciousness* is verbal-representational (inner speech), but other configurations are equally and uniquely human and abstract—just different.

4. Blood pressure cuff or vibration methods could be used to provide a direct test of this model. Subjects with especially poor balance should show body image anomalies and other dream disorganizations, while subjects with unusually good balance should be precipitated directly into lucid, archetypal, and/or integrated and pleasurable titanic dream forms. Average subjects should report increased levels of normative dream bizarreness. It is intriguing that such a simple experimental method might provide the test for a cognitive model of the visual-spatial aspects of dream formation.

References

Ablon, S. L., and Mack, J. E. (1980). Children's dreams reconsidered. *The psychoanalytic study of the child*, 35, 179–217.

Adelson, J. (1974). The dreams of creative college girls. In R. Woods and H. Greenhouse (Eds.), *The new world of dreaming: An anthology*. New York: Macmillan, pp. 17–21.

Alexander, C. N., Cranson, R. W., Boyer, R. W., and Orme-Johnson, D. W. (1987). Transcendental consciousness: A fourth state beyond sleep, dreaming, and waking. In J. Gackenbach (Ed.), *Sleep and dreams: A sourcebook*. New York: Garland Publishing, pp. 282–315.

Angyal, A. (1936). The experience of the body-self in schizophrenia. *Archives of Neurology and Psychiatry*, 35, 1029–53.

———. (1965). *Neurosis and treatment: A holistic theory*. New York: Wiley.

Angyal, A., and Blackman, N. (1940). Vestibular reactivity in schizophrenia. *Archives of Neurology and Psychiatry*, 44, 611–20.

Antrobus, J. (1977). The dream as metaphor. *Journal of Mental Imagery*, 2, 327—338.

———. (1978). Dreaming for cognition. In A. M. Arkin, J. S. Antrobus, and S. J. Ellman (Eds.), *The mind in sleep: Psychology and psychophysiology*. Hillsdale, N.J.: Lawrence Erlbaum, pp. 569–81.

———. (1983). REM and NREM sleep responses: Comparison of word frequencies by cognitve classes. *Psychophysiology*, 20, 562–68.

————. (1986). Dreaming: Cortical activation and perceptual thresholds. *Journal of Mind and Behaviour, 7*, 193–212.

————. (1987). Cortical hemisphere asymmetry and sleep mentation. *Psychological Review, 94*, 359–68.

Arenson, K. (1986). The metaliteral statement in dreams: A new tool. ASD *Newsletter, 3* (3), 8–9.

Aristotle (1936). *On the soul, parva naturalia, on breath*, trans. W. S. Hett. Cambridge: Harvard University Press.

Arkin, A. M. (1978). Sleeptalking. In A. M. Arkin, J. S. Antrobus, and S. J. Ellman (Eds.), *The mind in sleep: Psychology and psychophysiology*. Hillsdale, N.J.: Lawrence Erlbaum, pp. 513–32.

Arkin, A. M., and Antrobus, J. S. (1978). The effects of external stimuli applied prior to and during sleep. In A. M. Arkin, J. S. Antrobus, and S. J. Ellman (Eds.), *The mind in sleep: Psychology and psychophysiology*. Hillsdale, N.J.: Lawrence Erlbaum, pp. 357–91.

Armitage, R., Hoffmann, R., and Moffitt, A. (1988). Interhemispheric EEG activity in sleep and wakefulness: Individual differences in basic rest-activity cycle. In J. Antrobus (Ed.), *The mind in sleep*, vol. 2. Hillsdale, N.J.: Lawrence Erlbaum.

Arnheim, R. (1969). *Visual thinking*. Berkeley: University of California Press.

————. (1974). *Art and visual perception*. Berkeley: University of California Press.

Arnold-Forster, M. (1921). *Studies in dreams*. London: Allen and Unwin.

Artemidorus (1975). *The interpretation of dreams: Oneirocritica*, trans R. J. White. Park Ridge, N.J.: Noyes Press.

Asch, S. (1961). The metaphor: A psychological inquiry. In M. Henle (Ed.), *Documents of gestalt psychology*. Berkeley: University of California Press, pp. 324–33.

Aserinsky, E. (1986). Proportional jerk: A new measure of motion as applied to eye movements in sleep and waking. *Psychophysiology, 23*, 340–47.

Aserinsky, E., Lynch, J., Mack, M., Tzakoff, S., and Hurn, E. (1985). Comparison of eye motion in wakefulness and REM sleep. *Psychophysiology, 22*, 1–10.

Bakan, P. (1977). Dreaming, REM sleep and the right hemisphere: A theoretical integration. *Journal of Altered States of Consciousness, 3*, 285–307.

Barrett, D. (1987). Flying dreams and lucidity: An empirical study of their relationship. *Lucidity Letter, 6* (1), 37–38.

Barron, F. (1969). *Creative person and creative process*. New York: Holt, Rinehart, and Winston.

Bartlett, F. (1932). *Remembering*. Cambridge: Cambridge University Press.

Becker, P. T., and Thomas, E. B. (1981). Rapid eye movement storms in infants: Rate of occurrence at 6 months predicts mental development at 1 year. *Science, 212*, 1415–16.

Belicki, K. (1985). The assessment and prevalence of nightmare distress. *Sleep Research*, *14*, 145.

————. (1987). Recalling dreams: An examination of daily variation and individual differences. In J. Gackenbach (Ed.), *Sleep and dreams: A sourcebook*. New York: Garland.

Belicki, K., and Belicki, D. (1986). Predisposition for nightmares: A study of hypnotic ability, vividness of imagery, and absorption. *Journal of Clinical Psychology*, *42*, 714–18.

Belicki, K., and Bowers, P. (1982). The role of demand characteristics and hypnotic ability in dream change following a presleep instruction. *Journal of Abnormal Psychology*, *91*, 426–32.

Belvedere, E., and Foulkes, D. (1971). Telepathy and dreams: A failure to replicate, *Perceptual and Motor Skills*, *33*, 783–89.

Bergson, H. (1901). *The world of dreams*, trans. W. Baskin. New York: Philosophical Library, 1958.

Bertini, M., and Violani, C. (1984). Cerebral hemispheres, REM sleep, and dreaming. In M. Bosinelli and P. Cicogna (Eds.), *Psychology of dreaming*. Bologna, Italy: CLUEB, pp. 131–35.

Binswanger, L. (1963). Dream and existence. In J. Needleman (Ed.), *Being-in-the-world: Selected papers of Ludwig Binswanger*. New York: Basic Books, pp. 222–48.

Bion, W. R. (1962). *Learning from experience*. London: Heineman.

————. (1963). *Elements of psychoanalysis*. New York: Basic Books.

Birnholz, J. C. (1981). The development of human fetal eye movement patterns. *Science*, *213*, 680–81.

Block, V., Hennevin, E., and Leconte, P. (1981). The phenomenon of paradoxical sleep augmentation after learning. In W. Fishbein (Ed.), *Sleep, dreams and memory*. New York: Spectrum, pp. 1–18.

Boisen, A. (1962). *The exploration of the inner world*. New York: Harper.

Boss, M. (1958). *The analysis of dreams*. New York: Philosophical Library.

————. (1977). *I dreamt last night . . .* New York: Gardner Press.

Bourguignon, E. (1972). Dreams and altered states of consciousness in anthropological research. In F. L. Hsu (Ed.), *Psychological anthropology*. Cambridge, Mass.: Schenkman, pp. 403–34.

Bowers, M. (1974). *Retreat from sanity*. New York: Human Science Press.

Breger, L., Hunter, I., and Lane, R.W. (1971). The effect of stress on dreams. *Psychological Issues*, *7* (3), 1–213.

Brelich, A. (1966). The place of dreams in the religious world concept of the Greeks. In G. E. Van Grunebaum and R. Caillois (Eds.), *The dream and human societies*. Berkeley: University of California Press, pp. 293–301.

Brenneis, C. (1971). The features of the manifest dream in schizophrenia. *Journal of Nervous and Mental Disease*, *153*, 81–91.

Brink, T.L. (1979). Flying dreams: The relationship to creativeness, handedness, and locus of control factors. *Journal of Altered States of Consciousness, 5,* 153–57.

Broughton, R. (1968). Sleep disorders: Disorders of arousal? *Science, 159,* 1070–78.

Brown, J. N., and Cartwright, R. D. (1978). Locating NREM dreaming through instrumental responses. *Psychophysiology, 15,* 35–39.

Brown, M. (1987). Ropes of sand: Order and imagery in Aquaruna dreams. In B. Tedlock (Ed.), *Dreaming: Anthropological and psychological interpretations.* Cambridge: Cambridge University Press.

Brylowski, A. (1986). H-reflex in lucid dreams. *Lucidity Letter, 5* (1), 116–19.

Burd, L. (1984). Dreams after amputation. *British Journal of Psychiatry, 145,* 448.

Burke, K. (1966). *Language as symbolic action.* Berkeley: University of California Press.

Butler, S. F., and Watson, R. (1985). Individual differences in memory for dreams: The role of cognitive skills. *Perceptual and Motor Skills, 61,* 823–28.

Buzby, K., and de Koninck, J. (1980). Short-term effects of strategies for self regulation on personality dimensions and dream content. *Perceptual and Motor Skills, 50,* 751–65.

Calderon de la Barca, P. (1968). *Life's a dream,* trans. K. Raine and R. M. Nadal. London: Hamish Hamilton.

Cann, D. R., and Donderi, D. C. (1986). Jungian personality typology and the recall of everyday and archetypal dreams. *Journal of Personality and Social Psychology, 50,* 1021–30.

Carrington, P. (1972). Dreams and schizophrenia. *Archives of General Psychiatry, 26,* 343–50.

Cartwright, R. D. (1966). Dream and drug-induced fantasy behavior. *Archives of General Psychiatry, 15,* 7–15.

———. (1972). Sleep fantasy in normal and schizophrenic persons. *Journal of Abnormal Psychology, 80,* 275–79.

Cartwright, R. D., and Kaszniak, A. (1978). The social psychology of dream reporting. In A. M. Arkin, J. S. Antrobus, and S. J. Ellman (Eds.), *The mind in sleep: Psychology and psychophysiology.* Hillsdale, N.J.: Lawrence Erlbaum, pp. 277–91.

Castaneda, C. (1974). *Tales of power.* New York: Simon and Schuster.

Cattell, R. B. (1930). The subjective character of cognition and the presensational development of perception. *British Journal of Psychology,* Monograph no. 14.

Chang, G. C. (1963). *Teachings of Tibetan yoga.* New York: University Books.

Child, I. (1985). Psychology and anomalous observations: The question of ESP in dreams. *American Psychologist, 40,* 1219–30.

Claridge, G. (1972). The schizophrenias as nervous types. *British Journal of Psychiatry, 121,* 1–17.

Cohen, B. (1974). The vestibular-ocular reflex arc. In H. H. Kornhuber (Ed.), *Vestibular system, Part I: Basic mechanisms.* Berlin: Springer-Verlag, pp. 447–540.

Cohen, D. B. (1979). *Sleep and dreaming: Origins, nature, and functions.* Oxford: Pergamon Press.

Cravens, G. (1973). Talking to power and spinning with the ally. *Harpers Magazine,* February, 91–97.

Crick, F., and Mitchison, G. (1986). REM sleep and neural nets. *Journal of Mind and Behaviour, 7,* 229–50.

Crovitz, H. (1970). *Galton's walk.* New York: Harper and Row.

Cytowic, R. (1986). Cerebral blood flow in synaesthesia. American Association for the Advancement of Science, Annual Meeting, Philadelphia (May).

D'Andrade, R. G. (1961). Anthropological studies of dreams. In F. L. K. Hsu (Ed.), *Psychological anthropology.* Homewood, Ill.: Dorsey Press, pp. 296–332.

Dane, J. (1986). Non-REM lucid dreaming. *Lucidity Letter, 5* (1), 133–45.

Deikman, A. (1982). *The observing self.* Boston: Beacon Press.

Delaney, G. (1981). *Living your dreams.* New York: Harper and Row.

Dement, W. (1975). The mental experience during sleep. In G. Lairy and P. Salzarulo (Eds.), *The experimental study of human sleep.* Amsterdam: Elsevier, pp. 287–307.

DeMille, A. (1978). *Castaneda's journey.* Santa Barbara, Calif.: Capra Press.

Dentan, R. K. (1987). Ethnographic considerations of the cross cultural study of dreams. In J. Gackenbach (Ed.), *Sleep and dreams: A sourcebook.* New York: Garland.

Domhoff, G. W. (1985). *The mystique of dreams.* Berkeley: University of California Press.

Dorus, E., Dorus, W., and Rechtschaffen, A. (1971). The incidence of novelty in dreams. *Archives of General Psychiatry, 25,* 364–68.

Drucker-Colin, R. P. (1981). Neuroproteins, brain excitability and REM sleep. In W. Fishbein (Ed.), *Sleep, dreams and memory.* New York: Spectrum, pp. 73–94.

Ducey, C. P. (1979). The shaman's dream journey. *Psychoanalytic Study of Society, 8,* 71–118.

DuPrel, C. (1889). *Philosophy of mysticism,* trans. C. C. Massey. London: George Redway.

Dykes, M., and McGhie, A. (1976). A comparative study of attentional strategies of schizophrenic and highly creative normal subjects. *British Journal of Psychiatry, 128,* 50–56.

Edelson, M. (1972). Language and dreams: The interpretation of dreams revisited. *Psychoanalytic Study of the Child*, 27, 203–82.

Ehrlichman, H., Antrobus, J. S., and Wiener, M. S. (1985). EEG asymmetry and sleep mentation during REM and NREM. *Brain and Cognition*, 4, 447–85.

Ehrlichman, H., and Wiener, M.S. (1980). EEG asymmetry during covert mental activity. *Psychophysiology*, 17, 228–35.

Eliade, M. (1964). *Shamanism*. New York: Pantheon.

Ellenberger, H. (1970). *The discovery of the unconscious*. New York: Basic Books.

Ellis, H. (1897). A note on hypnagogic paramnesia. *Mind*, 6, 283–87.

———. (1913). *The world of dreams*. Boston: Houghton Mifflin.

Ellman, S. J., Spielman, A. J., Luck, D., Steiner, S. S., and Halperin, R. (1978). REM deprivation: A Review. In A. M. Arkin, J. S. Antrobus, and S. J. Ellman (Eds.), *The mind in sleep: Psychology and psychophysiology*. Hillsdale, N.J.: Lawrence Erlbaum.

Emde, R. N., Gaensbauer, T. J., and Harmon, R. J. (1976). Emotional expressions in infancy. *Psychological Issues*, 10 (1), 1–198.

Engell, J. (1981). *The creative imagination: Enlightenment to romanticism*. Cambridge: Harvard University Press.

Ephron, H. S., and Carrington, P. C. (1966). Rapid eye movement sleep and cortical homeostasis. *Psychological Review*, 73, 500–26.

Epstein, A. W. (1979). The effect of certain cerebral hemispheric diseases on dreaming. *Biological Psychiatry*, 14, 77–93.

———. (1985). The waking event-dream interval. *American Journal of Psychiatry*, 142, 123–24.

Epstein, A. W., and Simmons, N. N. (1983). Aphasia with reported loss of dreaming. *American Journal of Psychiatry*, 140, 108–09.

Erdelyi, H. (1985). *Psychoanalysis: Freud's cognitive psychology*. New York: W. H. Freeman.

Erickson, M. H. (1941). On the possible occurrence of a dream in an eight-month-old infant. *Psychoanalytic Quarterly*, 10, 382–84.

Faber, P. A., Saayman, G. S., Touyz, S. W. (1978). Meditation and archetypal content of nocturnal dreams. *Journal of Analytical Psychology*, 23, 1–22.

Farah, M. (1984). The neurological basis of mental imagery. *Cognition*, 18, 245–72.

———. (1985). Psychophysical evidence for a shared representational medium for mental images and percepts. *Journal of Experimental Psychology: General*, 114, 91–103.

———. (1987). The neurophysiology of imagery. Psychology Dept. Colloquium, Brock University, St. Catharines, Ontario.

Finke, R. (1980). Levels of equivalence in imagery and perception. *Psychological Review*, 87, 113–32.

Fischer, R. (1975). Cartography of inner space. In R. Siegel and L. West (Eds.), *Hallucinations: Behavior, experience, and theory*. New York: Wiley, pp. 197–239.

Fishbein, W., and Gutwein, B. M. (1981). Paradoxial sleep and a theory of long-term memory. In W. Fishbein (Ed.), *Sleep, dreams and memory*. New York: Spectrum, pp. 147–82.

Fisher, C. (1965). Psychoanalytic implications of recent research on sleep and dreaming. *Journal of the American Psychoanalytic Association*, 13, 197–303.

Fisher, C., Kahn, E., Edwards, A., and Davis, D. (1972). Total suppression of REM sleep with Nardil in a patient with intractable narcolepsy. *Sleep Research*, 1, 159.

Fiss, H. (1979). Current dream research: A psychobiological perspective. In B. B. Wolman (Ed.), *Handbook of dreams*. New York: Van Nostrand Reinhold, pp. 20–75.

Fordham, M. (1958). *The objective psyche*. London: Routledge and Kegan Paul.

Fort, C. (1974). Wild talents. In *The complete books of Charles Fort*. New York: Dover, pp. 843–1062.

Foucault, M. (1978). *The history of sexuality*, vol. 1. New York: Pantheon.

Foulkes, D. (1966). *The psychology of sleep*. New York: Charles Scribners.

———. (1978). *A grammar of dreams*. New York: Basic Books.

———. (1982a). A cognitive-psychological model of REM dream production. *Sleep*, 5, 169–87.

———. (1982b). *Children's dreams: Longitudinal studies*. New York: Wiley.

———. (1983a). Dream ontogeny and dream psychophysiology. In M. Chase and E. Weitzman (Eds.), *Sleep disorders: Basic and clinical research*. New York: Spectrum, pp. 347–62.

———. (1983b). Cognitive processes during sleep: Evolutionary aspects. In A. Mayes (Ed.), *Sleep mechanisms and functions in humans and animals*. Berkshire, Eng.: Van Nostrand Reinhold, pp. 313–37.

———. (1985). *Dreaming: A cognitive-psychological analysis*. Hillsdale, N.J.: Lawrence Erlbaum.

Foulkes, D., and Fleischer, S. (1975). Mental activity in relaxed wakefulness. *Journal of Abnormal Psychology*, 84, 66–75.

Foulkes, D., and Pope, R. (1973). Primary visual experience and secondary cognitive elaboration in stage REM: A modest confirmation and extension. *Perceptual and Motor Skills*, 37, 107–18.

Foulkes, D., and Schmidt, M. (1983). Temporal sequence and unit composition in dream reports from different stages of sleep. *Sleep*, 6, 265–80.

Foulkes, D., and Vogel, G. (1965). Mental activity at sleep onset. *Journal of Abnormal Psychology, 70,* 231–43.

Fox, O. (1975). *Astral projection: A record of out of the body experiences.* Secaucus, N.J.: Citadel Press.

French, T. M., and Fromm, E. (1964). *Dream interpretation.* New York: International Universities Press.

Freud, S. (1900). *The interpretation of dreams.* New York: Avon, 1965.

———. (1905). *Jokes and their relation to the unconscious,* trans J. Strachey. New York: W. W. Norton, 1963.

———. (1911). Psycho-analytic notes upon an autobiographical account of a case of paranoia. In *Sigmund Freud, Collected papers,* vol. 3, trans. J. Riviere. New York: Basic Books, 1959, pp. 387–470.

———. (1913). The occurrence in dreams of material from fairy-tales. In *Sigmund Freud, Collected papers,* vol. 4, trans. J. Riviere. New York: Basic Books, 1959, pp. 236–43.

———. (1915). The unconscious. In *Sigmund Freud, Collected Papers,* vol. 4, trans. J. Riviere. New York: Basic Books, 1959, pp. 98–136.

———. (1919a). *Beyond the pleasure principle,* trans. J. Strachey. London: Hogarth Press, 1950.

———. (1919b). The "uncanny." In *Sigmund Freud, Collected papers,* vol. 4, trans. J. Riviere. New York: Basic Books, 1959, pp. 368–407.

———. (1922). Dreams and telepathy. In *Sigmund Freud, Collected papers,* vol. 4, trans. J. Riviere. New York: Basic Books, 1959, p. 408–35.

———. (1933). *New introductory lectures on psycho-analysis,* trans. W. J. H. Sprott. New York: Norton.

———. (1954). *The origins of psycho-analysis,* trans. E. Mosbacher and J. Strachey. New York: Basic Books.

Gackenbach, J. (1986). The manifest content of self-reported lucid versus non-lucid dreams among college students. *Lucidity Letter, 5* (1), 160–80.

Gackenbach, J., Cranson, R., and Alexander, C. (1986). Lucid dreaming, witnessing dreaming, and the transcendental meditation technique. *Lucidity Letter, 5* (2), 34–40.

Gackenbach, J., Moorecraft, W., Alexander, C., and LaBerge, S. (1987). Physiological correlates of "consciousness" during sleep in a single TM practitioner. *Sleep Research, 16,* 230.

Gackenbach, J., Snyder, T. J., Rokes, L. M., and Sackau, D. (1986). Lucid dreaming frequency in relation to vestibular sensitivity as measured by caloric stimulation. *Journal of Mind and Behavior, 7,* 277–98.

Gaillard, S., and Laurian, P. L. (1984). EEG asymmetry during sleep. *Neuropsychobiology, 11,* 224–26.

Galin, D. (1974). Applications for psychiatry of left and right cerebral specialization. *Archives of General Psychiatry, 31,* 572–83.

Gallup, G. (1974). Animal hypnosis: Factual status of a fictional concept. *Psychological Bulletin, 81,* 836–53.

Gardner, H. (1975). *The shattered mind.* New York: Basic Books.

———. (1983). *Frames of mind.* New York: Basic Books.

———. (1985). *The mind's new science: A history of the cognitive revolution.* New York: Basic Books.

Garnham, A. (1983). What's wrong with story grammars. *Cognition, 15,* 145–54.

Gass, W. (1976). *On being blue.* Boston: David Godine.

Gendlin, E. (1981). *Focusing.* New York: Bantam.

———. (1986). *Let your body interpret your dreams.* Wilmette, Ill.: Chiron Publications.

Geschwind, N. (1965). Disconnection syndromes in animals and man. *Brain,* 88, 237–94, 585–644.

———. (1981). Anatomical and functional asymmetry of the brain. Association for the Psychophysiological Study of Sleep, Annual Meeting, Hyannis, Mass. (May).

Gillespie, G. (1984). The phenomenon of light in dreams: Personal observations. *Lucidity Letter,* 3 (4), 1–3.

———. (1987). Dream light: Categories of visual experience during lucid dreaming. *Lucidity Letter,* 6, 73–79.

Glenn, L. L. (1985). Brain stem and spinal control of lower limb motoneurons with special reference to phasic events and startle reflexes. In D. J. McGinty, R. Drucker-Colin, A. Morrison, and P. L. Parmeggiani (Eds.), *Brain mechanisms of sleep.* New York: Raven Press, pp. 81–95.

Globus, G. (1987). *Dream life, wake life: The human condition through dreams.* Albany: State University of New York Press.

Goodenough, D. R. (1978). Dream recall: History and current status of the field. In A. M. Arkin, J. S. Antrobus, and S. J. Ellman (Eds.), *The mind in sleep: Psychology and psychophysiology.* Hillsdale, N.J.: Lawrence Erlbaum, pp. 113–40.

Goodenough, D., Shapiro, A., Holden, M., and Steinschriben, L. (1959). A comparison of "dreamers" and "non-dreamers": eye movements, electroencephalograms, and the recall of dreams. *Journal of Abnormal Psychology,* 59, 295–302.

Govinda, A. (1960). *Foundations of Tibetan mysticism.* New York: Dutton.

Green C. (1968). *Lucid dreams.* London: Hamish Hamilton.

———. (1976). *The decline and fall of science.* London: Hamish Hamilton.

Green, C., and McCreery, C. (1975). *Apparitions.* London: Hamish Hamilton.

Greenberg, M. S., and Farah, M. J. (1986). The laterality of dreaming. *Brain and Cognition,* 5, 307–21.

Greenberg, R. (1981). Dreams and REM sleep—an integrative approach. In W. Fishbein (Ed.), *Sleep, dreams and memory*. New York: Spectrum, pp. 125–33.

Greenberg, R., and Pearlman, C. (1967). Delirium tremens and dreaming. *American Journal of Psychiatry, 124*, 133–42.

———. (1975). A psychoanalytic-dream continuum: The source and function of dreams. *International Review of Psycho-analysis, 2*, 441–48.

———. (1978). If Freud only knew: A reconsideration of psychoanalytic dream theory. *International Review of Psycho-analysis, 5*, 71–75.

Greenwood, P., Wilson, D. H., and Gazzaniga, M. S. (1977). Dream report following commissurotomy. *Cortex, 13*, 311–16.

Gregor, T. (1981). "Far, far away my shadow wandered . . ." The dream symbolism and dream theories of the Mehinaku Indians of Brazil. *American Ethologist, 8*, 709–20.

Griffin, D. (1976). *The question of animal awareness*. New York: Rockefeller University Press.

Grinstein, A. (1980). *Sigmund Freud's dreams*. New York: International Universities Press.

Grof, S. (1980). *LSD psychotherapy*. Pomona, Calif.: Hunter House.

Grunbaum, A. (1986). Précis of the foundations of psychoanalysis: A philosophical critique. *Behavioural and Brain Sciences, 9*, 217–84.

Guss, D. (1980). Steering for dream: Dream concepts of the Makiritare. *Journal of Latin American Lore, 6*, 297–312.

Halgren, E., Walter, R. D., Cherlow, D. G., and Crandal, P. H. (1978). Mental phenomena evoked by electrical stimulation of the human hippocampal formation and amygdala. *Brain, 101*, 83–117.

Halifax, J. (1979). *Shamanic voices*. New York: Dutton.

Hall, C. (1953). *The meaning of dreams*. New York: Dell.

Hall, C., and Lind, R. (1970). *Dreams, life, and literature: A study of Franz Kafka*. Chapel Hill: University of North Carolina Press.

Hall, C., and Van de Castle, R. (1966). *The content analysis of dreams*. New York: Appleton-Century-Crofts.

Hall, J. (1977). *Clinical uses of dreams*. New York: Grune and Stratton.

Hallpike, C. R. (1979). *The foundations of primitive thought*. Oxford: Clarendon Press.

Hartmann, E. (1968). The day residue: Time distribution of waking events. Association for the Psychophysiological Study of Sleep, Annual Meeting, Denver.

———. (1981). The functions of sleep and memory processing. In W. Fishbein (Ed.), *Sleep, dreams and memory*. New York: Spectrum, pp. 111–24.

———. (1982). From the biology of dreaming to the biology of the mind. *The Psychoanalytic Study of the Child, 37*, 303–35.

————. (1984). *The nightmare*. New York: Basic Books.

Harsh, J., and Burton, S. A. (1986). Cognitive activity and instrumental responding to stimuli presented during sleep. *Sleep Research, 15*, 83.

Haskell, R. E. (1986). Logical structure and the cognitive psychology of dreaming. *Journal of Mind and Behavior, 7*, 345–78.

Hauri, P. (1975). Categorization of sleep mental activity for psychophysiological studies. In G. Lairy and P. Salzarulo (Eds.), *The experimental study of human sleep*. Amsterdam: Elsevier, pp. 271–86.

Hauri, P., and Van de Castle, R. L. (1973). Psychophysiological parallelism in dreams. *Psychosomatic Medicine, 35*, 297–308.

Herman, J. H., Barker, D., Rampy, P., and Roffwarg, H. (1987). Further evidence confirming the similarity of eye movements in REM sleep and the awake state. *Sleep Research, 16*, 38.

Herman, J. H., Barker, D. R., and Roffwarg, H. P. (1983). Similarity of eye movement characteristics in REM sleep and the awake state. *Psychophysiology, 20*, 537–43.

Herman, J. H., Ellman, S. J., and Roffwarg, H. P. (1978). The problem of NREM recall re-examined. In A. M. Arkin, J. S. Antrobus, and S. J. Ellman (Eds.), *The mind in sleep: Psychology and psychophysiology*. Hillsdale, N.J.: Lawrence Erlbaum, pp. 59–92.

Herman, J. H., Erman, M., Boys, R., Peiser, L., Taylor, M. E., and Roffwarg, H. P. (1984). Evidence for a directional correspondence between eye movements and dream imagery in REM sleep. *Sleep, 7*, 52–63.

Heynick, F. (1981). Linguistic aspects of Freud's dream model. *International Review of Psycho-analysis, 8*, 299–314.

————. (1986). The dream-scriptor and the Freudian ego: "Pragmatic competence" and superordinate and subordinate cognitive systems in sleep. *Journal of Mind and Behavior, 7*, 299–331.

Hillman, J. (1977). An inquiry into image. *Spring*, 62–88.

————. (1978). Further notes on images. *Spring*, 152–82.

————. (1979a). *The dream and the underworld*. New York: Harper and Row.

————. (1979b). Image-sense. *Spring*, 130–43.

————. (1980). *Egalitarian typologies versus the perception of the unique*. Dallas: Spring Publications.

Hippocrates (1931). *Regimen*, trans. W. H. S. Jones. Cambridge: Harvard University Press.

Hobson, J. A., Hoffman, S. A., Helfand, R., and Kostner, D. (1987). Dream bizarreness and the activation-synthesis hypothesis. *Human Neurobiology, 6.*

Hobson, J. A., and McCarley, R. W. (1977). The brain as a dream state generator: An activation-synthesis hypothesis of the dream process. *American Journal of Psychiatry, 134*, 1335–48.

Hofstadter, D. (1979). *Gödel, Escher, Bach: An eternal golden braid.* New York: Basic Books.

Hollingworth, H. C. (1911). The psychology of drowsiness. *American Journal of Psychology,* 22, 99–111.

Homer (1963). *The Odyssey,* trans. R. Fitzgerald. New York: Doubleday.

Hoppe, K. (1977). Spilt brain and psychoanalysis. *Psychoanalytic Quarterly,* 46, 220–24.

Horne, J. A. (1978). Dreaming sleep in man: A reappraisal. *Perspectives in Biology and Medicine,* 21, 591–601.

———. (1983). Mammalian sleep function with particular reference to man. In A. Mayes (Ed.), *Sleep mechanisms and functions in humans and animals—an evolutionary perspective.* Berkshire, Eng.: Van Nostrand Reinhold, pp. 262–312.

Horowitz, M. (1970). *Image formation and cognition.* New York: Appleton-Century-Crofts.

Hoyt, M. F., and Singer, J. L. (1978). Psychological effects of REM ("dream") deprivation upon waking mentation. In A. M. Arkin, J. S. Antrobus, and S. J. Ellman. (Eds.), *The mind in sleep: Psychology and psychophysiology.* Hillsdale, N.J.: Lawrence Erlbaum, pp. 59–92.

Hudson, L. (1985). *Night life: The interpretation of dreams.* London: Weidenfeld and Nicolson.

Hunt, H. (1984). A cognitive psychology of mystical and altered state experience. *Perceptual and Motor Skills,* Monograph no. 58, pp. 467–513.

———. (1985a). Relations between the phenomena of religious mysticism and the psychology of thought: A cognitive psychology of states of consciousness and the necessity of subjective states for cognitive theory. *Perceptual and Motor Skills,* Monograph no. 61, pp. 911–61.

———. (1985b). Cognition and states of consciousness: The necessity of the empirical study of ordinary and non-ordinary consciousness for contemporary cognitive psychology. *Perceptual and Motor Skills,* Monograph no. 60, pp. 239–82.

———. (1986a). A cognitive reinterpretation of classical introspectionism: The relation between introspection and altered states of consciousness and their mutual relevance for a cognitive psychology of metaphor and felt meaning, with commentaries by D. Bakan, R. Evans, and P. Swartz, and response. *Annals of Theoretical Psychology,* 4, 245–313.

———. (1986b). Some relations between the cognitive psychology of dreams and dream phenomenology. *Journal of Mind and Behavior,* 7, 213–28.

———. (1987). Toward a cognitive psychology of dreams. In J. Gackenbach (Ed.), *Sleep and dreams: A sourcebook.* New York: Garland, pp. 251–81.

Hunt, H., and Chefurka, C. (1976). A test of the psychedelic model of consciousness. *Archives of General Psychiatry,* 33, 867–96.

Hunt, H. T., and McLeod, B. (1984). Lucid dreaming as a meditative state. Unpubl. MS., Psychology Department, Brock University.

Hunt, H., Ogilvie, R., Belicki, K., Belicki, D., and Atalick, E. (1982). Forms of dreaming. *Perceptual and Motor Skills, 54,* 559–633.

Hunt, H. T., and Popham, C. (1987). Metaphor and states of consciousness: A preliminary correlational study of presentational thinking. *Journal of Mind and Behaviour, 11,* 83–100.

Irwin, H. J. (1985). *Flight of mind: A psychological study of the out-of-body experience.* Metuchen, N.J.: Scarecrow Press.

Isaacs, S. (1952). The nature and function of phantasy. In M. Klein, P. Heimann, S. Isaacs, and J. Riviere (Eds.), *Developments in psychoanalysis.* London: Hogarth, pp 67–121.

Itil, T. (1970). Digital computer analysis of the electroencephalogram during rapid eye movement sleep state in man. *Journal of Nervous and Mental Disease, 150,* 201–08.

Jakobson, R., and Halle, M. (1956). *Fundamentals of language.* The Hague: Mouton.

James, W. (1902). *The varieties of religious experience.* Garden City, N.J.: Dolphin Books.

Jaynes, J. (1986). Consciousness and the voices of the mind. *Canadian Psychology, 27,* 128–48.

Jeannerod, M. (1975). Discussion. In G. Lairy and P. Salzarulo (Eds.), *The experimental study of sleep.* Amsterdam: Elsevier, p. 310.

Jones, R. M. (1970). *The new psychology of dreaming.* New York: Grune and Stratton.

———. (1980). *The dream poet.* Cambridge, Mass.: Schenkman.

Jouvet, M. (1967). The states of sleep. *Scientific American, 216,* 62–72.

Jung, C. G. (1916). The transcendent function. In *Collected works of C.G. Jung,* vol. 8, trans. R. F. C. Hull. Princeton: Bollingen, 1960, pp. 67–91.

———. (1952). *Answer to Job.* In *Collected works of C.G. Jung,* vol. 11, trans. R. F. C. Hull. Princeton: Bollingen, 1958, pp. 355–470.

———. (1944). Psychology and alchemy. *Collected works of C. G. Jung,* vol. 12, trans. R. F. C. Hull. Princeton: Bollingen, 1953.

———. (1948). On the nature of dreams. In *Collected works of C. G. Jung.* vol. 8, trans. R. F. C. Hull. Princeton: Bollingen, 1960, pp. 281–97.

———. (1934). The practical use of dream-analysis. In *Collected works of C.G. Jung,* vol. 16, trans. R. F. C. Hull. Princeton: Bollingen, 1954, pp. 139–61.

———. (1953). Two essays on analytical psychology. *Collected works of C.G. Jung,* vol. 7, trans. R. F. C. Hull. Princeton: Bollingen, 1960.

———. (1956). Symbols of transformation. *Collected works of C.G. Jung,* vol. 5, trans. R. F. C. Hull. Princeton: Bollingen, 1960.

———. (1959). Archetypes of the collective unconscious. In *Collected works of C.G. Jung*, vol. 9, trans. R. F. C. Hull. Princeton: Bollingen, 1960, pp. 3–41.

———. (1960). On the nature of the psyche. In *Collected works of C.G. Jung*, vol. 8, trans. R. F. C. Hull. Princeton: Bollingen, 1960, pp. 159–234.

———. (1961). *Memories, dreams, reflections.* New York: Pantheon Books.

———. (1964). Symbols and the interpretation of dreams. In *Collected works of C.G. Jung*, vol. 18, trans. R. F. C. Hull. Princeton: Bollingen, 1976, pp. 185–264.

Kales, A., Hoedemaker, F., Jacobson, A., Kales, J., Paulson, M., and Wilson, T. (1967). Mentation during sleep: REM and NREM recall reports. *Perceptual and Motor Skills*, 24, 556–60.

Karle, W., Corriere, R., Hart, J., and Woldenberg, L. (1980). The functional analysis of dreams: A new theory of dreaming. *Archives of the behavioral sciences*, 55, 1–78.

Kaufmann, G. (1980). *Imagery, language and cognition.* Bergen, Norway: Universitetsforlaget.

Kelley, G. A. (1955). *The psychology of personal contructs*, vol. 1. New York: Norton.

Kerr, B., Condon, S. M., and McDonald, L. A. (1985). Cognitive spatial processing and the regulation of posture. *Journal of Experimental Psychology: Human Perception and Performance*, 11, 617–22.

Kerr, N., and Foulkes, D. (1981). Right hemispheric mediation of dream visualization: A case study. *Cortex*, 17, 603–10.

Kerr, N., Foulkes, D., and Jurkovic, G. (1978). Reported absence of visual dream imagery in a normally sighted subject with Turner's Syndrome. *Journal of Mental Imagery*, 2, 247–63.

Kerr, N., Foulkes, D., and Schmidt, M. (1982). The structure of laboratory dream reports in blinded and sighted subjects. *Journal of Nervous and Mental Disease*, 170, 286–94.

Khan, M. M. R. (1974). The use and abuse of dream in psychic experience. *The privacy of the self.* New York: International Universities Press.

———. (1979). *Alienation in perversions.* New York: International Universities Press.

Klein, M., Heimann, P., Isaacs, S., and Riviere, J. (1952). *Developments in Psycho-analysis.* London: Hogarth Press.

Klinger, E. (1978). Modes of normal conscious flow. In K. S. Pope and J. L. Singer (Eds.), *The stream of consciousness.* New York: Plenum Press, pp. 226–54.

Kluger, H. Y. (1975). Archetypal dreams and "everyday" dreams. *Israel Annals of Psychiatry*, 13, 6–47.

Kluver, H. (1966). *Mescal and mechanisms of hallucination.* Chicago: University of Chicago Press.

Koch, S. (1985). The nature and limits of psychological knowledge. In S. Koch and D. Leary (Eds.), *A century of psychology as science.* New York: McGraw-Hill.

Kohut, H. (1971). *The analysis of the self.* New York: International Universities Press.

———. (1977). *The restoration of the self.* New York: International Universities Press.

Kosslyn, S. (1981). The medium and the message in mental imagery: A theory. *Psychological Review, 88,* 46–66.

Koukkou, M., and Lehmann, D. (1983). Dreaming: The functional state-shift hypothesis. *British Journal of Psychiatry, 142,* 221–31.

Kracke, W. (1979). Dreaming in Kagwahiv: Dream beliefs and their psychic uses in an Amazonian Indian culture. *Psychoanalytic Study of Society, 8,* 119–71.

———. (1987). Dream, myth, thought, and image: An Amazonian contribution to the psychoanalytic theory of primary process. In B. Tedlock (Ed.), *Dreaming: Anthropological and psychological interpretations.* Cambridge: Cambridge University Press.

Kramer, M. (1969). Manifest dream content in psychopathologic states. In M. Kramer (Ed.), *Dream psychology and the new biology of dreaming.* Springfield, Ill: C. C. Thomas, pp. 377–396.

Krishnan, R. (1984). Dreams of flying in narcoleptic patients. *Psychosomatics, 25,* 423–25.

Kugler, P. (1982). *The alchemy of discourse.* Lewisberg: Bucknell University Press.

Kuiken, D. (1987). Dreams and self-knowledge. In J. Gackenbach (Ed.), *Sleep and dreams: A sourcebook.* New York: Garland, pp. 225–50.

Kuiken, D., and Nielsen, T. (1983). Structural analysis of stories. Unpubl. MS, University of Alberta.

Kuiken, D., Nielsen, T., Thomas, S., & McTaggart, D. (1983). Comparison of the story structure of myths, extraordinary dreams, and mundane dreams. *Sleep Research, 12,* 196.

Kuper, A. (1979). A structural approach to dreams. *Mind, 14,* 645–62.

———. (1983). The structure of dream sequences. *Culture, Medicine, and Psychiatry, 7,* 153–15.

———. (1986). Structural anthropology and the psychology of dreams. *Journal of Mind and Behaviour, 7,* 333–44.

LaBerge, S. (1985). *Lucid dreaming.* Los Angeles: Jeremy Tarcher.

LaBerge, S. P., Nagel, L. E., Dement, W. C., and Zarcone, V. P. (1981). Lucid dreaming verified by volitional communication during REM sleep. *Perceptual and Motor Skills, 52,* 727–32.

Lachner, J. R., and Levine, M. S. (1979). Changes in apparent body orientation and sensory localization induced by vibration of postural muscles. *Aviation, Space and Environmental Medicine, 50,* 346–54.

Laing, R. D. (1982). *The voice of experience.* New York: Pantheon.

Langer, S. K. (1942). *Philosophy in a new key.* Cambridge: Harvard University Press.

———. (1972). *Mind: An essay on human feeling,* vol. 2. Baltimore: Johns Hopkins University Press.

Lavie, P., Metz, L., and Hefetz, A. (1983). Long-term effects of traumatic events on sleep and dreaming: Dissociation between physiologic and psychologic aspects of REM sleep. *Sleep Research, 12,* 208.

Lavie, P., and Tzischinsky, O. (1985). Cognitive asymmetry and dreaming: Lack of relationship. *American Journal of Psychology, 98,* 353–61.

Lavie, P., and Wollman, M. (1985). A case report of a dream-story teller. *Sleep Research, 14,* 114.

Leaning, F. E. (1925). An introductory study of hypnagogic phenomena. *Proceedings of the Society for Psychical Research, 35,* 289–409.

Leary, T., Metzner, R., and Alpert, R. (1964). *Psychedelic experience.* London: Academy Editions.

Lehmann, D. (1981). EEG during REM mentation. Association for the Psychophysiological Study of Sleep, Satellite Symposium on Dreaming, Hyannis, Mass., May.

Lévi-Strauss, C. (1966). *The savage mind.* Chicago: University of Chicago Press.

———. (1969). *The raw and the cooked,* trans. J. Weightman and D. Weightman. New York: Harper and Row.

Levitan, H. L. (1976). The significance of certain catastrophic dreams. *Psychotherapy and Psychosomatics, 27,* 1–7.

———. (1980). Traumatic events in dreams of psychiatric patients. *Psychotherapy and Psychosomatics, 33,* 226–32.

———. (1984). Dreams which culminate in migraine headaches. *Psychotherapy and Psychosomatics, 41,* 161–66.

Lewin, B. D. (1958). *Dreams and the uses of regression.* New York: International Universities Press.

Lincoln, J. S. (1935). *The dream in primitive cultures.* Baltimore: Williams and Wilkins.

Lovecraft, H. P. (1962). *Dreams and fancies.* Sauk City, Wis.: Arkham House.

Lowy, S. (1942). *Psychological and biological foundations of dream-interpretation.* London: Kegan Paul, Trench, and Trubner.

Luria, A. (1972). *The man with the shattered world,* trans. L. Solotaroff. New York: Basic Books.

———. (1973). *The working brain.* Harmondsworth, Eng.: Penguin Books.

Mack. J. E. (1965). Nightmares, conflict, and ego development in childhood. *International Journal of Psychoanalysis, 46*, 403–28.

Macrobius (1952). *Commentary on the dream of Scipio*, trans. W. Stahl. New York: Columbia University Press.

Mahl, G. F., Rothenberg, A., Delgado, J. M. R., and Hamlin, H. (1964). Psychological responses in the human to intracerebral electrical stimulation. *Psychosomatic Medicine, 26*, 337–68.

Mahrer, A. (1986). The depth of dreams: Some data and a model. Association for the Study of Dreams, Ottawa, Ont., June.

Maier, N. (1931). Reasoning in humans, pt. 2: The solution of a problem and its appearance in consciousness. *Journal of Comparative Psychology, 12*, 181–94.

———. (1964). Selector-integrator mechanisms in behavior. In N. Maier and T. Schneirla (Eds.), *Principles of animal psychology*. New York: Dover, pp. 621–49.

Malcolm, N. (1959). *Dreaming*. London: Routledge and Kegan Paul.

Marcel, A. J. (1983). Conscious and unconscious perception: An approach to the relations between phenomenal experience and perceptual processes. *Cognitive Psychology, 15*, 238–300.

Marks, L. (1978). *The unity of the senses*. New York: Academic Press.

Maslow, A. (1962). *Towards a psychology of being*. Princeton: Van Nostrand.

Masson, J. M. (1984). *The assault on truth: Freud's suppression of the seduction theory*. New York: Penguin Books.

Mayer, R. E. (1983). *Thinking, problem solving, cognition*. New York: W. H. Freeman.

McCarley, R. W., and Hobson, J.A. (1979). The form of dreams and the biology of sleep. In B. B. Wolman (Ed.), *Handbook of dreams*. New York: Van Nostrand Reinhold, pp. 76–130.

McKellar, P. (1957). *Imagiation and thinking*. London: Cohen and West.

McKellar, P., and Simpson, L. (1954). Between wakefulness and sleep: Hypnagogic imagery. *British Journal of Psychology, 45*, 266–76.

Mead, G. H. (1934). *Mind, self, and society*. Chicago, Ill. University of Chicago Press.

Meier, C. A. (1966). The dream in ancient Greece and its use in temple cures (incubation). In G. B. Von Grunebaum and R. Caillois (Eds.), *The dream and human societies*. Berkeley: University of California Press, pp. 303–20.

Merrill, W. R. (1981). The Raramuri stereotype of dreams. In B. Tedlock (Ed.), *Dreaming: Anthropological and psychological interpretations*. Cambridge: Cambridge University Press.

Milner, M. (1957). *On not being able to paint*. New York: International Universities Press.

Mitchell, S. W. (1890). Some disorders of sleep. *American Journal of Medical Sciences, 100*, 109–27.

Moffitt, A., and Hoffman, R. (1987). On the single-mindedness and isolation of dream psychophysiology. In J. Gackenbach (Ed.), *Sleep and dreams: A sourcebook.* New York: Garland, pp. 145–86.

Moffitt, A., Hoffmann, R., Wells, R., Armitage, R., Pigeau, R., and Shearer, J. (1982). Individual differences among pre and post awakening EEG correlates of dream reports following arousals from different stages of sleep. *Psychiatric Journal of the University of Ottawa, 7,* 111–25.

Molinari, S. (1984). Psychoanalysis, dream research, and the formation of dreams. In M. Bosinelli and P. Cicogna (Eds.), *Psychology of Dreams.* Bologna: CLUEB, pp. 93–108.

Molinari, S., and Foulkes, D. (1969). Tonic and phasic events during sleep: Psychological correlates and implications. *Perceptual and Motor Skills, 29,* 343–68.

Monroe, R. A. (1971). *Journeys out of body.* New York: Doubleday.

———. (1985). *Far journeys.* New York: Doubleday.

Morrison, A. R. (1983). Paradoxical sleep and alert wakefulness: Variations on a theme. In M. Chase and E. Weitzman (Eds.), *Sleep Disorders: Basic and Clinical Research.* New York: SP Medical and Scientific Books, pp. 95–122.

Morrison, A. R., and Reiner, P. B. (1985). A dissection of paradoxical sleep. In D. J. McGinty, R. Drucker-Colin, A. Morrison, and P. L. Parmeggiani (Eds.), *Brain Mechanisms of Sleep.* New York: Raven Press, pp. 97–110.

Moss, K. (1986). The dream lucidity continuum. *Lucidity Letter, 5* (2), 25–28.

Murray, E. A., and Mishkin, M. (1985). Amygdalectomy impairs crossmodal association in monkeys. *Science, 228,* 604–06.

Natsoulas, T. (1981). Basic problems of consciousness. *Journal of Personality and Social Psychology, 41,* 132–78.

Neisser, U. (1967). *Cognitive psychology.* New York: Appleton-Century-Crofts.

———. (1976). *Cognition and reality.* San Francisco: W. H. Freeman.

Niederland, W. G. (1957). The earliest dreams of a young child. *The psychoanalytic study of the child, 12,* 190–208.

Nielsen, T. (1986). Kinesthetic imagery as a quality of lucid awareness. *Lucidity Letter, 5* (1), 147–60.

Nielsen, T., and Kuiken, D. (1986). Effects of dream reflection on emotional arousal. Association for the Study of Dreams, Annual Meeting, University of Virginia, Charlottesville, June.

Nielsen, T., Kuiken, D., Moffitt, A., Hoffman, R., and Wells, R. (1983). Comparisons of the story structure of stage REM and stage 2 mentation reports. *Sleep Research, 12,* 181.

Nielsen, T. and Powell, R. (1988). Longitudinal dream incorporation. *Sleep Research, 17,* 112.

Nisbett, R., and Wilson, T. (1977). Telling more than we can know: Verbal reports on mental processes. *Psychological Review*, 5 (1), 147–60.

O'Flaherty, W. D. (1984). *Dreams, illusion, and other realities*. Chicago: University of Chicago Press.

O'Keefe, D. L. (1982). *Stolen lightning: The social theory of magic*. New York: Random House.

Ogilvie, R. D., Hunt, H. T., Sawicki, C., and McGowan, K. (1978). Searching for lucid dreams. *Sleep Research*, 7, 165.

Ogilvie, R. D., Hunt, H. T., Sawicki, C., and Samahalski, J. (1982). Psychological correlates of spontaneous middle ear muscle activity during sleep. *Sleep*, 5, 11–27.

Ogilvie, R. D., Hunt, H. T., Tyson, P. D., Lucescu, M. L., and Jeakins, D. B. (1982). Lucid dreaming and alpha activity. *Perceptual and Motor Skills*, 55, 795–808.

Olton, D. S. (1984). Comparative analysis of episodic memory. *Behavioural and Brain Sciences*, 7, 250–51.

Oppenheim, A. L. (1966). Mantic dreams in the ancient near east. In G. E. Von Grunebaum and R. Caillois (Eds.), *The dream and human societies*. Berkeley: University of California Press, pp. 341–50.

Orne, M. (1969). Demand characteristics and the concept of quasi-controls. In R. Rosenthal and R. L. Rosnow (Eds.), *Artifact in behavioral research*. New York: Academic Press, pp. 143–79.

Ornitz, E. M., and Ritvo, E. R. (1968). Perceptual inconstancy in early autism. *Archives of General Psychiatry*, 18, 78–98.

Osgood, C. E. (1964). Semantic differential techniques in the comparative study of cultures. *American Anthropologist*, 66, 171–200.

Oswald, I. (1962). *Sleeping and waking*. New York: Elsevier.

Otto, R. (1923). *The idea of the holy*. New York: Galaxy Books, 1958.

Ouspensky, P. D. (1934). *A new model of the universe*. New York: Knopf, 1961.

Palombo, S. R. (1978). *Dreaming and memory*. New York: Basic Books.

———. (1984). Recovery of early memories associated with reported dream imagery. *American Journal of Psychiatry*, 141, 1508–11.

Pasricha, S., and Stevenson, I. (1986). Near-death experiences in India. *Journal of Nervous and Mental Disease*, 174, 165–70.

Penfield, W., and Perot, P. (1963). The brain's record of auditory and visual experience. *Brain*, 86, 595–696.

Piaget, J. (1962). *Play, dreams, and imitation in childhood*. New York: Norton.

———. (1963). *The child's conception of the world*. Paterson, N.J.: Littlefield, Adams.

———. (1973). The affective unconscious and the cognitive unconscious. *American Psychoanalytic Association Journal*, 21, 249–61.

Pivak, R. T. (1978). Tonic states and phasic events in relation to sleep mentation. In A. M. Arkin, J. S. Antrobus, and S. J. Ellman (Eds.), *The mind in sleep: Psychology and psychophysiology.* Hillsdale, N.J.: Lawrence Erlbaum, pp. 245–71.

Pivak, R. T., Bylsma, F., Busby, K., & Sawyer, S. (1982). Interhemispheric EEG changes: Relationship to sleep and dreams in gifted adolescents. *Psychiatric Journal of the University of Ottawa, 7,* 56–76.

Plato (1961a). *Republic.* In *The collected dialogues of Plato,* trans. P. Shorey. Princeton, N.J.: Bollingen, pp. 575–844.

———. (1961b). *Theaetetus.* In *The collected dialogues of Plato,* trans. F. M. Cornford. Princeton, N.J.: Bollingen, pp. 845–919.

Pompeiano, O. (1970). Mechanisms of sensorimotor integration during sleep. In E. Stellar and J. M. Sprague (Eds.), *Progress in physiological psychology,* vol. 3. New York: Academic Press, pp. 3–179.

———. (1974). Vestibular influences during sleep. In H. H. Kornhuber (Ed.), *Vestibular system, Part I: Basic mechanisms.* Berlin: Springer-Verlag, pp. 583–622.

Pontalis, J. B. (1981). Between the dream as object and the dream text. In *Frontiers in psychoanalysis,* trans. C. Cullen and P. Cullen. New York: International Universities Press, pp. 23–55.

Porte, H. S., and Hobson, J. A. (1986). Bizarreness in REM and NREM sleep reports. *Sleep Research, 15,* 81.

Purcell, S., Mullington, J., Moffitt, A., Hoffmann, R., and Pigeau, R. (1986). Dream self-reflectiveness as a learned cognitive skill, *Sleep, 9,* 423–37.

Pylyshyn, Z. (1981). The imagery debate: Analogue media versus tacit knowledge. *Psychological Review, 88,* 16–45.

Ramm, P., and Frost (1986). Cerebral and local cerebral metabolism in the cat during slow wave and REM sleep. *Brain Research, 365,* 112–124.

Rank, O. (1950). *Psychology and the soul.* New York: A. S. Barnes.

Ravagnati, L., Halgren, E., Babb, T. L., and Crandell, P.H. (1979). Activity of human hippocampal formation and amygdala neurons during sleep. *Sleep, 2,* 161–73.

Rechtschaffen, A. (1973). The psychophysiology of mental activity during sleep. In F. McGuigan and R. Schoonover (Eds.), *The psychophysiology of thinking.* New York: Academic Press, pp. 153–205.

———. (1978). The single-mindedness of dreams. *Sleep, 1,* 97–109.

Rechtschaffen, A., and Buchignani, C. (1983). Visual dimensions of dream images. *Sleep Research, 12,* 189.

Reed, H. (1978). The Sundance experiment. *Sundance community dream journal,* 2 (2), 264.

Reichel-Dolmatoff, G. (1975). *The shaman and the jaguar: A study of narcotic drugs among the Indians of Colombia.* Philadelphia: Temple University Press.

Reinsel, R., Wollman, M., and Antrobus, J. S. (1986). Effects of environmental context and cortical activation on thought. *Journal of Mind and Behavior, 7*, 259–76.

Ricoeur, P. (1970). *Freud and philosophy.* New Haven: Yale University Press.

———. (1984–85). *Time and narrative,* 2 vols. Chicago: University of Chicago Press.

Roffwarg, H., Herman, J., Bowe-Anders, C., and Tauber, G. (1978). The effects of sustained alterations of waking visual input on dream content. In A. M. Arkin, J. S. Antrobus, and S. J. Ellman (Eds.), *The mind in sleep: Psychology and psychophysiology.* Hillsdale, N.J.: Lawrence Erlbaum, pp. 295–349.

Roffwarg, H., Muzio, J., and Dement, W. (1966). Ontogenetic development of the human sleep-dream cycle. *Science, 152*, 604–19.

Roheim, G. (1952). *The gates of the dream.* New York: International Universities Press.

Roscher, W. H., and Hillman, J. (1972). *Pan and the nightmare.* Zurich: Spring Publications.

Rycroft, C. (1979). *The innocence of dreams.* New York: Pantheon Books.

Sacks, O. (1983). *Awakenings.* New York: E. P. Dutton.

———. (1987). *The man who mistook his wife for a hat.* New York: Harper and Row.

Saint-Denys, H. de (1867). *Dreams and how to guide them,* trans. N. Fry. Great Britain: Duckworth.

Sampson, E. (1981). Cognitive psychology as ideology. *American Psychologist, 36*, 730–43.

Schacter, D. L. (1976). The hypnagogic state: A critical review of the literature. *Psychological Bulletin, 83*, 452–481.

Schecter, N., Schmeidler, G. R., and Staal, M. (1965). Dream reports and creative tendencies in students of the arts, sciences, and engineering. *Journal of Consulting Psychology, 29*, 415–21.

Schanfald, D., Pearlman, C., and Greenberg, R. (1985). Focal brain damage and dream recall. *Sleep Research, 14*, 116.

———. (1987). The capacity of stroke victims to report dreams. *Cortex, 21*, 1–15.

Schilder, P. (1924). *Medical Psychology.* New York: International Universities Press, 1953.

———. (1942). *Mind: Perception and thought in their constructive aspects.* New York: Columbia University Press.

Schwartz, D. G., Weinstein, L. N., and Arkin, A. M. (1978). Qualitative aspects of sleep mentation. In A. M. Arkin, J. S. Antrobus, and S. J. Ellman (Eds.), *The mind in sleep: Psychology and psychophysiology.* Hillsdale, N.J.: Lawrence Erlbaum, pp. 143–241.

Schweder, R. A., and LeVine, R. A. (1975). Dream concepts of Hausa children. *Ethos, 3*, 209–30.

Searles, H. (1965). The differentiation between concrete and metaphorical thinking in the recovering schizophrenic patient. In H. Searles, *Collected papers on schizophrenia and related subjects*. New York: International Universities Press, pp. 560–83.

Shepard, R. N. (1978). Externalization of mental images and the act of creation. In B. Randhawa and W. Coffman (Eds.), *Visual learning, thinking, and communication*. New York: Academic Press, pp. 133–89.

———. (1984). Ecological constraints on internal representation: Resonant kinematics of perceiving, imagining, thinking, and dreaming. *Psychological Review, 91*, 417–46.

Shukla, G. D., Sahu, S. C., Tripathi, R. P., and Gupta, D. K. (1982). Phantom limb: A phenomenological study. *British Journal of Psychiatry, 141*, 54–58.

Sidgwick, H. (1894). Report on the census of hallucinations. *Proceedings of the Society for Psychical Research, 10*.

Siegel, R. K. (1979). Dizziness as an altered state of consciousness. *Journal of Altered States of Consciousness, 5*, 87–107.

———. (1983). Teachings from psychoactive plants and intoxicated animals. In L. Grinspoon and J. B. Bakalar (Eds.), *Psychedelic reflections*. New York: Human Sciences Press, pp. 213–22.

Silberer, H. (1909). Report on a method of eliciting and observing certain symbolic hallucination-phenomena. In D. Rapaport (Ed.), *Organization and pathology of thought*. New York: Columbia University Press, 1951, pp. 195–207.

———. (1917). *Hidden symbolism of alchemy and the occult arts*, trans. S. E. Jelliffe. New York: Dover, 1971.

Singer, J. L. (1978). Experimental studies of daydreaming and the stream of thought. In K. S. Pope and J. L. Singer (Eds.), *The stream of consciousness*. New York: Plenum Press, pp. 187–223.

Slight, D. (1924). Hypnagogic phenomena. *Journal of Abnormal Psychology, 19*, 274–82.

Smith, C. (1981). Learning and sleep states in the rat. In W. Fishbein (Ed.), *Sleep, dreams and memory*. New York: Spectrum, pp. 19–35.

Smith, C., and Kelly, G. (1986). PS deprivation several days after the end of training retards learning. *Sleep Research, 15*, 77.

Smith, C., and Lapp, L. (1984). Prolonged increases in PS and number of REMs following shuttle box training. *Sleep Research, 13*, 98.

Smith, R. C. (1986). Evaluating dream function: Emphasizing the study of patients with organic disease. *Journal of Mind and Behaviour, 7*, 397–410.

Snyder, F. (1970). The phenomenology of dreaming. In L. Madow and L. Snow (Eds.), *The psychodynamic implications of the physiological studies on dreams*. Springfield, Ill.: Thomas, pp. 124–51.

Snyder, T. J., and Gackenbach, J. (1988). Individual differences associated with lucid dreaming ability. In J. Gackenbach and S. LaBerge (Eds.), *Lucid dreaming: New research on consciousness during sleep*. New York: Plenum.

Spadafora, A., and Hunt, H. (1988). "Correlates of lucid, archetypal, and nightmare dreaming." Paper presented at meeting of the Association for the Study of Dreams, Santa Cruz, June.

Sparrow, G. S. (1976). *Lucid dreaming: Dawning of the clear light*. Virginia Beach: A.R.E. Press.

Spitz, R. A. (1965). *The first year of life*. New York: International Universities Press.

Starker, S. (1978). Dreams and waking fantasy. In K. S. Pope and J. L. Singer (Eds.), *The stream of consciousness*. New York: Plenum, pp. 301–19.

———. (1982). Toward a psychophysiology of waking fantasy: EEG studies. *Perceptual and Motor Skills*, 55, 891–902.

Stern, W. C. (1981). REM sleep and behavioral plasticity: Evidence for involvement of brain catecholamines. In W. Fishbein (Ed.), *Sleep, dreams and memory*. New York: Spectrum, pp. 95–109.

Stevens, P. (1974). *Patterns in nature*. Boston: Little, Brown.

Stevenson, R. L. (1912). A chapter on dreams. In *Across the plains, with other memories and essays*. New York: Charles Scribner's Sons, pp. 206–30.

Sullivan, H. S. (1953). *The interpersonal theory of psychiatry*. New York: Norton.

Swartz, P., and Seginer, L. (1981). Response to body rotation and tendency to mystical experience. *Perceptual and Motor Skills*, 53, 683–88.

Sylvia, W., Clark, P., and Monroe, L. (1978). Dream reports of subjects high and low in creative ability. *Journal of General Psychology*, 99, 205–11.

Tart, C. (1979). From spontaneous event to lucidity. In B. B. Wolman (Ed.), *Handbook of dreams*. New York: Van Nostrand Reinhold, pp. 226–68.

Taub-Bynum, E. (1986). PSI, the shared dreamscope and the family unconscious. *ASD newsletter*, 3 (4), 226–68.

Tedlock, B. (1981). Quiche Maya dream interpretation. *Ethos*, 9, 313–30.

———. (1987). *Dreaming: Anthropological and psychological interpretations*. Cambridge: Cambridge University Press.

Tholey, P. (1983). Techniques for inducing and manipulating lucid dreams. *Perceptual and Motor Skills*, 57, 79–90.

Tolaas, J., and Ullman, M. (1979). Extrasensory communication and dreams. In B. B. Wolman (Ed.), *Handbook of dreams*. New York: Van Nostrand Reinhold, pp. 168–202.

Tulving, E. (1983). *Elements of episodic memory*. Oxford: Oxford University Press.

————. (1984). Relations among components and processes of memory. *Behavioral Brain Sciences*, 7, 257–68.

————. (1985). Memory and consciousness. *Canadian Psychology*, 26, 1–12.

Tylor, E. (1871). *Primitive culture*, vol. 1. New York: Gordon Press.

Valadez, S. (1986). An interview with Ulu Temay, Huichol Shaman. *Shaman's Drum*, 6, 18–23.

Van de Castle, R. (1971). *The psychology of dreaming*. New York: General Learning Press.

————. (1986). ESP in dreams: Comments on a replication "failure" by the "failing" subject. Association for the Study of Dreams, Annual Meeting, University of Virginia, Charlottesville, June.

Van den Hoed, J., Lucas, E. A., and Dement, W. C. (1979). Hallucinatory experiences during cataplexy in patients with narcolepsy. *American Journal of Psychiatry*, 136, 1210–11.

Van Dusen, W. (1972). *The natural depth in man*. New York: Harper and Row.

Van Eeden, F. (1913). A study of dreams. In C. Tart (Ed.), *Altered states of consciousness*. New York: Wiley, 1969, pp. 145–58.

Vogel, G.W. (1976). Mentation reported from naps of narcoleptics. In E. D. Weitzman (Ed.), *Advances in sleep research*, vol. 3: *Narcolepsy*. New York: Spectrum, pp. 161–68.

————. (1978a). An alternative view of the neurobiology of dreaming. *American Journal of Psychiatry*, 135, 1531–35.

————. (1978b). Sleep-onset mentation. In A. M. Arkin, J. S. Antrobus, and S. J. Ellman (Eds.), *The mind in sleep: Psychology and psychophysiology*. Hillsdale, N.J.: Lawrence Erlbaum, pp. 97–108.

Vogel, G., Foulkes, D., and Trosman, H. (1966). Ego functions and dreaming during sleep onset. *Archives of General Psychiatry*, 14, 238–48.

Vowles, D. (1970). Neuroethology, evolution, and grammar. In R. Aronson, E. Tobach, D. Lehrman, and J. Rosenblatt (Eds.), *Development and evolution of behavior: Essays in memory of T. C. Schneirla*. San Francisco: W. H. Freeman, pp. 194–215.

Vygotsky, L. (1962). *Thought and language*. Cambridge: M.I.T. Press.

Wallace, A. F. C. (1958). Dreams and the wishes of the soul: A type of psychoanalytic theory among the seventeenth century Iroquois. *American Anthropologist*, 60, 234–48.

Wasserman, M. D., Pressman, M. R., Pollak, C. P., Spielman, A. J., DeRosairo, L., and Weitzman, E.D. (1982). Nocturnal penile tumescence: Is it really a REM phenomenon? *Sleep Research*, 11, 44.

Watkins, M. M. (1976). *Waking dreams*. New York: Harper and Row.

Watson, R. K. (1972). Mental correlates of periorbital potentials during REM sleep. Ph.D. diss., University of Chicago.

Watson, R., Butler, S., and Liebmann, K. (1982). PIPS and the Rorschach. *Sleep Research*, 11, 33.

Weber, M. (1963). *The sociology of religion*. Boston: Beacon Press.

Werner, H. (1961). *Comparative psychology of mental development*. New York: Science Editions.

Werner, H., and Kaplan, B. (1963). *Symbol formation*. New York: Wiley.

West, L. J. (1962). A general theory of hallucinations and dreams. In L. J. West (Ed.), *Hallucinations*. New York: Grune and Stratton, pp. 275–91.

Wheeler, R., and Cutsforth, T. (1922). Synaesthesia and meaning. *American Journal of Psychology*, 33, 361–84.

Whiteman, J. H. M. (1961). *The mystical life*. London: Faber and Faber.

Wilber, K. (1984). The developmental spectrum and psychopathology, part 1: stages and types of pathology. *Journal of Transpersonal Psychology*, 16, 75–118.

Wilensky, R. (1983). Story grammars versus story points. *Behavioral and Brain Sciences*, 6, 579–623.

Wilmer, H. (1986). Combat nightmares. *Spring*, 120–39.

Winget, C., and Kramer, M. (1979). *Dimensions of dreams*. Gainesville, Fla.: University Presses of Florida.

Winnicot, D. W. (1971). *Playing and reality*. New York: Basic Books.

Winson, J. (1985). *Brain and Psyche*. New York: Vintage Books.

Wisdom, J. O. (1947). Three dreams of Descartes. *International Journal of Psychoanalysis*, 28, 11.

Wittgenstein, L. (1966). *Lectures and conversations on aesthetics, psychology, and religious belief*. Berkeley: University of California Press.

———. (1972). *On certainty*. New York: Harper Torchbooks.

———. (1979). *Remarks on Frazier's Golden Bough*. Atlantic Highlands, N.J.: Humanities Press.

Woody, E., and Claridge, G. (1977). Psychoticism and thinking. *British Journal of Social and Clinical Psychology*, 16, 241–48.

Woolfolk, R. (1975). Psychophysiological correlates of meditation. *Archives of General Psychiatry*, 32, 1326–33.

Yates, J. (1985). The content of awareness is a model of the world. *Psychological Review*, 92, 249–84.

Zimmerman, W. B. (1970). Sleep mentation and auditory awakening thresholds. *Psychophysiology*, 6, 540–49.

Ziskind, E. (1964). Significance of symptoms of sensory deprivation experiments due to methodological procedures. *Recent Advances in Biological Psychiatry*, 6, 111–18.

Zornetzer, S. F. (1981). The nucleus locus coeruleus and its involvement in memory processing. In W. Fishbein (Ed.), *Sleep, dreams and memory*. New York: Spectrum, pp. 47–72.

Zubek, J. (1969). *Sensory deprivation: Fifteen years of research.* New York: Appleton-Century-Crofts.

Zuckerman, M. (1970). Sensory deprivation. In W. Keup (Ed.), *Origin and mechanisms of hallucinations.* New York: Plenum Press, pp. 133–48.

Index

Action sequences, 165, 174
Active (sending) roles, 200–02
Adelson, J., 13
Adler, Alfred, 27, 86
Aesthetics, 8, 9, 12, 14, 15
Affect, 33, 42, 43, 44, 124
Aggression, 132, 136
Alexander, C. N., 121, 195
Altered states of consciousness, 4, 8, 198, 200; and symbolism, 14; and NREM / REM states, 24, 30; parallels with dreaming, 73–74; intensified integration or dissolution, 124; and brain hemisphericity, 169, 172; similarities with sleep onset, 181, 185–87, 188; and visual-spatial processes, 189, 191; and synesthesia, 190; as regression, 192–93
Amnesia, 58, 59, 61, 63
Amplification, 8, 129, 146, 178
Amputees: dreams of, 39
Amygdala, 27, 29, 58
Angyal, Andras, 137, 197
Animal dreams, 42–43, 132, 228n6
Animals: and dreaming, 42, 47–49; self-referential capacity, 62; episodic recall in, 62, 65
Animism, 154–55
Anthropology: and dreams, 81–86, 146–56. *See also* Culture pattern dreams
Anticipation: and dreams, 27, 30, 47–48
Antrobus, John, 4, 16, 21, 37; on memory and dreams, 60–61, 63, 64, 78, 208; definition of dreaming, 75; on dream bizarreness, 161,

163; on storylike quality of dreams, 162–63; and brain hemisphericity, 169, 170
Anxiety: and ability to dream, 53–54
Anxiety dreams, 30, 33
Aphasia: and dreaming, 103, 170, 171
Apparition dreams, 86, 181, 231n9. *See also* Visitation dreams
Archetypal dreams, 45, 64, 70, 79, 89, 198, 232n5, 233n1; in tribal societies, 82, 83; and dream diamond, 95, 96, 139; and lucid dreams, 119, 122, 123; contents and characteristics of, 128–31; and personal traits, 131; and meditation, 131, 132; self-referential awareness, 131–32, 152–53; self-curative qualities, 155–56; narratives vs. imagery in, 160, 168, 185. *See also* Jung, Carl; Titanic dreams
Arenson, Kenneth, 104
Aristotle, 78, 79, 87, 88, 89, 112, 211–12
Arkin, A. M., 181
Armitage, R., 169
Arnheim, Rudolph, 8, 15, 109, 173, 190, 213
Arnold-Foster, Mary, 80–81, 120, 226–27n6
Asch, Solomon, 109
Aserinsky, E., 40
Asociality: of dreams, 12, 84. *See also* Sociality
Assimilation: of traumas in dreams, 125
Association for the Study of Dreams, 4
Associationism, 61, 65, 78
Assonance, 103, 106–08, 207
Autosymbolism, 182, 188, 190
Awareness, animal, 48–49. *See also* Consciousness